Around the World without Wings

By George Williams

Revised with minor amendments 2021

ISBN: ISBN-13: 9781479266876

Contents

Planning and Preparation

Sector 1 - Southampton to San Francisco

Sector 2 - San Francisco to Sydney

Sector 3 – Sydney to Singapore

Sector 4 - Singapore to Dubai

Sector 5 – Dubai to Southampton

Dedication

This book is dedicated to the 600 or so other travellers who went around the world with us on board the MV Aurora in the spring of 2012

More especially it is for Brenda and Mick, Isabel and Jimmy, Laura and Roger, and Christine and Neil with who shared our adventures as friends.

Planning and Preparation

Introduction

On the first day of December 2011 I started my retirement.
A whole new way of life beckoned with all kinds of challenges,
possibilities, and choices. Retirement raised lots of possibilities
on which to ponder, but initially most of my time was spent
getting ready for January 4th 2012 when Deb (my amazingly
supportive wife, friend, and explorer) and I would be starting
an adventure that only relatively few people will ever
experience.
On that day we would be setting sail on the P&O Cruise ship
Aurora for a three-month cruise around the world.
During that cruise I kept and published a blog on the internet
to tell friends and family about where we were and what we
were doing as the voyage progressed around the world. My
blog was open for anyone to read and its 78 entries were
regularly looked at by 600 to 1,000 people, eventually getting
over 50,000 total hits.
Along with a diary that Deb kept, that blog became the basis of
this book which gives even more people a chance to read
about our adventure of a lifetime.

Shall We Do It?

The cruise cost us a small fortune, and many people expressed their surprise that we felt it was value for money when perhaps we should be consolidating our nest-egg for retirement. In all honesty there were times when I shared their sentiments and before we decided to go ahead, Deb and I thought long and hard. There was about a year during which we considered the financial aspects and balanced it against the thrill of where we would go, what we would see and the experiences we would gain. One of the major factors that eventually helped to swing the decision was the realisation that mortality is unpredictable, but certain, and this chance might never come again. Hence nearly three years in advance of the cruise we agreed that, subject to our financial situation being satisfactory, the world cruise was definitely going to happen.

As I put my fingers to the keyboard to create the blog's first entry there were just two weeks to go before we jumped into the car for the trip to Southampton. So what had happened in our lives that led us to make this decision?

Our very first cruise was in the year 2000 as a supposed one-off holiday of a lifetime for our Silver Wedding anniversary. This is captured in my earlier book, "A Cornishman goes Cruising", which chronicles not just the magic and thrill of the holiday but also choosing a cruise and the preparation stages. One of the most critical factors that led us to sample cruising was my utter fear of flying which conflicted with my desire to see distant lands and to feel the warmth of a summer that is not always a certainty in Britain.

By 2009 we had had been on more than ten cruises and the thrill had not diminished. How to celebrate my retirement was becoming a topic of discussion on Saturday evenings over glasses of wine as we watched old cruise holiday videos. We have quite a library of homemade and professionally produced cruise videos, but we often search out the original promotional videos that we used when deciding to go on that very first cruise. As well as the Mediterranean option, that we eventually chose, they show the exotic possibilities of the Caribbean and the ultimate adventure of a Round the World cruise. On one of those Saturday evenings, the conversation must have turned to the idea of such a cruise, and although perhaps just a joke suggestion at the time, the idea grew over the weeks until we eventually flicked through to the back of the brochure, to pages that we had never bothered to look at before.

We asked ourselves two questions before going any further.

"Was this something we really wanted to do"?
"How much would it cost, and could we afford it"?

The brochure was describing cruises that ticked so many of the boxes that we had mentally stored in our life wish-lists, so the first response was to carry on looking. Round the World cruises left the UK in January, meaning we would be missing the worst of the winter, and the ships used for these long cruises were certainly our favourites.

In terms of the cost, I already had a good idea of the lump sum I had coming to me along with my pension, so a mental figure of how much we could afford was inside my head.

At that time, the brochure we were looking at was for the spring of 2011 and the duration of the trips that we liked were between 80 and 90 days. We have always used a calculation that allowing £100 per day per person would give us a suitable cabin. Based on that calculation, the worst case figure for such a cruise was within budget.

Hence almost 2½ years before our target cruise date, the

decision was made that a Round the World adventure was viable as our introduction to retirement.

We shared our plans with friends and relations and there was a mixture of amazement, disbelief, and thrill at our decision. The immediate problem was that the cruise we would eventually book would not even be advertised for another twelve months. One Saturday during the summer of 2010 an advert finally appeared in the newspaper for World Cruises, and a couple of days later, a brochure from P&O dropped through the letter box. We eagerly scanned the pages and were initially shocked to see that the cruise durations for 2012 had increased, so our calculations were now subject to a review. Fortunately as my pension was getting closer I was able to make more accurate calculations of available money and the future still looked rosy. In the end the decision became quite simple. Aurora was offering a true Round the World circumnavigation and it offered a chance to have a balcony cabin within our budget. It was visiting virtually all the dream locations, and my mind started to swim and my legs trembled with the realisation that it was actually going to happen.

The cruise we chose would be leaving Southampton on the 4th January 2012 and returning home, after 99 days, on the 12th April. In our balcony cabin on 'C' deck we would be sailing west via the Caribbean, through the Panama Canal, with major stops at San Francisco, Sydney, Singapore, Mumbai, Dubai, and then through the Suez Canal before returning home via Istanbul, Athens and Lisbon.

The first dates when it would be possible to make a booking were a couple of weeks away, so we had time to scan the newspapers and internet offers to who see was offering the best deals. The chosen company were contacted for an estimated price, which was agreed in principle until the booking could be officially made. One magical Monday morning, I went to work knowing that Deb had a list of suitable cabins alongside the phone number of our travel agent, and she had promised to ring me as soon as a booking was made. Just after 9:00 my office phone rang and an excited Deb told me the confirmed cabin number and I immediately logged into the web page to spot where we would be living for 99 days of a dream to come.

Of course, there was still 18 months to go yet.

Making Our Trip Public

During the long gap between deciding to go around the world and the actual moment of setting off, life carried on as near to usual as was possible but it was difficult to ignore the excitement. At work I was starting to tell people about what was planned, and this resulted in some people expressing out-and-out jealousy while others doubted my sanity. Virtually all the people I worked with knew about my love of cruise ship holidays but this trip seemed to be a journey too far, especially when it came to answering their usual question:
"How much is this costing?"
It didn't take too much imagination for my colleagues to realise that I would be retiring to enable the cruise, and along with others of a similar age to myself, the complexity of pensions became a regular topic of conversations around the office. I had always been a source of advice about pensions as I'd studied my own position for several years. There were a handful of us in the same age profile so we often bored our younger colleagues whose minds were far from such discussions.

Deb was also planning the future and it was agreed that she would retire at the same time so that we both made a clean break from work to start a new phase of our lives at the end of 2011. Now she was similarly being interrogated about the cruise.

The plans also had to be explained to our families. Deb's mum and dad were totally blown away by the idea of their daughter sailing around the globe, although her brother seemed bemused by the costs involved. My brothers were equally intrigued with the idea, and understood my desire to do this while I could.

Our friends, outside of work, also exclaimed amazement at our plans. After a few weeks however I am sure their thoughts quickly became *"oh not again!"* as it required just a tenuous connection in a conversation to allow us to bring up the topic once more. We were determined to make sure everyone knew what we were going to do.

A lot of things happened in that 18-month period.

Sadly Deb's father died, and her mother went into a residential home in Ludlow. This resulted in regular trips to Shropshire, especially by Deb in order to see her mum and check she was happy.

Our 24-year-old cat also finally decided to call it a day and although this was sad, it solved one problem that had been worrying us about what to do with our little Twiglet when we went away. We also found a new home for our son by purchasing a flat as an investment for him to rent from us.

As the weeks passed we started tentative planning for various things to avoid last minute panics. Clothes were the most obvious items to be addressed with suits being tried on from my side of the wardrobe and dresses by Deb. Anything that no longer fitted or had not been worn for a long time was disposed of to make way for new. My shirts we carefully inspected to see which ones would see out my working days and if others were tidy enough to eventually be given a place in the holiday luggage. After all this the wardrobes started to look a little less cluttered, and although the search for new clothes was not urgent, we always kept a lookout out for bargains or things that caught the eye.

I wanted to change my camera and had planned to use some of my pension lump sum, but this was taken care of by Deb with some of the prize money she got for winning an episode of the BBC quiz 'The Weakest Link'. With the time ticking down, we also needed to plan getting to and from Southampton, and what to do with our cars. Retirement took away our need for two cars, so our solution was to trade both cars in as we left for the cruise, and have a new one waiting for us on our return. A hire car was then booked for when we left home, and another to drive back. To complete the travel plans a hotel in Southampton was sorted for an overnight stay before our departure.

Travel insurance took quite a while to arrange because of two snags. Firstly few companies like to offer insurance for such a long duration, and secondly both of us take a sweet-jar of prescription pills each day which puts a number of companies off. With around six months to go I finally got serious with my searching and eventually found a company willing (at a price) to cover us. This turned out to be an amusing half an hour on the phone with the salesman. He needed to record all the countries we would be visiting so as I gave him each destination port, we had to use the internet to establish what country it was in. This was easy for the obvious places but a few were unfamiliar and several islands came under the flags of countries far away. With the application finally completed I put the phone down and, for the first time, the enormity of the cruise actually struck home. Goose bumps reappeared on my arms along with a tingle at the back of the neck.

Another weekend was spent checking which countries needed visas immediately, and then applying for them at a considerable cost. Deb's passport also needed replacing which delayed her visa applications for another couple of weeks. Vaccinations had to be considered and eventually we decided that the only thing we ought to take were anti-malaria tablets. In the end we never used them but I was glad to have had them available.

House insurance was another thing to sort out as, and just like for travel, leaving a house empty for this length of time was not a standard insurance cover. Fortunately our company accepted the request, and didn't charge any extra premium as long as we met their criteria. We already had a friend who was willing to come in a couple of times a week and keep an eye on the house, and our son also came regularly while we were away.

The magic day came when an envelope from P&O dropped through the letter box with our luggage labels, and a notification that the tickets were available online. At that moment I certainly had just a twinge of concern about what was going to happen in just over two months.

My concerns didn't last long.

As months became weeks one of the last things we did was to actually submit our resignations to our respective employers. Deb left a little earlier than me to allow time to sort out the house and newly-bought flat, and to buy some of the last items we needed. After many questions from my manager, and my office mates, I finally emailed my resignation to take effect at the end of November. That gave me time to assist Deb with those last minute bits and pieces, as well as digging the allotment so that it could be put to bed until we returned home.

In a blink of an eye the farewell presentations, drinks, and goodbyes with our workmates were over.

One morning with perhaps three weeks to go, a surprise arrived via the internet. There was an email in Deb's in-box confirming our cruise but the information had changed, and it was now showing B144 as our cabin number. Confused, we looked at the cabin on the ship's plan and discovered that we had been given an upgrade to a significantly larger cabin at no extra cost. Rather pleased with the surprise, there was a minor issue that we didn't have the correct luggage labels but when Deb telephoned customer services, they assured us that simple home-printed ones would be sufficient. This upgrade was a major treat and completely unexpected. We had spoken to P&O several weeks earlier asking what the price would be to upgrade to this same standard, but then politely coughed and said *"no thanks"* to the £6,000 increase.

Now we had it for free!!

Our final challenge was to have Christmas with all the family. First there was a trip to Cornwall early in December to see my brothers for Christmas dinner number one. Next our daughter Lynsey came to have a brief stay with us, exchange presents, and to eat a Cornish pasty cooked by her mum. That was as good as a Christmas dinner to Lynsey! Deb's mum stayed with us over Christmas, and on the festive day itself we had a quiet time with our son Andrew arriving late in the morning to receive and open presents with us. That was followed by our own Christmas dinner and later in the afternoon Andrew wished us the best and returned to his own home. A couple of days later we had some old friends around for nibbles and a drink with a lovely evening of reminiscing and descriptions of what we were going to do, and why.

With Christmas over, and no more visitors expected, the decorations were quickly taken down and returned to the loft. Deb and I had a quiet New Year's Eve knowing that it was just two days left before we set off towards Southampton and the world.

Time To Go
Tuesday 3rd January 2012

The day had finally come. After months of planning and waiting, it was time to leave home to start the adventure of a lifetime. It was a wet and windy morning but our worst fears of snow and ice had not materialised so everything was full speed ahead. The cases were packed, apart from some last minute items that had to be tucked away in suitcase corners, and while Deb sorted out the house I took our car to the dealership. As organised with the garage, this car was being traded in against a new one that would be waiting for us on the day we returned home.

I drove into Stafford, parked, said a quiet farewell to the car, and went into the garage to drop off the car keys and to sign any paperwork that was needed. Time was not a major problem but the aim was to collect the hire car and be on the road as quickly as possible. We needed to get to the hotel in Southampton in time to unload, and then drive to Andover and see our daughter for an evening meal. Unfortunately plans hardly ever go smoothly when other people involved don't share the same urgency or excitement. It was early, the garage had only just opened, and I was the only customer sharing the showroom with a cleaner and a sleepy assistant at the service reception desk. The sales team were having a meeting, and more worryingly, I couldn't see the salesman that I had been dealing with inside the glass-plated office where salesmen and their manager were probably discussing targets and bonuses. That was far more urgent than a customer going on a three month cruise. I was told by the receptionist to sit and wait because they would not be long.

How many times had I heard that before?

After some ten minutes the meeting did indeed end, but no-one came to see me. I started poking and fiddling with the gleaming polished new cars and finally caught the interest of a junior assistant who was probably concerned that more polishing would be needed if I didn't stop soon. When asked if I needed any help I explained that I was waiting to trade in my car and this successfully initiated the short contractual obligations required. Soon keys had been handed back and I had a form to send off to complete the formalities of selling a car.

Stage one completed and it had not taken too long. There was still an hour to go before the car hire agreement started, so plenty of time to walk to the depot, sort out the paperwork, and drive the car home.

The walk (in the rain) to the hire car office was a healthy distance of perhaps a mile across the town, involving crossing several major roads before getting to the quieter backstreets and the industrial estate where I was heading. The wind was annoying, blowing the cold rain into my face, and continually flipping my now sodden hood off. Walking was made worse by the numerous puddles on the pavements meaning that I had to constantly make detours around them, or occasionally jumping over the smaller ones. At the same time I had to watch for the puddles at the side of the road, being careful to avoid getting splashed when a car came by. Unfortunately there was one such puddle which was so large that when a car appeared I could not escape. To maintain my faith in drivers, I have to believe that it was an accident and the driver was not aware of the effect of driving through water at speed.

The inevitable happened and I was drenched!

It was a moment of comedy for anyone watching. I realised what was about to happen so I turned my back away from the road just quickly enough to restrict the initial surge of water to the back of my legs. But, as if in slow motion, I then looked towards the heavens, and in disgust I saw a plume of water lifting up and over my head, before dropping down onto the rest of my body.

Now dripping from head to toes, I made a comment along the lines of *"never mind, you pesky driver"*...

... well something like that

The rest of my walk was without further disasters although I was continually embarrassed whenever I passed by other walkers who stared at my bedraggled state and tried to hide their sniggers as I squelched along the pavement.

Arriving early (still wet) at the hire car office I was greeted by a cheery assistant who queried my arrival when the car was not booked for another half an hour. I explained that I have always tried to be early so that the paperwork could be completed to allow a quick getaway. Despite my protestations that it would save time, he was having none of it. As there was nowhere to sit I squelched back outside and walked around for the next half an hour. Fortunately it had finally stopped raining so the outside of my damp clothes began to dry out, but they had become so wet that the clothes beneath my coat were soaked with no chance of improvement.

At the exact time required, I returned to the office to find a queue at the desk and the now less-than-cheery assistant, trying to attend to his customers with the slight problem that he had very few cars available to match their requirements. This was the first day after the Christmas break and the fleet of cars necessary were in transit from a nearby depot. I gave him a stare of *"I told you so"* from the back of the queue but I did not say anything as this was a special day, and he was not going to spoil it anymore.

Finally it was my turn at the desk, and he said he would upgrade me to a better car for my troubles.

... actually, it was the only one available.

Once the paperwork and show-around was completed I drove away almost an hour later than the time I had planned to be home.

Arriving back at the house to a confused Deb, I briefly explained the soggy saga and changed into some dry clothes. After a quick drink, we packed away the luggage. This was not easy as the upgraded car actually had less boot space than the anticipated one so once again our suitcases were spread all over the back seat as well as in the boot.

After several *"Did you remember to…"* panics, and *"Have you packed the…"* questions, we locked the door (checked twice), made ourselves comfortable in the car, and set off.

The drive to Southampton was not pleasant.

It was a normal Tuesday to thousands of travellers, and the spray from the busy wet roads was a constant obstacle to visibility. The car's controls were unfamiliar, and I had to consciously think when it came to wiping and cleaning the screen. Just getting used to driving a different car takes an hour or more before it becomes automatic. Hence I didn't enjoy the first part of the journey towards Birmingham, but as we finally left the M42 and joined the M40, the traffic decreased and I relaxed a little. I began to realise that my dreams of the last 18 months were really, **yes really**, coming true.

After a longer than usual trip to Southampton we arrived safely at the hotel. Once we had checked in and found our room, we set about bringing the eight suitcases in from the car to store away until the following morning. While we were going back and forth to the car, we spotted three other couples with a similar abundance of suitcases all displaying labels like our own. Would we see and recognise them again during the cruise… probably not.

Cases stored, we quickly found the one with our washing bits and pieces plus a change of clothes allowing us to freshen up. Within an hour of arriving we set off again through the Southampton rush hour traffic back the way we had come towards Andover and our daughter Lynsey.

The car was familiar now, and the journey less arduous, and soon we were giving Lynsey a hug, having a cup of tea and chatting about what we had done and what we were about to do. We had not eaten much during the day and our stomachs were demanding that it was time we went for a meal.

We walked into the town centre and had a pleasant meal in a newly-opened Italian restaurant that Lynsey wanted to try out. All too soon we had walked back to her home and bid our daughter a cuddled farewell before driving back to the hotel. It had been a long day and we needed our bed.

Sector 1 - Southampton to San Francisco

The Adventure Begins
Wednesday 4th January 2012

Deb and I were about to board a ship to travel over 35,000 miles around the world. This was special, so special that I woke up and could not believe that my life, that has been so ordinary, was about to turn a page to an adventure that few people ever experience.

Our plans for the morning were three-fold, and began with getting the hire car back to its owners. After that we could relax and look around the shopping centre where we had been on many previous occasions before the start of a cruise. Finally, we had to organise a taxi to take us and our luggage mountain to the cruise terminal and allow P&O to take over our lives for three months...

... simple!

We ate a hearty breakfast in the hotel knowing that it could be quite a while before the chance of food came along again. After a quick wash it was out to the car and a short drive along the road to the car-hire depot. This was easy as traffic was generally coming into the city rather than heading in the direction we were going.

At the depot we stripped the car of our last bits and went inside. We introduced ourselves and there was an instant flurry of computer activity resulting in being told that this was the wrong depot as there was one right next to the cruise terminal.

I protested that we had been told that the other depot was closed: the answer came back that it had only just opened and our booking had been changed (without us knowing).

After a few grunts of frustration we took directions and returned (with our bits) to the car and the now busy road back into the city. I must admit the other depot was ideal as it was at the back of the hotel where we were staying. Unfortunately this 100-metre journey had actually taken 30 minutes plus about three miles of driving to and from the other depot. Finally, where we should have been, the process was painless and before leaving we took a look at other possible cars that might have been more suitable for the luggage we struggled with on our journey to Southampton. Complete with a business card showing the number to call on our return we walked back to the hotel and onwards to the shopping centre. Plans now were to try and find me a pair of sunglasses to replace the ones I'd left at home, plus envelopes and a postage stamp for the document proving I had sold the car. Well, we found the postal bits, bought various other bits and pieces, even had coffee, but the sunglasses proved impossible. I have an eye problem which means I need very flat glasses with no transition of tint to avoid getting headaches. These are always difficult to find, but in mid-winter they are virtually unheard of, and those I did find were on special offer with a 50% mark up. I decided to wait for warmer climates as we sailed south.

Back at the hotel I sent off the car document and organised the taxi. Surprise, surprise, there were dozens of us with a taxi booked, as this hotel is very popular for cruise passengers. Time was nearly up so we set about bringing all the suitcases down to the lobby and camped ourselves on a settee along with around 30 other people with their piles of luggage awaiting their taxis.

I checked out at reception with butterflies starting to squirm in my stomach at the prospect for the remainder of the day and the rest of the winter.

Just a few minutes late, our taxi arrived. Its driver took a look at the suitcases, then his car, and exclaimed that it was going to be difficult. We were the only ones so far to have a traditional saloon car as our taxi, with the previous people getting estates or MPV vehicles. After a little coaxing our driver took on the challenge and soon, with one case perched on Deb's lap, we set off for the short journey to the Mayflower terminal where the MV Aurora was waiting for its 1800 (give or take a few) passengers.

Now everything became a smooth, well-planned, manoeuvre. First the suitcases moved from taxi to baggage trolley with little or no need for us to help. They were trundled off to a hole in the wall to be seen again in our cabin...

... hopefully

The taxi and its driver sped off for another appointment with a hotel lobby and we strolled into the terminal building with just hand luggage and a small package of documents. Normally we would have been able to use our 'Gold Loyalty Status' to get a priority check in, but today almost everyone was of the same status so we all queued together in a snake until we got to the front and a free desk welcomed us. Although the queuing had been a few minutes of mild frustration, it started the 'getting to know our fellow passengers' routine with the odd chat to those near us, and smiles all round. The process continued without a hitch and soon passports had been checked, forms had been signed, and we were directed towards the final security checks.

Security scanners are objects that should not cause any fear (to the innocent) but somehow they can produce just a tingle of concern that it might beep its disapproval and suspicion as you pass through. I had been caught out by the scanner on our previous trip by a metal strengthening strip in my trainers but this time the shoes would not be a problem. To save further embarrassment, and time, I quickly removed my belt, and transferred all the cash and metal objects from my pockets to my trolley bag. I walked straight through the machine (holding my trousers up by hand) without a beep and exclaiming success, restored belt and metal bits and pieces to where they came from. Deb scoffed at me as she also passed the scanner test, and we continued our way through the door, up the escalator, and onto the walkway to the ship.

Stepping into the atrium of Aurora we gave a mutual sigh and quiet giggle of excitement knowing that we had arrived, and the journey of a lifetime had begun.

Cruise passengers arrive at the ship over a period of several hours, either by car, or by coach from all over the country and, in this case, from several other countries. Some arrive early like us, while others get to the ship with only a few minutes to spare before it sets sail. Being early we nearly always have to wait for our cabin to be made ready, and get directed to somewhere to have a snack and wait for announcements.

We were confronted by a slight disappointment now with the realisation that the ship was still in the middle of a Norovirus outbreak. The ship had been struggling to rid itself of the virus on its previous cruise without success.

It was still operating under a strict regime of cleanliness, and avoiding unnecessary contact by passengers in eating areas until fresh cases ceased. We were directed to the Orangery buffet to find all the food was being served with a 'no touching' instruction for passengers. We quickly understood the situation, chose our snack and happily tucked into our first meal on board.

With the meal finished we took our bits of hand luggage and sat by the covered pool with a glass of wine to celebrate. We watched more people arrive, but by the time the wine was finished we heard the announcement that our cabin was ready. Five minutes later we arrived at cabin B144 that was to be our home for 14 weeks.

The holiday, that had taken years to plan, choose and prepare for, was finally beginning.

The First Evening and Settling In

We knew what the cabin was like so there were no surprises.
Well not for me, but Deb was delighted to find some flowers
and chocolates, plus a bottle of champagne cooling itself in the
fridge. I had ordered a welcome pack (at great expense) and
she soon found that it included a formal photograph and a
champagne breakfast on one morning when we fancied a treat.
Another card on the desk confirmed that Andrew and Lynsey
(our children) had arranged for some on board credit to be
added to our account, as a Christmas present. We had been so
delighted with such a thoughtful gift.

As yet there was no luggage to unpack except for my linen
jackets, cameras, laptop, and a few bits that had been put into
our hand luggage. So, the balcony was checked for comfort,
and below us we could see preparations for sail-away. The
familiar conveyor belts were transferring loads of suitcases to
the ship (where were ours?!) and mountains of food were
being moved around by fork lift trucks, but there were some
less familiar items at intervals along the quayside. Spotlights
sat on top of boxes alongside strange metal pipe structures,
and there were large inflatable red, white and blue material
tubes that were already being tested, waving around in the
breeze as air was pumped through them. Elsewhere there
were mysterious boxes with electrical connections that would
turn out to be a firework display.

.... This was not going to be the usual sail-away!

Our adventure was the first of a series of world cruises sailing
from Southampton over the coming week, and they were all
getting an extra special send off.

A quick check outside the door confirmed there was still no
luggage.

We went for a walk around the ship to remind ourselves of the already familiar layout and met several people who would become acquaintances for the next few weeks. Some looked lost and received a little helping direction whilst others were like us just checking out the bars and lounges to see if anything had changed. Deb went to the library in the hopes of getting a book or two but discovered it was not open quite yet. Bored with the walk we returned to the cabin in hopes of finding something to unpack but whilst many cabins had suitcases outside their door, ours remained deserted. Never mind, it was only the middle of the afternoon so we would just have to be patient.

Our steward made an appearance to introduce himself as Savio, and to ask if we wanted anything, as well as explaining the system that we already knew. We mentioned the lack of luggage but he seemed less than interested so we bid him farewell for now. A couple of minutes later there was another knock on the door – it was a waitress holding a bottle of champagne. Explaining that it was a mistake as we already had the one that I ordered, she insisted it was for us, and when I read the card, it turned out to be from my brother Ronald as a present for our retirement. Deb and I laughed and I rang my brother to thank him for the wonderful gift.

Still no luggage, so we went to the Orangery buffet for afternoon tea, just to stop us from getting bored of course, and to check out the sausage rolls.

On the way back Deb returned to the library and grabbed a couple of books to supplement the ones she had on her e-reader. It was nearly 4:00 now and the cabin was still bereft of any luggage. I went on a search to see if it was sitting in the service areas but there was no sign of it.

"Stay calm, it will turn up eventually".

A few minutes later the first case did appear, and although this reassured us that the luggage was actually on the ship, it was frustrating that so many other cabins seemed to be cluttered with cases. The first case was one with odd items such as underwear and socks which were quickly deposited in suitable drawers, but where were the other cases? I checked outside the door.... nothing, so I went on another search along the corridor and found one case in the stewards' service area. Scampering back to the cabin it felt like we were getting somewhere with clothes on hangers and drawers just starting to fill.

With the first cases emptied and their contents put away, we twiddled our thumbs until it was time for the welcome-on-board talk and the Muster Station drills. We have become very familiar with this 30-minute get together in a crowded room, listening to the same speech, and watching the same demonstration of how to put on a life jacket. We know it is imperative that everyone attends so we sat quietly through the procedure while spotting new cruisers who struggled putting the jacket on and insisted on blowing the whistle. It was soon over and we returned to the cabin.

It was getting dark now and sail-away was due soon. I desperately wanted a change of clothes before dinner but none of my shirts and less formal trousers were in the cases that had turned up so far. We had no real concerns as the dress code on the first evening was quite flexible, so we relaxed, opened the champagne, and went out on the balcony to check on progress with our first glass. We knew the routine with the band playing, and people hanging over the balcony rails chatting to their new neighbours and watching for the tell-tale signs of our departure.

Firstly the walkway from the terminal building was moved away from the ship with a *'beep beep'* to warn anyone in its path. Next an obvious clearing away of people from the ship except for the orange-coated stevedores ready to slip the mooring ropes into the water. All the activities were accompanied by the spotlights flashing across the ship and buildings plus the multi-coloured air tubes waving in the breeze like uncontrolled robotic limbs. The next surprise was that the strange metal pipes that I had seen earlier now sprayed a shower of glistening 'flutterfetti' into the sky producing a snowstorm effect over the side of the ship...

... absolutely magical

The captain then *'bing bonged'* his alert to let us know that all the departure formalities were completed, and that Aurora would shortly be setting sail for Madeira. The mooring ropes splashed into the water, and the ship's horn announced that we were free of the quay and ready to move away. After a few minutes of the band's final tune, the gap to the shore increased, and the fireworks started.

By now we were on our last glass of champagne and our slightly numbed minds were thrilled by the spectacular show of coloured sparkles, like thousands of diamonds, erupting from fizzing rockets accompanied by banshee squeals and thunderous explosions. It lasted no more than five to ten minutes by which time we were into the channel of the Solent and starting to move down towards the sea. Suitably impressed, and glasses empty, we returned to the cabin and found all the remaining suitcases outside the door.

Dinner time had arrived, but there was long enough to change into some clean clothes to feel just a little more respectable. It was time for the first of our 98 dinners on board, and to meet our new table mates. The rest of the unpacking could wait until we had eaten so we made our way to the Medina restaurant with the little card letting us know that our table was number 103.

The First Dinner

At the restaurant we were greeted by one of a pair of head waiters who first squirted disinfectant gel on our hands while looking at our table number. He then summoned the next waiter from a line to show us to our table, where we were courteously seated before he scampered away to re-join the queue of guides. It takes a while on the first evening to get through this exercise, but soon our personal waiter arrived and introduced himself as Paul. The other table guests soon appeared and as the napkins were flicked onto our laps, and the menus handed out by Paul's young assistant (Meghnath) we introduced ourselves. There was Jimmy and Isabel from Perth in Scotland, Mick and Brenda from Swindon, and Roger and Laura from Cornwall. The obvious question soon came along to find out how far we were all travelling, and much to our surprise, all four couples were completing the full world cruise. We had been led to believe that we would be on a table with passengers doing a mixture of journey lengths, but as long as we did not fall out with each other, the table guests would remain as it was for the complete cruise.
The conversations continued all through the meal with lots of questions about who had cruised on what ships to which destinations before. Everyone had cruised before, and all but Roger and Laura had been on a P&O ship. We were by far the most experienced cruisers but by no means the most travelled. All three of the other couples had travelled to different countries around the world, so whilst we had seen far more of the European destinations, the others had far more experience of the areas of the world we were about to visit. Work is rarely a subject that is brought up in conversations on a cruise but over the weeks we allowed ourselves to talk a little about our past, and our backgrounds were from differing areas of

business and different industries. Hence the table had a mix that turned out to be successful as we stayed together throughout the adventure. We did not eat together every night as we all took breaks from the formality of the dining room to use the Orangery buffet occasionally, or sampling the delights of the 'Select Dining' options in Café Bordeaux and the Pennant Grill. Most evenings we would catch up on our tours and experiences in the ports that we visited and laughed our way through the good, and sometimes not so good, days. During the meal an announcement from the captain (David Box) warned us that the weather was not going to be good during the night, with strong winds and a rough sea as we made our way down the Channel. This is one of the few times we can remember such a warning being made on board, so we knew that it was going to be a bad night. To be fair, we were on a ship, and it was mid-winter, so it was no real surprise that the weather was turning out to be rough.

The meal continued and the conversation did turn towards the state of the sea for a while, but it was soon forgotten. The menu and the food chosen were up to the standard we expected and the service from Paul and Meghnath was superb. Soon we were strolling along the corridor and saying a temporary cheerio to each other as we went our own ways around the ship. Deb and I returned to the cabin, where we found that Savio had prepared the bed, drawn the curtains, and left us our pillow chocolates. Our first task was to store the chocolates, and reopen the curtains before we set about the rest of the unpacking.

First evenings on a cruise tend not to have any significant entertainment shows as new passengers need to find their way around the venues, plus most people are tired from their journeys, and look toward an early night. Once we had finished unpacking, and squeezing the suitcases under the bed, our evening consisted of a stroll around the ship, popping into the different venues to see what was on offer. In Carmen's (the show lounge) there was some dance music being played, which we would be taking advantage of later in the cruise, but not tonight. Champions (pub-style bar) was quite busy but Andersons (quiet bar) was almost deserted, and even the Casino was not being very successful in attracting mugs to lose their money. With the ship already moving around erratically we avoided going up to the Crow's Nest bar high above the bridge at the bow end, where we knew the movement would be worse, and instead we returned to the cabin for a read and an early night.

As the light was turned off, my head was spinning with the excitement of being back on a ship again, as well as the anticipation of the days ahead. The sea was certainly letting us know that it was angry, as Aurora creaked and rocked its way down the Channel.

The crash each time the ship sank into the troughs of waves was quite dramatic, so this would not be a good night for weak stomachs. I took no chances, and swallowed a little white pill to comfort my stomach, and hopefully to allow me to sleep.

Into and Out of Biscay
5th to 7th January 2012

The first night had been a shocker. The wind blew at Force 10 from the moment we left the Solent, and although we did get some sleep, the constant booming of the sea against the hull plus the creaks and rattles constantly disturbed us. When we finally got up, the storm was still raging, but we had not reached the Bay of Biscay yet so the worst was perhaps still to come.

As the ship was still under Norovirus containment measures, the Orangery was not serving breakfast, so that had to be taken in the Medina restaurant with waiter service. This is a splendidly lazy way of eating but does not suit our style of grazing for the first meal of the day. We would have to put up with this for a day or two. To be quite honest we were not that enthusiastic about breakfast that day, as we were both still tired and, like many of the passengers, suffering from the side effects of sea sickness, and its remedies.

Aurora was very quiet on that first day at sea with people dozing in places where the noise was less dramatic, or the ship's motion less disturbing. Going out on the deck was not a good thing to do but the covered Crystal Pool made a reasonable compromise of getting some daylight whilst staying dry and warm. Unfortunately the water in the swimming pool was a constant reminder of the state of the sea as it moved around and splashed in sympathy with the sea's motion. We spent the day trying to catch up on lost sleep, and a high number of passengers just curled up in their cabins, with whatever remedy they chose, to see out the storm.

Deb did not want any lunch but I was feeling peckish so with the Orangery completely closed, and the Sidewalk snack bar similarly out of action I had to go to the restaurant again. The quality and choice of food is wonderful but formal seating and waiter service is just not my thing except for dinner.

By the afternoon we were into the Bay of Biscay but it seemed that the wind's force and the anger of the sea was reducing, although there was still a deep swell that was making the ship both pitch and roll. It was time to just lie and read or doze in the cabin.

We both went to dinner but there were a number of empty seats around the restaurant. Perhaps the weather was improving because we certainly felt more comfortable, and managed to enjoy the meal. The captain took the opportunity to make another announcement during dinner to advise us that some of the passengers were showing signs of suffering from the Norovirus so hygiene restrictions meant that the Orangery would be closed until further notice. I was a little confused how you can distinguish between sea sickness and Norovirus quite so accurately and quickly, but it was time to trust the experts and put up with the inconveniences if it meant not catching the illness.

After dinner we went to the main entertainment venue, the Curzon Theatre, to watch the evening cabaret by Jimmy James (without his Vagabonds) for a very enjoyable three quarters of an hour of his old songs. Deb is a serious Motown fan and was totally absorbed by the show.

When it was over we moved on to the Masquerade disco venue for a Motown themed quiz with one of the entertainment officers.

This stimulated the brain a little (well Deb's anyway) passing away an hour with a glass of wine, and almost winning a bottle. These evening post-show quizzes would become regular during the cruise as they reflected themed evenings or just posed 20 questions on general knowledge or musical topics. By the end of the quiz, lack of sleep was catching up on us so we had another early night. The ship was certainly less creaky and unpredictable in its progress now, so we were hoping for a better night.

Friday 6th January and we awoke after a much better night's sleep with the ship moving far more easily and comfortably. We'd completed our crossing of Biscay, and had started on the Atlantic crossing for real. The wind had dropped to a Force 3 or 4, and the sea state was rated as 'slight'. Even the temperature showed signs of improvement and reached about 12°C during the day.

What we didn't know until the reports being circulated got to us, was that there had been a major water leak during the night on E Deck with soaked carpets and puddles in the corridors and in a number of cabins. Whilst this was being fixed, the water supply had to be turned off and passengers had to leave their cabins as a temporary measure. These sorts of mishaps never get announced officially, but a cruise ship has a very efficient information-gathering system and communication channels.

Much of this process happens in the passenger launderettes, and stories that start as *"I think there has been a problem in......"* or *"Someone has fallen over and..."* are clarified (or not!) and suitably embellished before getting cascaded on to the rest of the passengers in lifts, queues, and bars.

The eventual stories can often have little or no similarity to the original mishap, and can result in *"The ship has hit a submarine and is returning to port"* or *"Three passengers tripped over a lady who fell down the stairs and one has died and two others are seriously ill"*. The officers on the Bridge also get to hear the stories and although many can be laughed at, some really have to be addressed and the truth (if there is anything that is true) has to eventually be announced.

On Aurora there were in the region of 1800 passengers looked after by a crew of about 900. The captain (sometimes called the Master) is in charge of everything, and everybody. He has a number of groups below him, starting with the bridge team who fundamentally get the ship safely from A to B. Alongside them is the engineering team who look after the mechanical aspects of Aurora, plus the electro technical team obviously dealing with electrical kit and gadgets.

The Chief Purser has a huge number of people under his control as he is in charge of the hotel aspects of the ship such as the reception, bedrooms, catering and cleaning. Also answering directly to the Purser is the entertainment team and they are led by the Cruise Director who has a group of talented people to organise and look after sports and exercise sessions, plus other activities such as quizzes, compering cabarets, and generally being around to talk to the guests. Aurora has a number of resident bands and musicians that play in the different venues. In the theatre there was the Miles Foreman Orchestra who occasionally played elsewhere, and a fantastic group called Caravan played a wide range of songs in the other venues, plus the Accent Duo and a trio called Kool Blue.

The cabaret and show acts are planned and booked in advance by P&O's Head Office ashore, and the Cruise Director normally introduces them when they come on stage in the theatre. These acts arrive on board at one of the ports and stay for a few days before being replaced by others. They normally perform two different shows, with two sessions for each, one for first sitting of dinner, and the other for second sitting. The final set of entertainers is the Headliners Theatre Company, and each P&O ship has one of these troupes supplied by an agency. The young singers and dancers are choreographed to perform perhaps ten different shows and reviews during a cruise. They are really talented and work hard to entertain the passengers. Occasionally they will help out the Entertainments team during other shows or games and sometimes one of them will accompany a port tour as representative of the ship to look after the passengers.

Back to our day at sea and we started with breakfast in the Medina again where we sat with some strangers and had a good chat about the usual *"How many cruises...."* and *"What is your favourite..."* questions. The breakfast was very nice, and we enjoyed the company, but we are looking forward to having the freedom to choose our breakfast style. The Norovirus was not affecting us in a physical way, but it was producing frustrations that were just niggling us a little.

During the morning we went to the first of the Port Talks delivered by Jo, who was the Port Presenter, and part of the Tours Team. The talk was on our first Caribbean stop of St. Lucia, and Jo was really very good and not at all like previous presenters we'd heard.

She gave a brief history of the island, a little about its culture, warned us about the poverty we might find, and described some of the island's highlights. She did not labour on the tours that she was ultimately employed to sell, but pointed out the things to see and then mentioned which tours would allow people to see these sights. For once this was not a *"sell, sell"* presentation but more of a *"what to do"*, no matter if you are going to do it yourselves, or by booking onto a tour through the ship. The talk gave us some ideas, but confirmed that the tour we had chosen and already booked was probably the one for us.

Following the talk we scuttled down to Carmen's, the cabaret lounge, where the dance teachers (Alan and Ginny) were attempting to show passengers the rudimentary steps of a Salsa. We were looking forward to improving our dancing during the cruise, and this was our first opportunity. After an hour we could certainly wiggle and step our way through the

Salsa with some co-ordination but I think we need a lot more practice before stepping out on the floor for real.

......well maybe we can give it a go one night.

The dancing gave us a little bit of exercise, but after lunch we ventured into the gym. There was a pleasant welcome from the staff that showed us the basics, before being let loose on the machines of torture. It was not very busy so we had a chance to try out the running machines, and the static bicycles, and after about twenty minutes we were both perspiring well. The machines are good and have a little video display where you can watch television channels or the speed of your efforts, calories burnt off and so on. We promised ourselves to go back to the gym as often and as regularly as we could manage.

Tonight was the first of the formal evenings meaning I was wearing a dinner jacket and Deb had the first of her posh frocks on. First stop was a 'Welcome on Board' party in the Crow's Nest, with the captain and his officers. These events are a chance to reduce P&O's profit by making the most of the free drinks, and we quickly discovered that along with the more visible wine, whisky, and gin, glasses of champagne were available, if you asked. We chatted to one of the officers as that can be a way of checking out rumours, and possibly getting more factual information, but importantly the waiters pay more attention to the officers with the most stripes. I seem to remember we were talking to a cadet officer on that occasion and struggled to get many drinks...

... we learnt to be choosier for later parties!

At these parties the captain makes a welcome speech and Captain David Box announced the usual overview of the cruise plus his hopes for good weather, but he was a little restricted on this occasion as Carol Marlow, P&O's Managing Director, was on board and, as his boss, she took over the speeches with her hopes for an enjoyable and wonderful cruise. She stayed on board until Madeira so at least shared the not-so-pleasant weather with us. Captain Box and Carol Marlow soon ended their show and disappeared at a high rate of knots towards the other party going in on in Carmen's. We carried on drinking until realisation dawned that it was dinner time.

We were last to arrive at our dinner table, slightly tipsy from the 30-minute binge but the others had also been to the party and had taken advantage of the drinks as well. The waiters put up with their slightly exuberant diners and the meal was very enjoyable.

After dinner we went to watch the first show from the Headliners in the Curzon Theatre. We had seen the show they were performing before but it was still worth watching as each troupe has a slightly different way of doing it. The theatre was full for the show, and the comments on the way out were very positive about this show and the entertainment in general. Throughout the trip, whenever the Headliners performed, the theatre was full and the passengers always came out with a positive acclaim for their spectacular shows.

With the theatre entertainment over, and still dressed up in our posh clothes, we bypassed the quiz in Masquerades and carried on to Carmen's, at the stern of the ship, to have a dance or two. The very popular band Caravan was playing and the dance instructors hosted the evening. These two were really very good, and as well as being good dance instructors, they offered an evening of fun for the passengers.

This had been a really pleasant day and we had relaxed into the holiday. Aurora had beaten the curse of Biscay, and was much steadier and quiet. Deb and I had great hopes of a good night's sleep.

Unfortunately, with less noise from the storm, we could now hear the wind blowing through the balcony door.

After putting up with it for an hour or more, we investigated where it was coming from without success, so returned to bed and slept fitfully for another night.

Saturday 7th January and I looked out of the balcony window where the sea has calmed significantly.

This view became our back garden for the next three months and it changed daily from an angry series of hills and valleys, to a smooth manicured lawn, or its colour varied from a cold dark expanse of water to a seemingly warm colourful garden pond sparkling in the sunshine.

We decided on a change of breakfast venue and went to Café Bordeaux for a waiter-served start to the day. Here there was a limited choice of tasty breakfast treats that were just that little bit more interesting than the traditional restaurant breakfast fare. It was such an enjoyable meal that we returned there for lunch as well.

In between the meals, I went to Reception to report the annoying balcony door, and Deb took the plunge and had a swim in the Crystal Pool that had finally had its nets removed. I lay nearby on a lounger with the sun coming through the glass roof and watched Deb who was alone in the pool enjoying the exercise. Some of the other early risers looked on in horror at someone actually swimming at speed, as most passengers used the pool as a place to cool down or perform very relaxed movements that roughly follow the principles of swimming. I know I should have joined her for a swim but my music occupied me as the ship came to life with an increase in the chatter, plus the 'tip tap' of the table tennis players. Soon most of the loungers were taken and with Deb by my side reading her book, the pool had new occupants.

This was the first opportunity for a pastime that I always love, and that it to just sit back and watch people. It could be someone passing by, or people around me talking, playing cards, reading, sleeping or just being in their own zone of meditation.

I am not perverted, I just like to see the differences in how we look, or speak, plus the smiles and little mannerisms we use when we communicate. It fascinates me.

Of course, a few of the people I watched were unusual in one way or another, and received a little more attention than the majority. These people all showed me something that was different, or special. Sometimes they were unique with strange dress sense or quirky hair styles, others had amusing traits, perhaps they were overly polite or extremely rude, and occasionally they were downright annoying. I considered most of them to be eccentrics making me smile when I saw them, and they all contributed to my holiday.

I will share a few of these people with you at intervals during this book but I must make it clear that we are all different, and what is eccentric to me may be quite normal for you, so nothing I write is meant to be insulting. If we were all the same, life would be predictable and the enjoyment of new things and experiences would be impossible.

Being lazy was one thing we spent a lot of time doing, but there were other things we could have done. Every morning and afternoon there were talks in the Curzon Theatre by either an expert in a particular subject, or passengers with a hobby or experiences to share. These were always well attended but I am a little choosy about what I listen to especially when the darkness of the theatre has been known to send me to sleep if the subject does not keep my attention.

Deb and I did go to a few and listened to several really very interesting talks, but the main presentations that both of us attended were by Jo with her Port Talks.

Mick from our dinner table was very interested in the talks and along with Roger was dripping in praise for one speaker who was giving a series of talks about air travel. He covered specific planes like Concorde, general history of the industry, air traffic control, or crashes. When they asked if I had attended them, I explained my total fear for flying and hence my disinterest in such subjects...

... they seemed rather surprised.

In the afternoon we returned to the gym and it was getting busier now that the ship was more stable, and attracting some of the less steady passengers to try out the machines. Deb found a bike which she favoured while I had no choice but to use the treadmill again. After about 20 minutes I had completed a little program that seriously pushed my pulse up, and made me drip with sweat. As I staggered over to Deb who had also finished and was waiting for me, I spotted a set of scales. This became a source of on-going amusement. While we attempted to use it to see if our weight was increasing with the abundance of food, we discovered that if you gently bounced on it repeatedly, the reading would change to whatever you preferred to see. Apparently I lost half a stone after 20 minutes on the treadmill on one day!

Late in the afternoon our routine was to have a shower and that day, as I rinsed off the results of the treadmill, Deb answered the door to two smiling engineers. They had come to look at the balcony door and proceeded to poke it, prod it, then spray and adjust it and were gone again before I finished my shower. Assuming they have done their job, the night should finally be quiet.

The evening entertainment was the second and final superb show by Jimmy James. He was leaving the ship when we landed in Madeira the next day. From the theatre we went to Carmen's and had a few dances. We were joined there by Brenda and Mick so had a pleasant chat over a drink or two. The entertainment team also put on a show based on the 'Deal or No Deal' TV show. Unfortunately it went on for a long time with an ever-decreasing audience, but the lucky passenger competitor stood her nerve and won £250 of on board credit. By then it was almost 11:00, and this was the latest we had stayed up so far and it confirmed my view that it takes two or three days to change from normal life to a relaxed holiday mode.

Tomorrow we would wake up to the Island of Madeira for the first of many stops on our adventure.

Norovirus

The first month of our cruise was badly affected by Norovirus. Because of its impact I feel it's a good idea to explain a little bit about what this virus is, and how it is spread from person to person as well as the measures that were put in place to contain it aboard Aurora.

As the name suggests it is a virus but it seems there are several different types or strains of Norovirus, but they all end up potentially causing Gastroenteritis.

In case you are not familiar with the name, gastroenteritis is an infection of the intestines that usually results in vomiting, diarrhoea, or both. I once had what my doctor thought was a dose of Norovirus that restricted itself to vomiting. In one night, I lost half a stone in weight.

Fortunately, it doesn't normally last very long and usually clears up within a few days. To an otherwise healthy adult, the only serious risk is becoming dehydrated.

Let's set the scene to explain how somebody catches it. Anyone who has the virus has the evil little bug in their stomach and intestines. When they go to the toilet and pass the diarrhoea, they also deposit thousands of particles of the bug. As the unfortunate person wipes their bottom, the bug may inadvertently pass to the hand, and it can also be sprayed into the air as the person flushes the toilet. The result is that particles of this living bug end up on the person's body. Hopefully the affected person will now thoroughly wash their hands with soap and water, and if they do, then the bug will probably be washed away. If hand washing is 'forgotten' or not performed adequately, that person will leave the virus particles on anything that they touch. For example, taps, door handles, stair banisters, furniture, crockery, cutlery, cruet sets, and very importantly food!

You can then catch Norovirus it in two ways.

Firstly you can eat the food that has been contaminated by the original poorly person. This tends to have dramatic effects with several people catching the virus at the same meal. Secondly you can touch a surface that is contaminated, and without thinking about it, transfer it to your mouth. You are probably the next victim. It only needs a few virus particles to spread its misery, and you can pass it to your mouth in simple ways such as touching or scratching your face, or smoking. You now discover a day or so later that you are ill, and then you become the potential means by which it passes to someone else.

This is a typical time line of the illness.

Initially you might just feel a little nauseous, with a headache perhaps. As time goes by you might get flu-like aches and pains. My own symptoms were feeling uncomfortable as if I had overeaten. The stomach now becomes the major player, and you might just vomit, and I promise you it will not be just once. Alternatively you might just have a stomach-ache and start a repeated dose of diarrhoea, or you might have both vomiting and diarrhoea.

This will probably last for a day or maybe two.

A major side effect is that you will become dehydrated and so the treatment is to drink often to maintain body fluid levels. If a doctor is consulted then they might prescribe some salts to enhance the drinks but this may not be necessary. It is unlikely that any other treatment is required unless the person has other underlying illnesses or conditions, but most people who are in that situation quickly know they need further assistance. To overcome an outbreak of Norovirus on a ship, the first challenge is to try and find the cause.

On a cruise ship it is most likely to be brought on board by a new passenger or crew member who has caught the virus elsewhere. Ships maintain very high standards of cleanliness in the food preparation and serving areas, but a rogue member of the crew can quickly start the ball rolling.

If the source of the outbreak is from food, there will be a rapid spread. The suspicion may focus on a member of the crew, and any of them feeling unwell will be looked for.

If the initial cause is a new passenger, then the spread will be much slower as it will not be in the food chain immediately. The major requirement to clear up an outbreak is for people who are ill to make themselves known. They can then be isolated to stop further contamination, and anyone close to them can be watched to see if they show similar symptoms. Once the 'offender' has been isolated, the next step is to have a cleaning program to wipe out standing sources of the virus. Equally important is to convince everyone to wash their hands thoroughly and regularly, especially after going to the toilet, and before eating.

As a passenger you have to trust that the ship's management and crew will do their best to clean the surfaces but YOU must do your bit to protect yourself, and avoid further spread of the evil bug.

Having seen Aurora under the influence of Norovirus I can tell you some of the visible things that happened during the outbreak.

The most obvious action affecting passengers was to stop them touching virtually everything involving food, or its service, until it was in front of the eater. The easiest way to achieve this is to shut down buffet outlets (the Orangery and Sidewalk café on Aurora) and not have any common or shared items such as condiments. Hence initially all the food was served by a waiter directly to the person eating it and if salt or pepper was required, then it would be added by a waiter.

Another visible action was to put signs all over the ship to remind people of the need to wash hands thoroughly after going to the toilet and before eating. Public toilet doors were also kept open so that there was no need to touch the handles. Every day there was an announcement by the captain or the senior doctor giving an update of the situation, plus emphasising the need to wash hands. At one point the doctor suggested that to be sure of washing your hands properly it should continue until you have sung 'happy birthday' which took about 20 seconds.

When they were not serving food, virtually all the available catering staff spent time cleaning every surface in the restaurants and hotel cleaners continually cleaned surfaces, bannisters and rails all over the ship. I assume this was happening with non-public spaces as well.

One measure that has become the routine on cruise ships is the squirt from a bottle of gel on the passengers' hands upon entering restaurant areas. A few years ago, when this first became common practice, there were many passengers who refused this simple safeguard (for whatever reason) but now it is very rare (and usually accidental) is someone misses the squirt.

At the time of writing this chapter, the medical experts were sceptical if this anti-bacterial gel had any effect on Norovirus contamination of hands, but a new ethanol-based product has shown positive results, but at this time it is not a commonly used substance.

If nothing else, the 'squirt' might cause the virus a bit of confusion and slow down its attack for a while, and it certainly helps to protect people from other bacterial bugs that might be present.

Anyone who did show signs of the virus were isolated in their cabins with food being brought to them until they were deemed safe to go out in public again. We knew a couple where the wife caught the virus and she found it very difficult to stay in the confined space of a cabin for two or three days. There was a surprise however as her husband was allowed to walk around the ship and eat as normal. I would have thought he was a very high risk at that time, but the experts presumably were confident with their actions, and as an aside he never did catch it.

There was a difficult period as we were approaching San Francisco with the American authorities being very much aware of the health status aboard the ship, and giving advice to help bring the outbreak to an end.

It was never said, but I suspect there might have been a difficult situation if the virus had not been beaten by the time we arrived in America, and speculation was suggesting we might not have been allowed to dock. We will never know as the ship was clean by the time we passed under the Golden Gate Bridge.

Strangely we had to return to Norovirus precautions after we left San Francisco as the virus is common in the city, and we had a lot of new passengers joining the ship and possible bringing new cases on board. Fortunately, we only had a few more days of the regime to endure before the all-clear was given, and the ship remained healthy (from Norovirus that is) for the remainder of the cruise.

Madeira
Sunday 8th January 2012

On this sleepy January morning we arrived in the capital city of Madeira at the port of Funchal.

Probably a high percentage of the passengers (like us) had been here before as there was no urgent stampede to get off the ship when we docked. It was Sunday, and it was still winter so Madeira would not offer much of interest at 9:00 in the morning. This was a chance for the passengers to stretch their legs after three days at sea, and some of the crew were probably also quite keen to get onto land again.

Once the Captain and his second in command had announced our arrival, and given the all-clear to go ashore (*"take careful to avoid the uneven surfaces and pot holes on the quayside"*) a slow but steady number of passengers bounced their way down the gangplank to go on an organised tour or just go for a stroll.

As for us, well we had woken from a wonderfully quiet (balcony door repaired) and calm night so we both enjoyed a really good sleep. The morning was bright with sunshine reminding us that we had sailed many hundreds of miles south from Britain and Madeira rarely suffers the same degree of cold as we have at home. So firstly we had a leisurely breakfast, in the Alexandra restaurant for a change, and while waiting for some toast we chatted to a couple going as far as Sydney. Our discussions lasted some time as for whatever reason the toast seemed to take an eternity to arrive, and as per usual it shattered as soon as you bit into it.

P&O do not seem to be able to make toast, and having spoken with Paul (our dinner table waiter) it seems the toast is made in one of the conveyer belt machines, but to avoid burning it, the guys use the machine at a low temperature and send the bread through several times. In other words, this is not toast; it is baked bread, and closer to being a biscuit. By the time we left the restaurant and had a wash, all the tours had left, and queues to get off the ship were short. So we each put on a warm jumper, grabbed cameras, maps, and money and we went ashore to catch the shuttle bus into the central area of Funchal.

As I said, we have been to Madeira a number of times so the plan today was to find some shops, for the things we forgot to pick up at home, and also to go on the cable car to the top of the island. What we didn't expect was the army of taxi drivers waiting outside the shuttle bus assuring us that we needed to have a guided tour of the area in their superb vehicles. After explaining several times, to several different drivers, at ever increasing volume, that we did not want their service we finally got free of this distraction and headed into the shopping area. By now the unexpected warmth had resulted in my jumper being tied around my waist and Deb's similarly removed and stuffed into her bag.

It really shouldn't be this warm in early January!

With sunshine dazzling us we reached a Christmas market with festive decorated trees, fake igloos, and shops selling hot mulled wine and various seasonal food and gifts. This was now totally surreal, with us in short-sleeved tee-shirts walking down this road which looked like a typical winter Christmas scene. Four days ago, we had left a chilly Britain where there was still frost in the mornings and a threat of snow, but now we were considering sitting in the sunshine to start a tan.

We didn't get anything in the Christmas market except for a few photographs and some happy memories of the scene. It took a few minutes now to walk to the cable car terminal where we met Jimmy and Isabel who were having a cup of coffee with their friends from Scotland. After a chat we went into the terminal and consulted the prices. That convinced us to change our plans as we could have bought an all-day bus pass for three Euros whilst a ride to the top of the hill and back would set us back fifteen Euros.

Outside the terminal we spotted a sign pointing to the Madeira Museum across the road, so off we went for a bit of historical culture. It was not expensive and we soon found out why. To be polite, it was boring, and the highlight was the roof garden with a view of the city, plus being amazed by various spring flowers. The Bird of Paradise plants were in full bloom (it was January, remember) along with others flowers that require full summer warmth in Britain. Photos were taken to prove to friends and family when we get back.

The only other thing that tickled our chuckle-muscles was the ride in the lift which we spotted was manufactured by a company called 'Schindler'. I know it is a childish word thing, but we both instantly laughed to be riding in 'Schindler's Lift'. It can't be just us that think that way as even the spellcheck on my laptop tried to convince me that I should have typed 'List' instead of 'Lift'.

Leaving the museum we found a supermarket where Deb managed to get some nail varnish remover (left at home) and I found a cheap pair of sunglasses in a tourist 'tat' shop nearby. A little further along the road we came to a peaceful park where we strolled (hand in hand if I remember correctly) amongst more flowers in bloom, lush vegetation to confuse our seasonal expectations, and trees in full leaf. Another laughable sight was one of the trees that had some form of fruit hanging from it that looked like an overgrown sweet potato (or was it a haggis?). The little sign simply described the tree as 'African Sub Tropical' so we had a jokey discussion with our Scottish friends to clarify that haggis does not grow on trees.

The walk in the sunshine, and on terra firma, was extremely welcome after being on board Aurora for three days, especially considering the bad weather we had suffered for most of those days. We were tiring now and the time spent in the gym was making my legs ache so we agreed that it was time to give up the walk and head back to the ship for lunch.

Café Bordeaux was chosen for our lunchtime snack, and afterwards we actually went to the open air Riviera Pool and stripped off in the sunshine. Deb went for a swim, and from then on, the Riviera Pool was her preferred one for swimming. The covered Crystal Pool was too hot as she used the swimming as exercise, whilst the Riviera Pool was far more suitable and usually less occupied as well. I personally found the open air pool just a little too chilly for my aging body, but I did use it a few times during the cruise and enjoyed the workout that swimming provided. It had been a long time since I swam, and those little 20-minute sessions reminded me of how good it feels to be in the water.

By the late afternoon Aurora was preparing to sail again and we knew there would be another week at sea before we got to our next port. There was no rush tonight as the dress code was 'Smart Casual' so we took the chance to have a go at the Individual Quiz in Champions bar, with 20 general knowledge questions. I know my limits when it comes to quizzes and although I enjoy the challenge, my aim is to get as close to the score that Deb gets rather than contemplating winning. The ship appeared full of intelligent people who are fans of quizzes like us and they regularly seemed able to just pip Deb by the odd question.

While we were having dinner and discussing our day on land, the captain announced that the Orangery would be opening the next morning for breakfast.

Cheers all around the restaurant.

The breakfast service would still not be self-service, as although it appeared the Norovirus situation was improving, the risk was still present so the waiters would serve the food on request.

After dinner we had a new act in the Curzon Theatre who came on in Madeira. His name was Bobby Knutt, and as well as appearing regularly on The Comedians TV show, he was also the voice of the Tetley Tea adverts. It was an entertaining act and even if some of the jokes were just a little familiar, he kept the laughs coming and worked his audience like a true professional. There was no abusive or blue material and comments overheard as we left the theatre (and the next day around the ship) confirmed my view that he was very good. It had been a busy day and an enjoyable one with the walk around Madeira plus the sun giving just a little more warmth than we expected. That was the first of many ports of call we would visit, and the only one we had visited before, until the places we would get to in the final ten days of the cruise. The adventure really began now as we were to sail across the Atlantic Ocean towards the Caribbean before seeing land again. We had never experienced a run of so many sea days before, so now we would discover if the on-board entertainment was enough to keep us all occupied.

Five Days Alone in The Atlantic
9th to 13th January 2012

We were on the first of five full days at sea with over 2,500 miles to go before we reached St. Lucia. We would now discover if we truly enjoy the complete cruise experience. Most travellers have a fortnight's cruise with just a handful of sea days, and the longest we have been continuously at sea in the past is probably three days. We have always enjoyed the sea-day element of a cruise so there were no immediate concerns, but for some passengers it could prove to be a problem.

Peace and tranquillity send me into meditation mode, and during one of those daydreams I tried to decide what the modern term is for what most people describe as 'sailing'. Aurora has no sails, and does not use steam as for propulsion so that can be discounted as well. Suggesting that we might be 'dieseling' takes away much of the poetic magic of a ship's journey, and again it would be wrong, as the actual method of turning the propeller is an electric motor. After considering it for some time I decided that a possible term could only be a combination phrase.

Hence for the rest of the week we would be 'diesel-generated electrically propelled' towards the Caribbean. The sailors I spoke to were not convinced and preferred simply 'sailing'. Anyway, back to reality and we discovered that by choosing a cabin on the port side of the ship, we had made a very fine decision. As we sailed a south-westerly course, the rising sun shone on our cabin balcony from dawn through to late afternoon. It meant that we were greeted by its warmth and brightness each morning as we got up and checked on the 'back garden' before going to breakfast. So we had the alternative of relaxing on the sun-baked balcony for a read (or more likely a doze in my case) rather than always searching for a suitable spot on deck.

Saying that, we usually went on deck for an hour after breakfast, and then again after lunch, but the balcony was an excellent place to go later in the afternoon. This meant that while continuing to worship the sun, if it became too hot we could pop back into the air-conditioned cabin and grab a cool drink from the fridge. This was a regular routine as I quite enjoyed staying in the sunshine but Deb preferred the cool of the cabin in the afternoon, so the balcony was the perfect compromise whilst still being in each other's company.

It was soon apparent that the climate in Britain was not what we would be subjected to during this cruise. The temperature soon rose to over 20°C and it was gradually getting warmer each day as we moved southwards. For some people this was proving a shock as they sunbathed to excess without appreciating the power of the sun. There were a few walking lobsters, and it was easy to start to dehydrate. Personally I was careful, whilst being thrilled with the unseasonal warmth. I can see why so many people like to get away from home at this time of the year. Chatting to strangers we heard that some passengers had been on over 20 world cruises, and there were also several people who had completed more than a million miles at sea. Without being stupid about it, I was envious of people who had the freedom and funds to do this, but looking at some of these seasoned travellers, they didn't seem to have the same thrill on their faces at the new sights and experiences as us 'virgins' of long distance cruising.

So other than sunbathing, what else do passengers do to keep themselves amused on sea days?

Well maybe it is not an amusing task, but washing clothes became necessary. We took enough clothes to last us a couple of weeks before a visit to the laundry became necessary, but by then we were running short of underwear. For passengers who were on just one or two sectors, and hence having to fly home, the weight limits for air travel seriously restricted clothing and for them doing the laundry became a regular necessity.

Now the cruise ship launderettes are not an ideal place for men. They are small rooms where the women passengers gather to listen to, and discuss stories or comments that have been overheard...

... well almost heard.

When the washing has been completed, the ladies return to their friends and family to spread the (enhanced and exaggerated) gossip and rumours. I had a major guilt trip about leaving Deb to do all the washing, but I really felt like an unwanted interloper when I entered the room. The talking reduced in volume and whispers behind cupped hands with looks in my direction gave the impression that I was not to hear the rumours as I was not experienced in the art of 'gossip'. Deb on the other hand just listened and ignored without any problem and I just popped back and forth to gather completed washing and hang it up in the cabin.

The launderette gossip was a major news-gathering and communication channel, and even the captain was forced to comment on the gossip there during some of his speeches, although usually it was to dispel the rumours...

... and there were a lot of rumours in those 14 weeks!

The laundry was done for another few days, so what else? Sea-day mornings and afternoons included regular talks or presentations in the theatre or the cinema. Usually they started with a mid-morning port presentation in the Curzon Theatre by Jo, and we both attended virtually every one of these talks. This was a major necessity as many of the places being visited were just names of cities or countries that we have only seen in books or on television. We were spending huge sums of money to visit these places, so it was vital to know something about them before deciding what to do in the short time available at each port. Long before setting off on our journey, we had tours pre-booked at virtually every port.

Our choices were partly based on the brochure information but there was also a serious amount of 'pot luck' involved. The port presentations became the decision-maker to either stay with our first choice tour or change to something else. Generally the talks supported most of our initial choices but also enhanced them by giving us a lot of things to look out for, as well as suggestions to occupy the rest of our time when the tour was over. Of course sometimes we realised that our choice was not the best so we would trot along to the tours office and change it for something more suitable.

There were also other daily talks by professional speakers, or passengers with a passion for a subject that they could pass on to the rest of us. These talks usually resulted in the theatre being almost full of willing listeners, but I have to say that only a handful of talks appealed to me throughout the cruise.

There were three or four celebrity speakers who came on board for a few days during the cruise and gave talks about their lives and work.

These were really popular, and good seats were always at a premium. The first such guest was former MP and broadcaster Martin Bell in his white suit. We had seen him on our previous trip on Aurora and knew his talks about his career in news broadcasting would be popular but we avoided them as we'd heard them before.

Elsewhere on the ship passengers had the opportunity to join in with games, classes and competitions.

For the thinking and creative people there were classes on bridge, cribbage, painting, and handicrafts, plus talks on jewellery, cosmetics, skin care, and weight loss. If you were a little more energetic there were dancing lessons, walk a mile sessions, Pilates, and aerobics. Other passengers had the Aurora Choir hour each day, and there was even amateur dramatics available for some of the cruise.

For the competitive, prizes could be won by playing deck quoits, shuffleboard, and table tennis every morning and afternoon, as well as daily sessions on the golf simulator. Organised games of cricket attracted a few aging passengers each afternoon in the netted court, where you could also play tennis, football, or basketball. The three swimming pools attracted a small band of aquatic fanatics as well as other passengers who used them to cool down in at regular intervals.

There were also a few more specialised get together meetings. Solo travellers had a coffee-and-chat hour in the mornings, and multi-denomination religious services were held each Sunday, with daily services for those with a more devout faith. Freemasons also had private meetings, and one or two other groups with strange cryptic names occasionally locked themselves away in the Uganda function room.

Finally of course the sun shone for most of the sea days and a lot of people simply enjoyed many hours of absorbing its warmth and getting a tan while they read a book, or listened to music.

... absolutely wonderful.

A major aspect of relaxing at sea is the amount of time passengers spend just looking at the water. It changes according to the weather, perhaps smiling in sunshine or sulking in the shade. We always watch the oceans for that thrill of spotting turtles, dolphins, whales or other marine creatures, plus seeing the different ships that come into view.

Only after the first couple of days did I realise that I had not seen another ship since Madeira, and the reality of the vastness of the ocean humbled me. One morning at breakfast there was a *'bing bong'* and the officer on watch announced that on the starboard side there was a ship. Yes, they were as excited as we were spotting another vessel, and the officer went a little over the top by telling us all about the bulk carrier informing us of its name, where it was from and going, what it was carrying and even the Captain's name...

... they must have been very bored on the bridge.

That just about covers the daytime activities, except those meals need to be factored in as they are an important break from the culture, sport, or serious relaxation.

In the evening there were quizzes galore to suit most people's tastes and intellectual standards. Music played in at least three venues as well as the theatre having a show of some sort each night. Dancing was normally hosted in Carmen's for ballroom and sequence fanatics and Masquerades had a late night disco. The ballroom dancing was very popular but I never saw the disco crowded, though this reflected the age profile of the ship which was a little towards the older end of the scale. Although I can only comment on my own memories, I don't believe I was ever bored, in fact sometimes there just weren't enough sea days to fit in all the things I wanted to try out. So, for this first five-day period, and many more to come, Deb and I sampled what we fancied, and hardly ever asked the question *"What shall we do now?"*

Landfall at St Lucia
Saturday 14th January 2012

Land again as we had arrived at the Port of Castries on the island of St Lucia. This was our first-ever time in the Caribbean and initial impressions were pretty positive. It was dry and warm with an expected maximum temperature of just below 30°C, although there was a warning that showers are always possible at this time of year.

We had a tour booked and it meant getting up early to be on time. I had set the alarm for 7:00 am, but it was not needed as we had neighbours who struggled with the idea of changing time zones as we sailed westwards. When we went to bed at night (typically 11:00 pm) the couple next door must have been in bed for some time as one of them was already snoring. He (or maybe she!) was very good at snoring and could possibly have won prizes for it, but our routine read before lights out usually pushed us from being tired to exhausted and sleep was rarely a problem. Anyway, as a result of our neighbours going to bed early, it also meant they woke up early, usually by 6:00. This got worse as the clocks continued to move backwards, and their early wake-ups drove me slightly insane until they left us in San Francisco.

Getting up early meant less of a rush for us, and we had time to look at the view from the balcony before breakfast. This was probably how I would have described a Caribbean scene with a sandy beach and palm trees in one direction and the city beyond the harbour in the other.

Around us were small houses of different colours, plus lush vegetation on the distant hills that overlooked Castries. The harbour itself was typical of so many that we have seen and sadly the container terminal destroyed some of the magic of the scene.

With breakfast over we cleaned our teeth and grabbed cameras and bottles of water. The port was literally in the middle of the city and we had a short walk from the quay to where the minibus was waiting for us. Our tour would take us to see a few highlights of St Lucia and would be stopping at a local craft factory, but the main stop would be at a nature reserve in a small rain forest. We set off with a local guide who seemed to be related to the bus driver, and at times they broke into the local Creole language. This seemed to be when the driver decided that the guide had not mentioned something he felt was important. After some clucking and probably abuse she usually expanded the description accordingly. We were introduced to some unusual sights as we drove along the narrow twisting roads and after two schools and a college, we realised that the islanders are very proud of their education system. The importance of education would be a common theme in most of the small islands we visited but it came as a shock initially to have (as far as we were concerned) mundane business-as-usual buildings pointed out to us.

As we drove away from Castries, and up into the hills we started to see real poverty, with ramshackle tin-roofed huts that were sometimes in serious need of repair, alongside rusting cars or vans needing similar major attention.

The local people stood around in far from new clothes, and watched as we passed with no sign of joy or laughter on their faces. We had been warned that the cruise would take us to communities where life is far simpler and things we take for granted are just not available, and St Lucia brought this home to us.

After a few miles we arrived at the Caribelle Batik craft factory where children surrounded us as we got out of the bus. They tempted us (unsuccessfully) to buy small posies of flowers, but we ignored them as our group concentrated on following the guide. Down in the garden we heard the sounds of a local man playing a steel drum to entertain us. Inside the Colonial-style building local ladies proudly showed us how Batik printing was achieved to decorate material. This is a typically Caribbean craft consisting of pouring hot wax onto the material as a pattern and then soaking it in a dye to colour the material except wherever the wax has been applied. The process is repeated several times to build up some complicated and very attractive patterned clothing such as dresses or shirts. The factory shop gave us the opportunity to buy the clothes, or other souvenirs to boost the local economy. Yes, several items were purchased, to the delight of the local ladies, and soon it was time to return to the minibus to continue to the nature reserve.

Everything seemed to move at a slow and relaxed pace on the island and our guide educated us about St Lucian life as we wound our way further into the hill side.

The only thing that seemed to move with any urgency was the teenage boys on their high-powered motorbikes. Our driver *"tutted"* his disapproval as each one roared past him or cut him up coming from the other direction.

Some things really are the same the world over!

We arrived at the 'Lushan Country Life' nature reserve and like all things in St Lucia it was understated. A small gateway with a crude hand painted sign hanging by a rusty chain, welcomed us to this oasis of tranquillity in an island that was already laid-back. Stepping inside we were greeted by our guide, a knowledgeable teenage girl, who handed out smooth tree branches as long walking sticks to help us keep our balance on the steep and sometimes slippery paths to come. Making sure we were all ready for some exercise we set off along a well-worn track into the woodland.

Our guide was well-versed with a script including jokes to keep our attention, but she also showed a natural passion for the forest and its environmental importance. After pointing out and naming different trees, she focussed our attention on a ginger plant and explained how the root is used as a natural remedy for all kinds of ailments, and gave us all a small sample to smell or taste. We went deeper into the forest with the canopy closing over a little more.

All around us unseen birds were warning each other of our approach.

... although I preferred to think they were saying hello.

Before long we were smelling plants again, and this time it was Aloe Vera, and we were taught about its medicinal and beauty properties. We were then shown a sign displaying the Creole name of a tree and a volunteer was asked to try and pronounce it to the amusement of the rest of us. We never did find out the purpose in life of the 'Turtle Testicle' tree.

... I've no doubt it has medicinal benefits for something.

After a good stroll we were given a demonstration of traditional cooking by a typical Caribbean matriarchal woman with a chance to taste some of her delightful fish nibbles. Thanks and applause given we set off again to see and smell more herbs before coming to a display of locally grown fruits with a chance to sample the intense taste of freshly picked Caribbean fruits. This was turning out to be a magical place and the hour or so we spent there made us forget the poverty and to concentrate on the island's beauty and innocence.

On the way out many accepted the chance to taste a local speciality – banana ketchup. To our surprise it was not strongly banana flavoured, and more a spicy version of its tomato cousin. Yes of course we bought some, and several of our group also purchased other items in the small shop. Time to go and we returned to Aurora down the winding lanes with more

schools pointed out by the friendly tour guide and her driver.
It had been an eye-opening tour and I was beginning to
understand the appeal of Caribbean life with its laid-back
approach to seemingly everything.

The climate encourages relaxation, and the natural plant life
gives the taste buds a thrill long forgotten by western society
with its supermarket shelves full of fruit or vegetables which
have travelled long distances, and cool stored whilst unripe.
Back on board our air-conditioned luxury ship Deb and I
reflected on a wonderful morning of an experience that
Mediterranean destinations have not quite matched. St Lucia
was making us realise that this world cruise was going to open
our eyes on so many new places and that surprises would wait
to excite us for the rest of the winter.

Lunch over, we quickly returned ashore to look around a little
of the town of Castries and more importantly to find
somewhere to buy some souvenirs. We found a street with
stalls on either side selling fruit and vegetables, together with
household items and a sprinkling of souvenirs. Reggae music
played everywhere and Rastafarian men smiled as we passed
them. Many appeared under the influence of something, and a
sweet herbal-based smell hung in the air from the large
cigarettes being smoked. One gentleman appreciated us
gently swaying and jigging to the music and with some heavily
Creole-based verbal encouragement grabbed my hand to have
a dance. I was out of my depth here and after a smile and a
tug of my arm we carried on down the street laughing and a
just a little relieved to be free.

The street market was dominated by stall holders making a
living by selling their produce, but every now and again there
would be a little old lady with a newspaper spread on the road
to display her small pile of local fruit or sweet potatoes.
She was not there to make a living; she was there to make

enough money for her family to live another day. It was such a confusing mixture of business and survival.

With no souvenirs as yet, we went into a large covered market building where there were far more stalls designed to tempt tourists with all kinds of local items, plus imported tat of course. There was Batik clothing like we had seen earlier on our tour, and more interestingly carved wooden objects that took our fancy. Deb bought a summer dress and a small wooden dancer. Hopefully they were locally produced but even if they are not, they will remind us of that day.

The only disconcerting thing about the market was the abundance of stalls selling liquids in second-hand bottles with the original labels left on, and certainly not describing the current contents. As the sellers were usually locals speaking in Creole, we never did find out what they were trying to get us to buy but I don't think it would ever meet our Western standards of hygiene, and probably not our taste either.

We had one last purchase to make and that was to replenish our cola stock for our fridge, and this meant going into a local supermarket. The drink was found and as we approached the till, I realised that we had no local currency and no small value US Dollar bills. We ended up with a lot of local change that could not be used or converted, so we had to accept that it was an expensive bottle of coke. Fortunately on the way back along the road we met Mick and Brenda who were out to get a local beer but needed some local currency. Success, we handed over our coins in return for a drink on the ship at a later date.

Mick and Brenda were just retired like ourselves, and had travelled all over the world. They had set themselves an objective to have a drink of the local beer at every place we stopped as long as the local religion allowed. Apparently they achieved this except at the very first stop in Madeira where

Mick didn't have the confidence to take on the Portuguese language. The four of us spent many evenings together in the bars chatting, laughing and attempting quizzes. Mick had an amazing memory for musical topics, and he and Deb made a team that was hard to beat.

Hot and tired we returned to Aurora and relaxed in the sunshine and reflected on our memories for the rest of the afternoon. Soon the ship was pushing away from the dock and we set a westerly course again for our next stop.

There was a buzz around the ship with many passengers shocked at the news that the Costa ship Concordia had run aground during the previous night, then capsized and sank. A small number of passengers were dead and others missing. It was a reminder to everyone, that although cruise ships are inherently safe, things can still go wrong.

With our ship back at sea again, life returned to normal with dinner and a show by Colin 'Fingers' Henry. He is a comic pianist (hence the 'Fingers') and it was his second and final show. He had a good mix of jokes and music with a trademark trick of playing the piano while standing on his head... *weird*. After the show we went up on deck at the Riviera Pool where there was to be the late night Tropical Party. This turned out to be really entertaining, and having each been draped with a plastic flower 'lei' we danced for a while to the best band on board (Caravan) accompanied by a few glasses of wine.

Although lots of people were dancing, one young woman who loved to dance stood out and caught most people's attention. Her style was energetic, involving serious shaking, hopping, twirling, and flicking of her skirt. During the cruise several men attempted to dance with her, but she never accepted their offers, preferring to entertain herself by herself. We often saw her at the back of the dance classes but no matter what tempo we were attempting, she would adapt it to match her personal style. When music was being played on the open decks, she appeared and bopped around to virtually any beat.

'Dancing Girl' was one of the characters of the cruise until she left us in New Zealand. The mere mention of *"did you see the girl dancing….."* and most of us pictured her instantly. She did nobody any harm, and entertained us.

Unfortunately for the Tropical Party, the weather turned nasty and it started to rain after about half an hour. Undeterred, the entertainment team tried to keep us happy with a series of songs with some connection to rain.

There really are a lot of songs about rain, and the audience groaned as each new one blasted out to annoy us. The rain continued and after about a half an hour the last soggy dancer gave in and retired to shelter, and a halt was called to the evening.

It had been a funny evening in the rain and we laughed our way to Café Bordeaux for a late night cup of hot chocolate. It was served really milky and sweet, and became a regular drink to finish the nights over the next couple of months.

St Lucia was the first new place we visited and turned out to be spectacular because of its warmth, and beauty, but also because of its innocence. It is typically Caribbean and not totally spoilt by the greed that taints so many places.

Perhaps being someone already immersed in the lifestyle of material greed I might sound as if I am trying to hold back progress but I hope this innocence continues for as long as possible. Unfortunately, based on what we were to see as the cruise continued, it will be difficult to maintain that sweet simplicity for long.

Just Another Sea Day
Sunday 15th January 2012

We had a day at sea again before our next stop but as well as
the routine activities that I have already mentioned there were
a couple of special treats.

Now I had been having concerns that someone in the crew was
using a catapult to fire little lumps of food into the sea from
somewhere below us on the ship. I was constantly seeing
something fly from the side of the ship and skim along the
surface of the sea before dropping into the water. This was the
day when the mystery was cleared up.

It was not man-made but a magical creature called a flying fish.
In the warm waters that we were now in, flying fish abound
and as their swimming was disturbed by our large ship they
leapt from the sea and flew (or more accurately glided, I
believe) for a significant distance before returning to their
natural environment. So what I was seeing was the fish
escaping from Aurora. This became apparent because of some
more creatures paying us a visit, which were identified by the
ship's officers as masked booby birds.

While I was lazing on our balcony I noticed a group of these
birds flying alongside Aurora in formation like a squadron of
fighter planes. Occasionally they would suddenly screech in
excitement and dive into the sea. Getting curious I woke up a
little and watched their display with more enthusiasm. The
birds were flying along again peacefully when I just caught a
glimpse of something shooting away from the ship and then
the birds performed their screeching dive in that direction.

I was wide awake now and my men-with-catapults theory was
quickly destroyed as I saw another flying object and this time I
could see the shape of a fish with fins fluttering as it hugged
the contours of the waves. Down came the birds stalking the

poor flying fish and then diving on their prey. If successful (and they often were) the birds would quickly bob up to the surface again and swallow their meal in an instant so that they could flap their way back into the air to continue the raid on these very unusual fish.

This display of escaping fish and well-fed birds continued for over an hour with the birds circling the ship looking for shoals of the creatures from above and then coming in for attacks as the ship caused the flying fish to leave the water. We had several days when flying fish were giving their show, but the birds were less common and only appeared when the numbers of fish were high.

Our other treat that day was a guest speaker who filled the theatre for his first talk. This was John Challis who played 'Boycie' in the BBC's Only Fools and Horses, and the follow up show, The Green Green Grass.

John Challis talked about his early career in many programmes such as Z Cars, Dr Who, and Citizen Smith. I felt embarrassed to admit I had never spotted him before he showed the footage. He made his major mark with Only Fools and Horses and his catch phrase of *"Marlene"* in that slow deliberate way, plus the facial expressions copied by anyone who remembers his character. Of course, he milked it in the talk but the audience never ceased to laugh at him. He also talked about the spin-off show (The Green Green Grass) which was set at his own estate in Shropshire, but perhaps this was not quite as well known by some of the passengers.

John stayed on the ship for several days and made a number of appearances with more talks plus numerous visits to other activities around the ship. Although having a holiday with his wife, he was quite amenable to having a chat and seemed to be at home with the passengers, and not aloof as is the case with some of the celebrities we've encountered.

In the evening we listened to a male singer by the name of Mark O' Malley, even though normally we avoid watching singers. He was luckier because the write-up for him mentioned that he had been in Les Misérables and Deb is very taken with that show. Unfortunately he let us down and spoke too much about his life between songs. He didn't sing anything from Les Misérables either and that really disappointed Deb. After his show we had another go at a music quiz in Masquerades and we were successful winning a bottle of wine. Let me correct that last statement now to come clean and say that 'Deb won a bottle of wine' as I just sat and encouraged her by agreeing with the answers she dragged out of nowhere. There was just time enough for another hot chocolate in Café Bordeaux to round off another day before our second Caribbean Island the next morning.

Captivating Curacao
Monday 16th January 2012

Today we were visiting the Dutch-controlled island of Curacao. I got up and put the kettle on to make a cup of tea in my normal way and opened the curtains in time to see our approach to the port of Willemstad. My first impressions were that this was a more organised island with a purpose-built cruise terminal, compared to the simplicity of St Lucia. There were tents erected presumably to be used to tempt us to buy local items.

Off we went for breakfast as we had another tour booked, so an early start was required. Today we'd be looking at the sights of the island, with stops at a museum, some caves, and a liqueur distillery.

Our instructions were to meet on the quayside at 08:30, but as we prepared to queue it started to rain and it rained like I had rarely seen it before. This tropical storm consisted of large drops, many of them hitting the ground and splashing up with such ferocity that it looked like a layer of water had formed just above the ground. The visibility also dropped as if it was fog, and there was no sign of the rain stopping. We had our pakamacs with us and these were put on in readiness.

Strangely we were at the front of the queue to leave the ship with most people hanging back waiting for the rain to ease. There was no time to hang about so when the gangplank was declared open, Deb took a deep breath and went for it. I followed still trying to do up the zip on my pakamac as Deb reached the quay and was splashing her way for 50 metres or so to the tents and shelter.

I soon arrived as well, but looking back there was reluctance by most of the passengers to join us for a moment or two.

As the tent eventually filled with damp passengers, the rain stopped and we were directed to our respective coaches according to our tickets. Today we had coaches rather than the minibuses we had in St Lucia. Our guide announced herself as 'Wha-Wha' and explained that this was not her real name, but that she had adopted it for her job as it was as close as her young niece could get to her real name. At least we all remembered what to call out if we wanted to attract her attention.

Off we went and once again we had the local schools pointed out as well as more major landmarks. Our first stop was the Curacao Museum which sounded impressive and although small was actually a very pleasant place. The museum and its grounds were once a military hospital and the main building was a beautiful Colonial-style mansion with steps leading up to the entrance, and imposing windows covered by shutters. Wha-Wha educated us with the history of the building as we went from room to room, and also pointed out and described some of the more significant artwork. Many of the paintings were a little abstract and not really my taste, but it was obvious that the collection was of a high standard, and reflected island life as well as the occupants of the house. One item of some rarity was an instrument called the 'Carillon', which consisted of a keyboard connected to a series of bells that hung around the outside of the building. Although very old and in need of repair, our guide gave us a quick rendition of *'Oh when the saints come marching in'* to show how it sounded. Our laughter and applause made her smile with delight.

Outside in the grounds there was a further building housing another major exhibit – the cockpit and engine of one of the original Dutch planes that serviced the island many years ago. With no interest in planes or flying this was not my cup of tea so I quickly returned outside. The grounds had a number of statues and sculptures along with traditional grass-roofed houses...

... much more interesting!

Back aboard our tour coach we moved on to the next stop via more schools, accompanied by descriptions of the larger hotels, the island's oil refinery, airport, and several examples of middle and upper class housing......*not very interesting!*

We were on our way to some caves but Wha-Wha made a diversion in the route to check out some old disused salt lakes where a colony of flamingos often visited. Our lovely guide made her money for the day at this unplanned stop thrilling us with a wonderful sight. There were upwards of a hundred flamingos seemingly grazing the lake, but more importantly, they were pink! The ones I have seen in parks in Britain have never been fully pink, so this was special.

Onwards again and we arrived at the Hato Caves with their entrance about half way up a cliff. Long ago the caves had been at sea level and were used as a hiding place by escaping slaves. The indigenous population were frightened to go into the caves and so the slaves had a safe (if unusually dark) place to live. Over the years the water level has reduced significantly leaving the caves now high above sea level.

OK, the caves were interesting, but I have seen more spectacular ones in Britain. It was cool, and the underground lakes (still above sea level remember) were quite dramatic, and the walls had all kinds of colours from minerals and the algae growing upon them. We were also treated to a look at some bats asleep on the roof. It was good to see that the local people are trying to safeguard the caves by not allowing flash photography to prevent the algae being destroyed, and also to avoid disturbing the bats too much.

At one point there was a hole in the roof of the cave to the sky above and we realised it was raining again. As we walked across that area of the cave we received a cool shower from outside.

Once outside the atmosphere had freshened up from the rain and there was obviously more bird song than when we went in. An added bonus was the sight of iguanas crawling around in the trees and back down at ground level we were delighted by the sight of one paddling in a puddle. The obligatory souvenir shop sold a few cooling drinks but little else so we were quickly back on the bus and away again.

The final stop on the tour was the Chobolobo Curacao Liqueur Distillery. This is the place where the famous liqueur is distilled and packaged, but our visit was restricted to the accompanying shop and seeing pictures describing the process. Never mind, they gave us a very pleasant tasting session and a chance to buy some of the drink to take home. Several people took advantage of the cheap prices but Deb and I realised it was not something we would drink at home, so we just browsed.

From there the tour took us back to Willemstad and a drive around the city to see more schools, and now universities as well. One major landmark was a huge road-bridge that was made in Holland and shipped in pieces to Curacao for assembly.

As we neared the centre of the city our guide showed us the market, and the Post Office to help us later if we decided to look around. This seemed a good option so at the end of the tour we thanked and said goodbye to Wha-Wha and set off on foot to soak up the culture, sounds and smells of the commercial side of Curacao.

When I said sounds and smells I was not being silly as music played almost everywhere, especially as it was the lunchtime and the cafes and bars were busy, and this was where the smells came from. Caribbean food aromas wafted into the streets and mingled with coffee and different food smells from all over the world, making our nasal senses tingle. Hunger is not a common condition on a cruise ship so we didn't give in to the food, but instead set about buying some postcards and getting them sent home to our family, especially to Deb's mum.

Wherever you go on holiday in the world, postcards are easy to find so once chosen and written we went to the Post Office to get stamps. Just like at home the Post Office suffered from too few staff to service the customers, but rather than a snaking queue we simply grabbed a numbered ticket (like in our supermarkets) and waited for our turn. This was less annoying than in Britain, but it only worked because the building was huge and had seats all over the place.

On the way back to the ship we visited the market and saw similar stalls to those we encountered in St Lucia. Wooden souvenirs and summer dresses were beautiful but didn't tempt us that day. We again saw a mix of large commercial outlets along with old ladies and their small bundles of fruit and vegetables. There were also more second-hand bottles of unrecognisable liquids that we continued to avoid.

Time to get back to Aurora now and the route took us over the harbour. The primary crossing method is a swing bridge, but we arrived during one of the many instances when it was open to allow ships to enter and leave. Instead we took a ferry over the waterway and squeezed into the boat with crowds of other commuters.

As I jumped off the ferry I broke the sunglasses that I had bought in Madeira.

Deb laughed at my clumsiness but I was annoyed. Making our way back towards the cruise terminal it appeared impossible to find a suitable shop where I could get another pair, but I did buy a tropical shirt to wear on party nights. Having just about given up, and resigned to buying expensive sunglasses on board the ship, we turned into the last street and there was an advert for sunglasses in a shop window. They were not exactly what I wanted, but the pair I found was cheap and would keep the headaches away until I could find something more suitable. Our visit to Willemstad finished with an ice cream as we looked out over the water towards Aurora dominating the terminal. Curacao was different to St Lucia: it was more modern, commercialised, and more prepared for the tourists that arrived every day from cruise ships and the airport.

Was it better?

To be honest I really enjoyed Curacao and felt comfortable, but I preferred the slow pace, the chaos, and innocence of St Lucia. Of course that might be because I was just visiting it for one day, and did not have to suffer the poverty of many of its people. Curacao still had poverty but it was not so apparent and so the people appeared happier, and certainly the people we saw were smiling and laughing more. Maybe I was being selfish, wanting to experience simplicity, whereas perhaps I should be applauding how Curacao and its people have developed with a desire to be more like the rest of the commercialised world.

On our wish list, Deb and I wanted to paddle in the Caribbean but we never managed it. It was one of many dreams and wishes that didn't come true on the cruise, so we will just have to go back one day and try again!

Back on board we settled into ship life again with a delicious dinner followed by a show in the theatre by a magician called Thomas Anthony. Later we took part in another quiz and won a second bottle of wine.

The Caribbean islands were behind us and we continued on towards one of the highlights of the cruise. After another day at sea, we would arrive at the Panama Canal and transit from the Caribbean Sea to the Pacific Ocean.

Farewell To the Atlantic
Tuesday 17th January 2012

Next day, our last day on the Atlantic side of America, was wonderful with dawn-to-dusk blue sky and hot sunshine beaming down on a flat calm sea. We made the most of the weather to further change our skin colour and to enjoy the sensation of heat. It wasn't totally lazy as we both swam in the morning, and both had a session in the gym after lunch. It really felt like we were on holiday now.

As I walked along the deck I spotted another of the characters who became a part of my cruise. He looked like and acted like the perfect gentleman and I named him Mr Dapper almost immediately. He was a Scot of quite senior years, and someone who was well travelled and had been on many cruises including several world trips. He was never scruffy, and wore tailored shorts and crisply ironed summer shirts by day, and a jacket and tie, or dinner jacket as appropriate in the evening.

In the daytime he was often alone sitting on a chair (without slouching) with his shirt on and usually asleep for much of the time. I never saw him using a lounger to get more comfortable, and never actually saw him doing anything else while on the open decks.

There were a number of men, who were like this, but Mr Dapper had something different, he appeared to have a harem. I know it wasn't actually a harem, but he regularly had the company of female companions of similar age, and usually it was two or three of them at the same time.

Almost every night they sat together in Carmen's and danced – and Mr Dapper was a very accomplished dancer. During the evening he took each lady politely onto the dance floor in turn no matter what style of ballroom or sequence dance was being played.

At breakfast he always attempted to sit at the same round table in the Orangery with his back to the sea surveying the room in front of him. The ladies would come and sit around him as if they were giving protection. Sometimes the scene reminded me of King Arthur with his modern-day female knights of the round table.

I once sat in his seat by accident and his ladies appeared as normal, made polite conversation with me but eyed me with suspicion. Mr Dapper eventually arrived but of course he was not able to have his normal seat and I quickly felt embarrassed as I realised my error. Eventually I made an excuse for him to change seats to avoid the sun shining into his eyes. Normal service was thus restored but I was not allowed to join in with the conversation even after complimenting him on his dancing. I have no doubt that the obvious friendship between Mr Dapper and the ladies was perfectly innocent, with nothing in the slightest bit 'naughty' going on. They looked after him and he gave them the company of a man who danced better than most of the younger men, but I wonder if, just maybe, the ladies were hoping for a little bit more.

Mr Dapper was what I would call a true gentleman......I think. After a beautiful day, the evening turned out to be one of the best as well. First there was a spectacular show by a tribute band called 'The Beatles Experience' who were fantastic musically, and extremely similar in looks and voices to the original.

The only minor weaknesses were that the 'Paul' character was not playing left handed, and 'Ringo' had put on a significant amount of weight. The audience lapped them up as almost everyone knew the songs, so we sang, hummed, or tapped our feet throughout the show. Probably the best act we had seen so far.

After that the evening continued with Deb and me taking part in the ship's version of 'The Weakest Link'. The Ent's team girl hosting the game had no idea we were husband and wife, and was certainly in ignorance to the fact that Deb had won the real thing during the previous summer. There were about eight of us playing in total, and I was lucky not to have been voted off early in the game, but I survived to the last three. In the final vote off Deb kept me in the game, so I had to take her on in the head to head to find the winner of the bottle of wine prize.

... of course I lost.

Afterwards the host had a chat to us and then realised we were together, and was totally flabbergasted to find out that Deb had met Anne Robinson in the real game, coming away with a winner's cheque.

In just three days, Deb had managed to win three bottles of wine. A couple of them were shared with our friends at the dinner table, where our wine waiter was definitely getting annoyed that we never seem to buy anything from him.

We rounded off the evening with a cup of hot chocolate in Café Bordeaux and went to bed in anticipation and excitement and about the day to come.

Pure Magic of The Panama Canal

Wednesday 18th January 2012

What an incredible, jaw dropping, amazing day!

An early wake-up was required, but the 5:15 alarm from next door was a little unnecessary. We were soon up, and dressed in scruffs so that we could face a cool morning. The three top cabin decks (A, B and C) all have small observations areas at the bow end, and the plan was to go to ours where we would get a glimpse of the canal as early as possible. So by 6:15 we stood in the dark with perhaps another 30 or 40 passengers looking forwards at a series of red and green marker lights guiding us into the Panama Canal. Above us on 'A' deck and below on 'C' deck were similar numbers of people straining to catch their first glimpse of the lock that would take us into the canal. The only slight snag was that few of us actually knew what we were looking for yet.

In the port talks we had been given a history of the canal, plus an overview of what would happen, and what we would be seeing on our day-long transit to the Pacific Ocean. We would not be stopping to get off the ship, although some of the photography team were allowed to go ashore and capture the moments from the banks. It was a cool morning but I was shivering with excitement as well, and as we turned into the approach to the first lock, its lights, plus the first brightening of the sky with the dawn, allowed me to make out the two sets of gates to the pair of huge locks. We would be directed into one lock with another vessel going in the same direction in the other. The markers indicated that we heading for the right hand channel.

As the growing number of passengers around us chattered and exclaimed amazement, the light of the sky increased enough that we could see a bridge running across the channel in the front of the lock gates, and now some scale could be put against the scene we were seeing. On this bridge there were cars, trucks and buses so for the first time the sheer size of the gates became apparent. It was obvious really, but I had not considered that the gates had to be significantly higher than the change of water level within the lock, and that was several metres.

We had a pilot on board from the canal team to assist the captain with the seriously difficult task of bringing Aurora to the gates accurately enough for the land teams to secure it with ropes to the huge 'mule' engines that would tow us through. The clearance is only a few feet on either side in the locks, and the paintwork was not meant to get scratched. To give it some scale, Aurora is 32 metres wide, and the lock chamber is just 33.5 metres wide.

By 7:00 the pilot was giving us a commentary as we started to enter the lock. The process starts very crudely with a small rowing boat pulling a rope out to connect to the ship to tie it to the first mule. Eventually there were a total of eight of the mules – two at the front and rear on either side. They ran on rails like a train engine and worked together to pull the ship through, but just as importantly to keep it in the middle of the chamber. As we slowly entered the chamber the noise of cameras increased and we could see the ship's photographers waving at us to smile into their lenses.

A horrid loud grinding sound told us that Aurora was not quite in the middle of the chamber, and the paintwork had indeed been damaged.

Mules stopped, men shouted, mules reversed, more shouting, and then we edged forwards again without any further problems. After a few minutes we were completely inside the lock and the gates shut behind us. We now started the lift from the Atlantic Ocean to the level of the canal lake. In total this is around 26 metres (depending on tides) and is achieved by three sets of locks that are grouped under the names of the Gatun Locks. It took around 15 minutes to manoeuvre into and out of each lock, and another 10 minutes or so to fill them. So, for the next hour and a bit the 90,000 tons of Aurora was lifted up and towed into the Gatun Lake which is the main waterway of the canal.

Although we missed very little of the action, we had moved back to our cabin to have a champagne breakfast on the balcony. This was another part of the gift pack I had bought before we left home. It was a superb dreamlike experience to sit in glorious sunshine, drinking glasses of Bucks Fizz, eating croissants, Danish Pastries, fruit, and cheese while we watched an incredible engineering feat going on so close that we could have a conversation with the workers on the side of the locks. By the way, we started drinking the champagne neat, but it was really too much so the freshly squeezed orange juice was added to avoid getting inebriated before 9:00 in the morning. Once through the first set of locks, we had several hours to slowly make our way across the Gatun Lake to the next set of locks on the other side. A third set of locks would then the drop us down to the Pacific Ocean.

In the meantime the pilot continued his description of the canal with more history, facts and figures, plus things to look out for.

He was totally obsessed with his job and occasionally gave seriously boring details of the other ships around us, but this was backed up by lots of fascinating stuff about the wildlife, plus an overview of the construction project underway to widen the canal locks. Up until now there was a maximum width of ship that could use it (and we were just about that wide) but soon wider ships such as the latest cruise monster-ships will be able to pass through as well. This will open up the route for the 5,000+ passenger ships to follow the likes of Aurora on similar world circumnavigations.

The water in the lake is ultimately supplied by a rain forest on either side of it and an ecological balance of the forest has to be maintained to keep the canal operational. The new locks have to be far more efficient with their use of water, as bigger ships mean bigger locks, and bigger locks will need more water. We spent the hours looking at the forest and watching birds soaring above it in the thermals. I believe there might have been condors at one point, but there were definitely frigate birds and masked boobies again, and pelicans were sitting on the banks watching us. There were many others that I could not describe let alone put a name to. We were always hopeful of seeing crocodiles and possibly monkeys but no-one reported any sightings.

 There were ships of various sizes and types passing in the other direction as well as pleasure-craft taking visitors from end to end. On the banks we also saw the railway line that follows the canal and a couple of huge multi-engine freight trains crossing from ocean to ocean like ourselves.

We had short breaks for coffee to allow time for Savio to spruce up our cabin, and also to look around at the view from the other side of the ship, but almost all of the day was spent either on our balcony or at the front observation area.

A few hours later we arrived at the narrow section of the canal known as the Culebra Cut where hundreds of the construction team lost their lives as they blasted and dug their way through a solid mountain of rock. Many were killed in accidents but just as many died from diseases such as malaria. We passed under a huge road bridge that spans the canal at this point; joining Panama to North America, and it brought the reality of the magnitude of the canal into perspective. A little while after the bridge we came to the second lock set (Pedro Miguel Lock) dropping us down into the smaller Miraflores Lake and soon we approached the final set of locks (Miraflores Locks) to complete the canal transit.

This was less spectacular than the Gatun complex but made all the more interesting by having a tourist and exhibition centre at the side of the lock where hundreds of people watched our passage enthusiastically with a commentary by the exhibition centre's staff. As we entered and left the final lock they cheered and waved and cameras worked overtime both on the ship and the shore, and we waved back frantically in appreciation.

It was about 4:30 in the afternoon, we were now in the Pacific Ocean and picking up speed as we moved into open water. The modern skyscrapers of Panama City could just be seen in the distance from our balcony and as the city disappeared from view the breeze got up to show that we were leaving the land and setting out again to the open waters.

The day had been so special, and it needed adjectives and superlatives that I don't have in my vocabulary to describe just how special it was. All I can say is that if anyone is thinking of paying a visit to the Panama Canal either on a cruise, or as a package, then do it. I know of nobody on the ship who was disappointed with the day, and most enthused about it for days to come. It has both history and is an example of incredible engineering. The lives of many hundreds of people were lost creating a solution to save days of travel, and hence millions of dollars, but it also has the natural beauty of the rain forest, hills, and wildlife, to look at and gasp in awe.

Dinner time beckoned and we chatted with our friends about the sights we had seen. The smiles on all our faces and the enthusiasm told the story of what a wonderful day we had all had. After eating we succumbed to tiredness, and spent an hour just sitting and dozing on loungers out on the Promenade deck. By 9:30 we had given in to exhaustion and were tucked up in bed fast asleep. I expect there was a contented grin on our faces as well.

We now had six days at sea before landfall again in San Francisco. There was a change of direction for the first time since we left Southampton and instead of sailing south and west, we were now heading north. The temperature would soon drop back again and the sea would stop being quite as calm as we moved towards California and the end of the first sector of the cruise.

Northwards To California
19th to 24th January 2012

We had enjoyed a few days with land to look at but now
Aurora was sailing north at almost full speed to keep her
appointment in San Francisco. The Pacific Ocean was
reminding us that the sea is not always friendly, and the ship
was buffeted around for most of the journey. The winds
increased to Force 8 for some of the trip, and the sea state was
not as calm as we had become used to in the Caribbean. Over
the days the temperature dropped from 29°C to the teens but
it was a gradual decrease getting us ready for our next stop.
The increase in movement had brought back a strange dance
that occurs as passengers walk along the decks and corridors.
Like some odd mating ritual, people walk straight for a while
then move first one way and then back again. Peculiarly even
when in pairs, they do not seem to be aware of their
coordinated changes of direction and continue to chat to each
other. This ritual is made more complicated according to how
able the person is to cope with the motion of the sea. Those
who are more used to the tantrums of the sea are able to
remain in control of their movements and walk in straight lines
down a corridor, others dance from side to side as described,
and then the totally uncontrolled career from wall to wall as
they progress slowly to the next place to sit down.
Where do I fit in with my descriptions? Well I think I am
somewhere between the controlled and dancers. I seem to
end up walking down a corridor avoiding gossiping women zig-
zagging towards me oblivious to the pandemonium they are
causing.
Even worse is attempting to overtake these people, as along
with the loss of balance they also become blinkered to
anything other than straight ahead. A number of times I

quietly "*tutted*" in disgust as I moved to the side of one of these people, only to be suddenly shoved against the wall as they 'tacked' in my direction.

It's very amusing to just sit and watch the antics, rather than trying to move around too much when the sea gets a little rough.

For some of the passengers, this was the last week of their holiday as they'd be leaving us at the end of the sector. But for us, and several hundred others, San Francisco was just the end of part one and the splendid daily routine would continue. During the first few days the sun was still warm and the ship was stable enough to be able to relax. The swimming pool was the perfect place to start the day with some exercise, followed by encouraging the tan to improve. Deb described these daily activities in her diary so sweetly, comparing them to a recipe:

"Immerse in cool water and keep moving for 20 to 25 minutes. Remove and pat dry. Spray liberally with oil and toast gently for 30 minutes on each side, or until feeling warm to touch. Add water at regular intervals to prevent drying out."

Keeping us occupied for the rest of the day there were more talks about aircraft based topics, but I still didn't go to them. There were others that Deb and I did go to, including stories from the ex-coxswain of the Bembridge Lifeboat who now works in the maritime salvage business.

His work has included trying to locate the crash site of Glenn Miller's plane, and this was another talk I attended.

Another strange presentation that I went to was about the musicians who played instruments for TV's 'The Muppet Show'. I'm afraid it just seemed an excuse to show clips from the show after an introduction to inform us who was really playing 'Animal's drums.

There were port talks of course, and John Challis packed the theatre again with a lively session where he was interviewed by Jason Dean who was a very accomplished and popular member of the entertainment team. The questions from Jason were scripted but 'Boycie' also had to answer questions from his fans in the audience, and that was good fun.

More amazing daytime entertainment came courtesy of the flying fish, and large predatory Kamikaze squadrons of birds. During the early warm and calm days of this journey, they appeared virtually every day, but for a few minutes on one morning the action was tremendous. The water flashed with hundreds of the fish star-bursting away from the ship, and the hunting pack of booby birds squawked, dived and fed to the delight of the watching passengers. Just when we thought it could not get any better a huge splash drew our attention to a pod of dolphins passing by the ship in the sea below us. Some gracefully rose up clear of the water and then returned with hardly a splash but others turned somersaults and even stood on the tails for a moment before noisily *'belly flopping'* back into the sea. Aurora moved on and left them playing but this was a moment when you felt blessed to have been witness to a show by the fish and birds, but especially by such athletic and sociable mammals.

Up on deck in the sunshine I enjoyed my people-watching and started to become fascinated by some of my fellow passengers. One lady with a good appetite proved a theory that I was taught whilst training to be a swimming teacher. If the body of a swimmer has lots of fat, he or she will float far easier than someone who is muscular. The lady in question had more than a generous amount of fat. One morning she decided to take a dip in the pool, and every time she lay in the water to try and float on her back, her ample bosom floated to the surface like huge flotation balloons (sorry) and quickly pulled her up vertically again. It was a scene I had to watch for a while to confirm what was happening until I began to feel just a little nauseous from its absurdity. I recounted the tale to Deb and christened the lady 'Mrs Self-Righting'.

We continued to attempt the Individual Quiz on most afternoons, and met a couple who became friends with us throughout the cruise. Neil and Christine enjoyed the challenge of the quiz in the same way as us, and saw it as a competition between husband and wife primarily rather than winning prizes. Neil had not been lucky, having a leg amputated following a failed knee replacement, but he never complained and always attempted to do things without any help. He had a mobility scooter with him but rarely used it, relying on a pair of crutches instead. They were a lovely couple who laughed at every opportunity.

Another day brought excitement as the captain announced that there was going to be a bomb alert exercise where the passengers could get involved.

The exercise was primarily targeted at the crew who had to respond with a well-rehearsed procedure, but we were asked to go to our cabins and look for any mysterious packages. For the one or two cabins where a 'suspicious' package had been hidden, the finders received a bottle of champagne. The response was amazing and the sounds of cabin drawers and wardrobes being opened and closed could be heard all over the ship.

We didn't find anything.

On the same day we received a special gift to commemorate the fact that we were going all around the world. It was an engraved Veritas tea set, and rather splendid. The only problem was that it was not expected and a number of passengers took it to Reception to claim their bottle of champagne thinking it was the suspicious package!

In the three weeks we had been away, the water leaks I

mentioned that occurred during the first couple of nights had continued to plague the ship. A rumour was that a new piece of plumbing equipment had been installed in Southampton and this was producing a higher than normal water pressure. Aurora's pipework was twelve years old now and was obviously shocked by this extra pressure. Consequently, bits of pipe or joints were bursting with drastic results. As the engineers fixed one leak, the problem just moved to another piece of pipe or joint further on in the system.

We were lucky and had no soggy carpets near us, but evidence was apparent all over the ship with plastic buckets in the middle of corridors on virtually every deck.

The buckets were even in the main walkways in the public areas, and in the Champions bar. Passengers got used to looking out for the buckets and side stepping them with confidence, but it was a little concerning that there seemed to be no solution to the problem.

In the evening the quizzes continued to amuse us, and dancing gave us a chance to waltz and cha-cha around Carmen's. The nightly cabaret entertainment was quite varied, but there did seem to be an abundance of vocalists. Maxine Mazumer was quite good with her Dusty Springfield tribute act but we never went to her Lulu show. We don't like the real Lulu and so we had no intention to listen to an impression.

The Beatles Experience thrilled us again, and we had the first show from Bruce Morrison who gave several entertaining evenings with a range of musical genre but mainly musical theatre. He was one of the best vocalists we saw during the cruise. Mark O'Malley was another singer we had watched and listened to earlier and was good enough for us to see him again. He spoke too much, like many other singers, but he gave an enjoyable show, right up until the point where he sang a jazz version of 'Bo Jangles'. I love this song, but Mr O'Malley murdered it and my support for him immediately disappeared. Another singer called Robbie Allen was one that we avoided twice. His pre-show write up on the first show did not inspire us, and following a lot of criticism about him from other passengers we gave his second performance a miss as well. On one or two nights the Headliners Theatre Company put on their glitzy productions, and they really were good, at both singing and dancing. As a change from singing, there was a second show from Thomas Anthony (magician) but this non-vocal act was a rarity. Feedback from around the ship was that there were just too many singers, and even some of the singers themselves were complaining that it was difficult trying to find out if a planned song had already been sung by a previous act. As we neared San Francisco we started to get warnings about the impending visit by people from the US Immigration Department. The announcements were to ensure we completed the necessary paperwork carefully, but also to stress that they would interview everybody on board (passengers and crew) before anyone would be allowed to leave the ship. This was going to take a long time to complete, and so we were warned to prepare for a delay before going ashore. There was also a serious instruction to not complain or joke about how long it was taking. On a previous cruise, someone started singing *"Why are we waiting..."* to which the US officials responded by doing everything exactly by the book, taking over five hours to complete the process. Normally it was over and done in less than three hours.

Six days at sea sounds a long time, but only one story came from the laundry communications team of anybody getting really bored. The comment was that a passenger stated *"If I had known there would be so many sea days, I would never have booked this cruise".* All I can say is that the sector was advertised as 21 days, with four ports of call, so what did she expect to be doing on the other days?

To be honest, I was quite looking forward to getting to San Francisco and to have a walk on solid ground again. It was always going to be one of the major highlights of the trip, and the anticipation was making me tingle. I was still enjoying life on board Aurora however, and each day brought new things to look at and gasp at in amazement, or laugh at in delight. It was still a magical dream from waking up to going back to bed, and the dream had a long time to go yet.

Sensational San Francisco
Wednesday 25th January 2012

This morning we had an even more ridiculously early 4:45 wake-up call from our neighbours. They were making sure they did not miss sailing under the Golden Gate Bridge but that was not going to happen for a while yet. I dozed off again but woke suddenly to peoples' voices and camera flashes coming through the balcony curtain. Jumping up and opening the curtains I could see the bridge and we were literally seconds away from passing beneath it.

Deb was up as well and the balcony door was opened, cameras grabbed and pointed in the general direction of the bridge. It was still night-time, and pitch black outside except for the street lights and aircraft warning beacons on the structure. It may only have been a shadowy image but that bridge is iconic and awe inspiring even when you are shivering on a balcony with nothing more than pyjama trousers.

... but that was more than Deb was wearing!

Very little of my video, and few of Deb's pictures were of any value, which to be honest was not surprising as I could hardly see the viewfinder let alone distinguish what the camera was pointing at.

Any more sleep was out of the question so we had our tea and pills, got dressed and went to breakfast at 06:30 (still in darkness) and to watch the sun rise over the beautiful city. What a sight!!

The view from the stern was amazing with the Golden Gate Bridge that we had sailed under to our left, and the Bay Bridge to our right.

All around the Bay the glass of the skyscrapers glistened in the rising sun, and lights twinkled as the workers of the city arrived at their offices. Around us there were very few people visible as yet except for the usual quayside workers, but there were numerous gulls and pelicans watching us in the hope of a free meal.

Aurora had berthed at Pier 35 and looking around us we were able to see a busy scene with ferries coming and going from lower-numbered piers to one side. In the other direction Pier 39 and Fisherman's Wharf was the immediate sight, and it dominated the view with its glitzy décor. Beyond it were shops and other buildings on either side of the busy road going as far as we could see. Below us there was a wide pavement – sorry, sidewalk – with an ever-increasing number of commuters on their way to and from the ferries and wherever they were going to work.

Back in our cabin we surveyed our view from the balcony as the sun finally lit up the scene. We had a view of the Bay Bridge which was seriously damaged by an earthquake in 1989 with many people killed. It was immediately repaired in less than a month but is now being replaced by a newer and presumably less earthquake-susceptible bridge. Between the bridge and our berth, the bay curved around with mainly older buildings near the waterfront but merging into the towering metropolis of the skyscraper city.

Although it is predominantly steel, concrete and glass, the city is truly beautiful and each day thousands of visitors gasp as they stare.

Some memories were coming back of my short visit 30 years ago when I was in total awe of the sights, sounds, and smells. My return had already begun to rekindle those memories, and I was itching to get out there and be absorbed by the city again. Before anyone could leave the ship, there was a three-hour wait while the US Immigration Authorities went through their processes and procedures to 'immigrate' nearly 3,000 passengers and crew. This was tedious as we knew it would be, but generally it was a relaxed period. Everyone had their passports checked and a short visual once-over by the officers. Most of us decided that as part of the Immigration Officer job-description they must be required to lose any sense of humour or character they might have had. There was never a hint of a smile, or a flicker of emotion, and saying hello to them was never greeted with anything more than a grunt of acknowledgement...

... at best.

Finally, just before 11:00 we had the all clear and some 1,500 passengers, grabbed their cameras and bags to go ashore. We formed a massive queue towards the gangways blocking stairwells and corridors, and it was approaching 30 minutes before we finally got our feet on solid ground for the first time in over a week.

I was officially 'immigrated', so welcome to America!!

Our decision for the day was to walk and sight-see for the rest of the morning and the afternoon before our organised tour to Chinatown in the evening. So we started off at a canter towards Fisherman's Wharf remarking on the sights we saw as we went. Overtaking us we recognised one of the younger single men from the ship.

He was always on the lookout for female company and joined in with everything designed for singles, or where single women gathered. Be it in the swimming pool, at one of the classes, or on the dance floor, he always turned up and tried to make friends with unattached ladies. One of his chats with the ladies must have raised the subject of jogging, and in particular a fad of running across the Golden Gate Bridge...

... but backwards!

Maybe it fascinated his sense of a challenge, or perhaps it was to get noticed, but he decided that running backwards across the said bridge would be the first thing he did in San Francisco.

He achieved his ambition, and I hope he got the recognition he deserved from his female friends. Many others of us thought he was just a little bit silly.

Running Backwards Man did have some success with the ladies later in the cruise and we saw him dancing with the same lady several times until he left Aurora at one of the later ports. Good luck to you sir, but consider what you look like before taking up too many dubious challenges!

We carried on down the sidewalk towards Fisherman's Wharf and were amused at some of the sights and other times just gasped in amazement. There were booths selling 'corndogs' (never did find out what they were), candy floss, or ice creams. Every other outlet seemed to be a tourist shop selling all the usual 'tat' but somehow it all seemed a little less tacky simply because this was America. Reversible waterproof jackets appeared to be the 'in thing' and at very good prices, but we were not expecting rain, or chilly temperatures.

I had started the day wearing trousers, shirt and jumper, but within a few minutes I was regretting the jumper. It ended up as a nuisance that had to be carried as the weather became pleasantly warm, and I also really wished I had chosen shorts. The locals were still in winter dress, but this was far from what we call winter.

Our first purchases were a fridge magnet for the growing collection on our cabin wall, plus the obligatory postcards. We were having a mass postcard-sending session that day to give a number of friends and family a reminder of who we were and where we had got to. A few steps further on and we met Jimmy and Isabel, and just like in Madeira they were having a cup of coffee. We had a few minutes of banter with them, and then moved on in the direction of the cable car terminus to complete one of the 'must do' items on our list.

It was taking a while getting used to crossing the streets, as we had been warned to avoid 'jay walking', or risk being arrested. So, we always waited for the little green man sign to indicate it was safe to cross, but the locals scoffed at us and crossed with confidence in the smallest gaps.

Eventually we arrived at the Aquatic Park near Ghirardelli Square where the Powell-Hyde cable car started its run. We joined a small queue which included some other Aurora passengers, though we couldn't work out how to get tickets as the booth was closed and there was no indication of where else to buy them. Jimmy, Isabel, and their friend Doreen had also joined us and we eventually decided to plead ignorance and piled onto the car waiting for someone to pounce on us because we had no tickets.

... just enjoy the ride.

I was one of the last to climb on board and without a seat I clung on to the leather straps. Clanking, jolting, and with the bell ringing we rumbled away up and down the city. I did the same thing 30 years ago and stood then as well! It is difficult to maintain your balance in those conditions, and quite honestly this was more of a fairground ride than commuting, and I do not really like fairground rides! Undeterred, I was actually feeling quite excited by the experience and the enjoyment exceeded the discomfort. Finally, the guard came to us and I bought the tickets for me and Deb, but Jimmy and co had already decided to make their escape before he got to them, so had a free ride.

We got off at Union Square to marvel at the high-rise shopping stores and the surrounding skyscrapers. Who should we meet but Jimmy, Isabel and Doreen deciding what they were going to do. Isabel and Doreen were off to go shopping in Macys Department Store, while Jimmy was simply going to amuse himself looking at the sights. We exercised our cameras taking pictures of the square and the high rise 'designer' department stores and buildings around us. We didn't bother with any retail therapy, and after consulting our map, strolled off in the approximate direction back towards the harbour area again. Our intention was to find somewhere to have a snack and the choice was vast, but by now the business community of San Francisco were already having their lunch, and the likely-looking places were packed. We dithered and decided to delay food for a while.

With the map opened again, a friendly local took pity on us and showed us where we were, plus explaining that some streets have names while others (at right angles to them) just have numbers. Slightly less confused (or not!) we thanked him and quickly walked onwards. We just walked, and looked at this wonderful city on our hike to the Old Ferry Terminal buildings on the water front. When we finally got there, we realised that it had been a major walking session for the morning, and certainly several miles. We now found ourselves at the Bay Bridge end of the harbour and a long way from where we started over two hours earlier.

Inside the Old Ferry Terminal building we found scores of food outlets and bars but once again they were generally all packed. Looking for somewhere to get to the counter and just see the food was difficult, but eventually we found a promising outlet. Called 'Spicy Pig Parts' it was a busy stall but was serving quickly and the assistant made time to describe what it was they were selling. After a moment to make a decision, we went for an unusually spicy and tasty pork roll. The name of the outlet may have been a little suspect, but the food was delicious.

Back to walking again, and we had to complete our circular trek by going along the waterfront to Pier 35 where Aurora was berthed. That was approaching another hour of walking in the glorious sunshine, taking in the breath-taking sights of San

Francisco. The people of the city were making the most of this rare spring-like day strolling along the palm tree-lined pavement.

Some were walking or trotting with dogs, and we saw several breeds and sizes. I did suspect that sometimes these animals were fashion trophies for the designer-clad walkers who were out to see and be seen. Joggers were also out in numbers and in general they looked like they knew what they were doing. Most were slim, if not well toned, and their pace was not a stroll.

There were of course vagrants in many different forms. Some were purely sitting and begging, whilst others were trying to appear more human by having cards expressing their honest need for a drink or drugs. A more unusual method of begging was to cover themselves with tree branches and then roar, or jump out, at unsuspecting passers-by. This was supposed to encourage people to drop coins into their tin cans. I found them rather annoying, and quite disturbing, compared to the more obvious beggars who in general did not cause a problem to those not in a giving mood.

One thing I remember from my visit oh so many years ago was the street theatre. At that time as well as the music acts there were jugglers and clowns, but now it just appeared to be musicians. The majority of them worked around Fisherman's Wharf but we did see one or two on our walk back towards our ship. They ranged from a single acoustic guitar busker to electronic backing-tracked singing, and then multiple singers with multiple instruments. My favourites were the classical guitarists who always attracted a good-sized crowd with perhaps a more discerning taste. All these performers were good, and some combined the music with a well-practiced patter to encourage visitors to chat as well as listen, in the hope of rattling some money into their tins.

Finally back at Aurora we changed from our misjudged cool weather clothing back into full summer kit. After a quick drink we rushed off the ship again towards Fisherman's Wharf and Pier 39 to absorb some more of the atmosphere.

One stop we had to make was to see the famous colony of sea lions. They didn't let us down and several hundred were sunning themselves and showing off to packed rows of visitors. They 'honked' both to your ears and your noses!

We carried on our very touristy stroll, and although we had a small list of items to buy, this was not a good day for traditional shopping as the outlets were virtually all tourist based. We eventually found a small supermarket where we replenished our Coca Cola but our other needs were left wanting. The stroll was just so sweet (if a little tiring by now) and there were moments when we just held hands or cuddled as we allowed the atmosphere to soak into our souls. I did not remember much of what I saw 30 years ago and this visit felt like coming to a completely new place again. I do recall that I fell just a little under the spell of San Francisco all those years ago, and it was happening in the same way again, and the look on Deb's face suggested the feeling was mutual.

Late in the afternoon we returned to the ship with a real glow of enjoyment from the experience of a sunny day in a beautiful vibrant city where people were generally happy, polite and friendly. The day was not over yet however as we had a tour of Chinatown coming up in the evening. There was just time for a quick snack in Café Bordeaux, plus another change of clothes more suitable for a walk in the dark and cooling evening.

The tour we had booked involved a scenic coach drive around the city highlights but more importantly a walk through the Chinatown area. Off we went without any pre-conception of what we were doing, but I must admit having some concerns that this was the middle of the Chinese New Year holiday period. The drive around in the coach was very relaxing and a pleasant reminder of many of the sights that we had walked by during the day plus some of the route we travelled in the cable car.

When we arrived at the Chinatown area and piled out of the coach, it became apparent that this was not going to be a fast walk, as we had some disabled passengers in our group. That is not a complaint but I was wondering how they would deal with the hills, quite high kerbs, plus the narrow dark alleys that seemed to be where we were heading. When it comes to passengers with mobility problems, the guides generally do their best to accommodate their needs, but they often fail. Guides have to stick to a tight timetable with a script in their heads to educate and amuse the visitors. Unfortunately for them, fifty people will spread themselves out according to the speed they walk at, and usually only those at the front of the group get the full advantage of the guide's commentary. Our friend Neil was on this tour with his crutches and generally ended up at the back. What made it worse for him was the number of dark streets where he struggled to see where he was walking, and to avoid potholes, unexpected kerbs and items of rubbish. I was not over-excited by the guide's patter and spent a lot of my time keeping an eye on Neil and occasionally having a chat with him.

As I suspected with the New Year celebrations continuing, most of the outlets were closed unless they were restaurants and perhaps the guide was having a more difficult than usual time finding things to talk about. As we went down narrow lanes or more interesting streets, we had some good explanations of how the Chinese build their homes with the higher end of society living at the top. We also learnt about the earthquake damage precaution of leaving a small gap between buildings to allow them to move independently of each other. A very old building that was once a temple (now a bank) was described, highlighting the narrow area of roof at the top with roof sizes increasing as it goes down to street level. This is to allow evil spirits to slide away from the building. If a building had lions outside, they would stop any approaching evil spirits walking in.

... quite interesting!

We had a quick visit to a 'fortune cookie' factory. It was actually a fortune cookie shop with a machine that shaped and baked the biscuit dough. An old lady mumbled in Chinese while she placed messages on the dough shape and then folded it before placing it into the baking oven. Several cookies were oddly shaped or damaged, and these were offered to us to taste. After we had shuffled through the small shop and returned to the street, there were some comments being made suggesting the tour was a waste of time, and the area not being that pleasant to walk around at night. I was not too concerned about the safety of the area, but I certainly felt disappointed by the tour's content.

Cookies eaten, we continued with the tour with more walks down dark lanes with dark buildings for a total of about three quarters of an hour. There were one or two interesting gems of wisdom during the walk but it would have been far better if it had been light enough to see, and perhaps something to taste other than the crumpled cookies.

At the end we visited an area called Portsmouth Square which is very much within Chinatown. It serves as a community area where adults meet, talk, gamble at cards, and where the children can play games. Even though it was only lit by street lamps it was still quite busy with groups of grownups and children happily enjoying the warm evening. A bonus (from my point of view) was the view over the city so the guide was able to point out some of the major buildings. He showed us the statues or artistic features that have been included in new buildings: these are incorporated in the planning stage to aid agreement for new sites. Even in the darkness the commercial centre of San Francisco is still lit up to display the cultural treats that makes the city so beautiful.

With the tour of Chinatown over we returned to the coach and continued our sightseeing journey around the city and a trip across the Bay Bridge to what is referred to as Treasure Island which lies in the centre of the two spans of the bridge. From here we had another spectacular view of the city. Aurora was visible and normally a cruise ship dominates a skyline of a city, but San Francisco won the 'view battle' this time. The return journey to the ship allowed us to see more high profile or memorable buildings including one that is a lookalike of the Washington Senate Building.

The city tour had been really enjoyable but the Chinatown element had been of little interest to me and several others. Even if it had been in the middle of the day, I don't think it would have excited me as much as the architecture and glitz of the city.

By the time that we arrived back on Aurora it was after 9:30 and Deb and I were starving having had little more than a pork sandwich and a deformed fortune cookie since breakfast. Food was no longer available unless we ordered room service but we were in too much of a hurry for that. Instead we scuttled along to Champion's bar, which was surprisingly deserted, had a soft drink and a packet of crisps...

... delicious!

A number of passengers passing by stared at us, and must have thought we were slightly mad as we literally gobbled the crisps like a pair of hungry pigs, with grins of satisfaction when they were finished. That was enough for us and we staggered back to the cabin too weary for anything except sleep. We had been walking for over five hours during the day and must have covered several miles of the streets of San Francisco...

... real tourists at last!

That night was the first time we had stayed in a port overnight since we visited Istanbul on our first cruise in 2000. An overnight stay is a rare time when the ship does not rock, or makes strange rattling noises, and we slept extremely well before awaking to our second day of adventures in this amazing city.

San Francisco (Day 2)
Thursday 26th January 2012

Today we woke up in one of the most beautiful cities in the world. We had another full day to soak up San Francisco, but more especially a tour to Alcatraz and Sausalito starting late in the morning that would take up most of the day.

The hustle and bustle of the ship was just a little more hustled and bustled this morning as excited passengers were getting ready for tours, but also some 500 people were leaving the cruise here at the end of the first segment. We had never witnessed people getting off in such numbers without us being a part of the process and it made me feel even more of a seasoned cruiser.

Rumours had been circulated from the laundry channel. Apparently three handcuffed passengers were seen being escorted from the ship by armed US police. The laundry information reports suggested that they were caught fighting in a bar, and that one had punched the ship's DJ. This was totally unconfirmed of course but there are usually some grounds for a rumour, so the ship awaited further information. While our cabin was having its morning spruce up, we sat in a quiet area of the ship called Charlie's to watch the world go by, and where I regularly caught up on my blog entries, while Deb read a book. It was not so quiet this morning as those leaving Aurora were using it as a waiting area before being called to go.

Having given Savio sufficient time to tidy up our room, we returned to the cabin to get our bits together for the day and to consider what we would do about food as our tour started at 11:00 and there would be no snacks available. For breakfast we had indulged in a rare hot meal but we decided to go back to the Orangery and have cup of coffee with a Danish pastry as a mid-morning snack. To avoid yesterday's panic eating, Deb made up a pair of ham rolls for emergency supplies to hide in the cabin. In America you are not allowed to take any food off the ship so the snack was our only option to avoid a repeat of the crisps meal of yesterday.

Everything ready and cameras fully charged we set off for Alcatraz. From the balcony we could see the terminal for the Alcatraz ferries, and it was literally a five-minute walk from our own berth. So to our surprise there was a coach waiting for us as we left Aurora. Slightly confused we got on the coach and sat down. We were now treated to another drive around the city and passed by Fisherman's Wharf down to the cable car terminus before following our route of yesterday to Union Square. This was the third time along these streets, and we were beginning to feel like locals. The drive continued to the Old Ferry Terminal and then back along the road where we walked the day before, and finally stopped alongside the berth for the Alcatraz ferry.

Hence we spent 20 minutes in the coach going four or five miles, before coming back to within 100 yards of the ship... *um!* Onto the ferry and a fifteen-minute ride later we were among a group of about 100 tourists getting off at the infamous Island of Alcatraz. The experience starts immediately with a talk by one of the Rangers to state the rules, and to set the scene for the visit.

These Rangers were available all over the site to help the tourists get the best from their visit as well as cleverly controlling the pace of the groups moving to avoid congestion. This is done by giving little five-minute talks at a spot where something significant happened. Some of the groups stop to listen while others do not bother with the talk and carry on with their tour. This spreads the groups out as well as giving a little more information to those who want it.

The visit lasted about two hours in total, and I have to say it is probably the best-organised visit to a historical site that I have ever experienced. I could never use words to describe and explain the tour of Alcatraz sufficiently to express its sinister atmosphere and the history that comes to life as you walk around the buildings. I simply offer a short resume of our time there and hope that it whets your appetite to make a visit to this fascinating place.

After the introductory talk, the well-planned and signposted route starts in a cinema showing a history video of the island, with some exhibits to see in the adjoining rooms. After that you are directed to a walk up a hill to the cell block that is the main attraction. Everyone is given an audio player in their particular language that both guides and informs you of the prison layout and cells. It gives a history of the prison, brings the different areas to life with sounds that would have been typical and has a mixed commentary from an ex-prisoner, former guard, and a lady who grew up on the island from childhood.

As you walk along the eerie cell block corridors, there are photographs of particular prisoners such as Al Capone, and the 'Bird Man' on the wall to bring the history to life. The cells could be mistaken for zoo cages, having a barred front with no privacy from the warders. They have been kept as they were with some being completely empty while others have bedding and the personal knick-knacks of the prisoners. Many were locked away in Alcatraz for a long time and tried to make their cells just a little less of a small cage by having personal possessions such as pictures, musical instruments and games. The tour takes you from block to block and area to area including a chance to see solitary confinement cells where there are photo opportunities to go inside a cell and have a picture taken while staring out through the bars. Deb could not do this as she found the isolation of these cells made her feel physically ill.

As well as the description of the prison and its cells, the commentary includes personal stories from inmates and warders. These stories bring Alcatraz to life with memories of the exercise yard and the visitor room, but eventually move on to talk about escape attempts. In particular a major one is recounted where hand grenades had to eventually be used to halt a riot as the escape attempt failed. This really brings the experience to a finale with a look at the hand grenade-damaged cell area where the prisoners and a warder died. The tour ends in the canteen area with its tear gas canisters on the walls and more light-heartedly the menu for Christmas dinner that actually sounded quite good.

Tour over; we had a little time to look at the souvenirs in the shop. They were better than the average 'tat' and we chose a couple of items as memory-jogging objects. From pencils, enamel cups to DVDs and logoed clothing there were things to tempt most people to open their wallets, and Deb was fascinated by the range of books to enhance the stories and history that visitors had just experienced.

We walked back down from the cell block to the ferry area looking at the tranquillity of the unspoilt grounds surrounding the prison and realised our time was nearly up. It had gone so quickly which only proves how good it was. We were soon back on the ferry and with hardly time to eat a cone of nachos covered in a revolting fluorescent cheese sauce, we were back on the mainland again.

That was a wonderful tour, but for anyone who is going to do this one day, leave yourself more time to really experience the atmosphere and sights of the island.

Once off the ferry we re-joined our coach and drove through the city again in the afternoon sunshine. We climbed our way up a few of the hills and eventually started to cross the disappointingly fog-immersed Golden Gate Bridge to the area on the other side of the bay called Sausalito. As we arrived in this little town the fog lifted and the sun came out to say hello to some more British tourists. It is a sweet and sleepy town with a marina and a shaded rocky beach area from which to gaze at the water of the bay. The shops were small and mainly for tourists and we soon found a café where we had a delicious cinnamon and caramel flavoured ice-cream.

Many of the shops here, as in the city, were selling large statuettes of animals. The quality of the statues was really very good, and they were not small. There were two-metre high giraffes, monkeys, frogs, in fact most of the known animal kingdom. Undoubtedly spectacular but not many tourists would be able to hide one of these in a cupboard as a souvenir when they get home.

In the distance we could see that the Golden Gate Bridge was clearing of fog slightly, and by the time we left, the tips of the towers were just showing above the annoying blanket of mist. Our coach took us back to the city and we had our final drive around the sights with more examples of the amazingly steep hills that have been used by Hollywood for car chases in so many films. After an absolutely splendid day trip with all kinds of experiences, we were getting off the coach at Aurora's berth.

Without returning to the ship we made the most of the remaining time and repeated our walk along the waterfront to be sure that as much of the San Francisco atmosphere was absorbed and remembered.

This day had been so sweet.

Eventually back on board Aurora we unloaded our bits and pieces, freshened ourselves up a little, and almost immediately it was time for dinner...

... the ham rolls were never eaten and ended up in the bin. After dinner we went up on deck to watch and savour sail-away. We don't often do this but San Francisco was special and needed to be said goodbye to. The infamous San Francisco fog rolled in and out and although most of the sights were visible at some time during that trip away from the city, the Golden Gate Bridge remained obscured.

A new entertainment officer was playing some background music so we had a chat to her as the ship prepared to leave. With passengers sipping drinks and leaning on the ships' rails, the inevitable Tony Bennett song *"I left my heart in San Francisco"* came on to bid farewell to the city. I don't think I lost my heart to the city, but I certainly believe that a little bit of San Francisco remains in my heart.

As we sailed slowly out into the Bay the evening air was getting cooler so we went inside to warm up, and to see if anything was of interest. There was nothing happening to capture our imagination so we finished the day with a cup of hot chocolate. It was time for bed and a chance to dream of the wonderful last couple of days as the ship started to rock and roll again. We were going west for four days now towards Hawaii and had a new captain to take us there - Neil Turnbull. There were also several hundred new passengers from USA, Australia, and New Zealand, and we all had expectations of lots of new experiences to come.

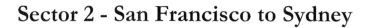

Sector 2 - San Francisco to Sydney

Westwards Across the Pacific
27th to 30th January 2012

The weather during our four-day crossing to Hawaii was warm but the sea was not as calm as in the Caribbean. Initially the sea state had been described as 'Moderate' which means 'reasonably rough' to non-sailors. It had calmed down to a more pleasant 'Slight' on the last day of this transit, which translates as 'still rough enough to upset some people'. The motion was very similar to being on a roller coaster going very slowly. Sideways rolling can be controlled by stabilisers but the bow-to-stern pitching we were experiencing has to be put up with. I have come to accept most of the different motions that the sea offers, but this is the one that gives me the worst problems. Fortunately, all was well as we made our way across the Pacific, and there was time to enjoy Aurora's facilities and entertainment again.

The Norovirus problems were finally declared to be over. The public toilet doors were free to close again, and we could all enjoy our own dining preferences, choosing what, and how much, we had to eat. We nearly always took breakfast and lunch in the Orangery, except for the occasional midday treat of a burger and chips in the Sidewalk Café. We usually had dinner in the Medina restaurant, but again had a change now and again with a buffet in the Orangery plus a couple of visits to Café Bordeaux for a special meal.

Another bonus of being virus free was that we were now allowed to shake hands with the crew and entertainers. This was especially significant for the dance teachers who could dance with the passengers for the first time. Up until now they could only dance with each other when demonstrating the steps.

Elsewhere the water leaks continued, and we were all very

familiar with red, green, and blue buckets in the middle of corridors catching the drips from above. There were rarely more than a couple of days without a report from Radio Laundrette announcing that someone had a sodden cabin carpet. On more than one evening while having a drink in Champions I felt the drip of a new leak from the ceiling, and the waiters reacting quite 'matter of fact' by directing us to another seat and finding another bucket. The most disturbing thing was that repairs were taking several days, and at times it felt as if there was no answer to the problem, with the buckets becoming permanent features.

A new facility that has come along since we started cruising is the use of the internet while at sea. It is not a fast service, but it allows people to stay in touch with home by email, and on a longer cruise to keep watch on the banking situation. During the first segment we had regularly used the internet service in that way, plus submitting a daily report for my blog.

Although horrendously expensive and painfully slow, it did what we wanted of it. After leaving San Francisco however, the internet service became very poor, and there were days when it was just not available at all.

Initially I thought that the satellite channel was failing, but eventually I chatted to the IT man who explained the problem. It seemed that the number of passengers with iPhone and iPad had increased significantly and these amazing machines automatically log onto an internet service when it finds one and stays there. In effect they had monopolised the channels available, meaning that us casual laptop users could never get a signal. The situation did improve after the ship's newspaper asked people to log off when they didn't need it, but I also changed my habits and used the internet in the evening or early in the morning rather than during the peak times of the day.

Somebody had been checking on the internet to see if there was an explanation for the passengers going off in handcuffs in San Francisco. No longer a rumour, we now had a quite sinister reason for the episode and the cruise started to become rather unusual.

The customs officials in San Francisco had found that an Australian passenger leaving the ship was carrying some cocaine. He was immediately arrested and brought back onto the ship while the officials searched his cabin. They found some more, and the gentleman came clean and identified his accomplices as two New Zealanders in another cabin. Moving to investigate this cabin, the occupants were busy flushing cocaine down the toilet and refused to open the door so the customs officials broke in. They seized another significant amount of the drug, and arrested the other two offenders. Courtesy of Radio Laundrette the early reports suggested the drugs came on board the ship while we were in St Lucia but newspapers eventually reported that Curacao was the source. There were no sniffer dogs or suitable scanners at either of these ports to look for drugs as the smugglers returned to the ship with their packets of death. Another story said that the drugs had been smuggled aboard inside a teddy bear. I find this hard to believe as the total amount was thirteen kilogrammes of cocaine. For those trying to work out how much that is, imagine thirteen bags of sugar in a supermarket. That would have meant either a very large teddy bear or a serious number of them. The final embellishment to the story was that the buckets dotted around the ship were not to catch leaks, but to allow sniffer dogs a drink as they searched the decks!

This story attempted to become a rumour but it was too far-fetched even for the laundry.

Nothing was officially announced about the drug smuggling on board the ship, and even when I questioned an officer at the 'Welcome on Board' party he carefully side-stepped the subject.

While talking about officers, I can't ignore the new Captain. He made himself known to the passengers very quickly, and he was a real breath of fresh air with his humorous style of making announcements.

Captain Neil Turnbull usually came over the PA system each morning *("this is the Captayne")* to let us know where we were, plus giving a weather forecast. He walked around the ship (as did his predecessor) and got to know anyone who made conversation with him. He became a regular in many of the photographs we had taken at the various 'Welcome on Board' and 'Portunas' parties we attended for the rest of the cruise. Sadly, our visits to the gym became less regular, and swimming similarly lost some of its appeal but we continued to do our best to stay active. The thought of sinking into a spiral of over-eating without exercise horrified us when we looked at the numerous overweight and downright obese passengers who reminded us of Weeble dolls.

We continued to go to port talks for the stops ahead of us, and enjoyed several evenings in the theatre for the shows and cabaret artists. There were still too many vocalists compared to other types of entertainment, and although the comedians we saw were amusing, virtually all of them could boast that they had a bus pass and pension on their CVs. The best act was Bruce Morrison (yes a vocalist) with a show based on Les Misérables which I enjoyed immensely and Deb was over the moon with. He did another show (his last on board) one afternoon dedicated to the life of Queen Victoria and was assisted by Cruise Director Christine Noble who played the part of the queen quite brilliantly.

Deb and I were happy with the sea days, and completely

relaxed into a delicious routine of a beautiful ship, good food, lovely people, the weather warming up again, and still lots to do. Our expectations for the ports to come were getting greater as we closed in on our next stop in the Hawaiian Islands.

The Hawaiian Island of Oahu, and Honolulu
Tuesday 31st January 2012

We docked in the port of Honolulu which is the commercial centre of the Hawaiian Islands, but more importantly for us, it is close to another port called Pearl Harbour. It was going to be a day when history was brought to life for me, and it left me with memories that I doubt will ever fade.

It became apparent just how far we had travelled when we woke up with the clocks now ten hours behind Britain, knowing that by early afternoon for us, it will nearly be tomorrow back home.

Our stop today was one of the special ones where we had booked the tour almost as soon as we had booked the cruise. Our visit to Pearl Harbour was a major 'must do' of the adventure. We had both read articles, seen television programmes, and watched films about 7th December 1941 when Japan finally convinced America to join in with the Second World War.

Unlike our ventures on shore so far, today we had to dress in a respectful way as the Pearl Harbour site is a memorial to the soldiers and sailors who died that day. Wearing trousers and a shirt was a shock especially as the weather was hot with clear blue skies, but I had no problem complying with the 'no shoulders or knees showing' rule.

Breakfast over, we collected our tour stickers from the theatre and made our way on to the coach. Once we had spotted who was talking to us, we realised that the driver was doubling up as the guide to get us to and from Pearl Harbour. He was a very outgoing man by the name of David, well more accurately 'Cousin David'.

During the short drive to the museum site we were educated about the landmarks of Honolulu along with history and a cultural overview of the island. He also insisted we responded with a loud *"Aloha!"* when he shouted the word to us as a welcome.

We had already been given a pretty good idea of how the day would unfold by Jo (our port lecturer) and we knew there would be some free time to look around the museum as well as the formal tour of the monument to the USS Arizona.

We arrived at the car park at around 9:00 and it was already crammed with coaches and hundreds of tourists were milling around. Cousin David handed out our tickets for the 11:45 tour of the USS Arizona, warning us that the site was a US Navy establishment and subject to quite strict security. Once inside the site we looked around at what was on offer and decided to buy tickets to go aboard the USS Bowfin which is a Second World War submarine. Just like the Alcatraz tour, we were given little audio players to guide and inform us as we walked around the submarine, and this certainly helped to explain its history.

Even with my concerns about claustrophobia, the visit turned out to be quite a treat as we never expected to get a chance to see inside a submarine. It really showed how difficult a life these sailors had. Bowfin was no more than a metal tube with just a narrow walkway going from bow to stern surrounded by engines, galleys, bunks, pumps and valves, plus the control area, and its weapons room. The torpedoes were not restricted to that weapons room and could be found stored under bunks.

It was uncomfortably enclosed and cramped, bringing home the horrific lives of submariners who had to survive for weeks on end with rarely a chance to stand upright. They also knew that if things went wrong, their last breath would be very sudden and probably of water.

After straightening up again and back in the open air we

followed up what we had seen with a look around the accompanying museum that featured the illustrious history of Bowfin, plus other submarines and their crew. There was another audio show as we walked around the memorabilia, with descriptions of submarine exploits through the ages. The last exhibit was just a little frightening and was an unused nuclear missile that was 2 metres in diameter and probably some 15 to 20 metres in length. It was designed to obliterate non-military targets...

... yes, that will have been us then!

The exhibition site was absolutely packed with both adults and youngsters, and although Americans were in the majority there were people from all over the world. This included a high number of Japanese visitors which to us was slightly confusing, considering the part they played at Pearl Harbour, so we asked a guide about them. The response was that many of the older Japanese come to silently say "sorry" while the young ones are just there to see a tourist sight.

Time to eat and we had a hot dog with onions, ketchup and chilli sauce. When in America it just has to be done at least once! This time I didn't go near the nachos and the strange radioactive-looking cheese sauce.

Suitably replenished we looked around another museum which dealt with the history of Pearl Harbour and its day of horror on 7th December 1941.

Our informal time at Pearl Harbour was up and we joined the queue for the main attraction of the USS Arizona memorial. Whilst we were in the queue an inquisitive American asked what the *"pretty yellow stickers with number 5 on"* was all about. I explained that we were from the cruise ship and this initiated a discussion on where we had come from and where we were going. On discovering the nature of our trip he was most impressed and invited Deb and me to give him a *"five on the knuckles"*. I was now amazed, and slightly concerned, at the size of his hand and knuckles...they were huge!

He was a big man, but not fat, and it looks like whatever sport he grew up on produced strong powerful hands. Anyway, having made our mark he bade farewell and turned to all those around him to let them know about us... fame!!

As our time arrived the choreographed experience started in a cinema. It was a moving video and its introduction from a young US female sailor had an impact on all who were watching and there was total silence as the historical material started. Most of the footage was captured at the time of the Japanese attack on Pearl Harbour, originating from both American and Japanese sources. There was a potted history including the mistakes that stopped the US Navy realising they were about to be humbled by the Japanese.

It may be very bad of me to have preconceptions of Americans but they often come across as big, loud and rarely silent, but everyone behaved with dignity and respect at that moment, and yes, you could have heard a pin drop.

Immediately as the video ended, doors opened at the side of the cinema to allow us to leave and board a US Navel boat that took us across the bay to the memorial building built over the almost-submerged remains of the USS Arizona battleship. This was the flagship of the US Pacific Fleet and took a direct hit by a penetration bomb into the ammunition store and exploded instantly killing, or more accurately vaporising, some 1,100 of the crew with fewer than about 20 survivors. The ship sank, and has been allowed to stay where it was as a tomb for the sailors and has stood ever since as a memorial to their memory. It remains as a symbol of that infamous attack that resulted in the USA becoming fully involved in the Second World War.

This was an amazing, thought-provoking, and for many, a tear-jerking, experience. As with memorials of the European conflicts in Belgium and France, the names on the wall bring the magnitude of this single ship's demise into reality. Here were the names of 1,100 sons, brothers, fathers and husbands who never knew if it had all been worth it. One of the Rangers told us of a recent burial at the site when two of the survivors had died with their wishes to be returned to the sunken ship as their resting place. They now lie with their mates again with a most poignant symbol of the fuel oil still leaking from the vessel forming rainbows on the surface of the water. People refer to this oil as the tears of the sailors below.

The whole exhibition is as good as it can be and organised so well by the US Navy. Just to show how efficiently the tour operates, the site opens with the first tour at 7:15 in the morning with another tour starting every 15 minutes. We were due into the cinema at 11:45 and it was exactly that time as we entered so there had been no delays or slippages.

As with the Panama Canal, and Alcatraz, this visit is worth every dollar we spent on it and I urge anyone who has a conscience, or just an interest in history to go and see it if you ever get a chance.

The remainder of our tour then took us on a drive around the city and included a visit to the veterans' cemetery which just cemented the memories of the day into my mind. Honolulu is beautiful, and a pleasure to be in, with friendly people who tried to make our stay a happy one. I will remember it as such a place but I don't think I will ever forget the Pearl Harbour experience.

Before we returned to Aurora we spent an hour or so looking around the shops and sampling Hawaiian ice cream. We didn't buy much as it quickly became clear that most of the souvenirs were manufactured in China, and hence fell into my category of 'tat'.

The entertainment on board that evening was a Headliners' show, followed by a weird quiz themed on alcohol. No prizes for us that night but we still had a glass or two of wine plus a bit of a dance in Carmen's before our bed beckoned to us.

Hilo and the Big Island of Hawaii
Wednesday 1st February 2012

As we approached the Port of Hilo, Deb and I had the thrill of fulfilling another ambition by spotting a small pod of whales swimming and spouting as they passed close by the ship. After 17 cruises, this was the first time we had seen these magnificent animals, and it was a delightful early morning surprise.

We were now visiting the island actually called Hawaii, also referred to as 'The Big Island'. Whilst Honolulu is the commercial centre, and most populated, this is the largest of the islands and historically the birth place of Hawaii. It is where King Kamehameha united the islands after years of conflict, thus becoming known as the 'Father' of Hawaii.

On our arrival, the weather was dull but it was still hot and humid as it would be in most of the places we would visit in the next month or so. Our day was going to be occupied with a long tour looking at a whole range of attractions around the island, so once breakfast was over we gathered together our cameras, drinks, and sun screen lotions, and went to the Curzon Theatre to await the call to our bus.

Today's driver and guide was an American from Minneapolis who had decided to swap the mainland rat-race and cold winters for the relaxed life and moderate climate of Hawaii. He initially had a winter holiday there but moved permanently a little while later. Hawaii has a lot of rain each year but rarely gets hotter than 30°C and never drops below 16°C. I can see why he likes it.

He spoke about his house and his passion for growing flowers and fruit in his large garden. To enhance his job he has learnt a lot about Hawaiian history and the attractions of the island, especially the volcano that we would be visiting today. To top it off he had a dry but quick humour that far exceeded many of the comedy acts we had on the ship so he was a major hit with us.

We set off with the usual *"here are the shops and..."*

It soon got much more interesting as we drove down a road lined with banyan trees planted by celebrities or dignitaries who had visited the island over the decades. Each tree had a plaque with the date it was planted and by whom. The trees are very distinguishable as they have tendril-roots which grow down from the branches until they find the ground where they take root and grow both thick and strong. On established trees there are so many of these roots that they surround the centre of the tree making its girth enormous. I have seen examples of the banyan tree before but never a whole road lined with them.

Our guide was giving us a very good commentary about the trees and plants that we were passing, but he also made sure we realised that this was a tsunami area and had been severely affected by them in the recent past. He showed us the extent of the latest tsunami damage and how much of the land had been covered by the flooding. He pointed out one area that has been flooded so many times that the people have given up protecting it, and it is now left as a public park area.

As we left the port we started a steady climb from sea level to the mountain area of the island formed by volcanic action over hundreds of years. The region we were going to was the Volcanic National Park, and in particular Mount Kilauea. This is a major volcano that has been continually erupting for several decades and is thus one of the most active ones in the world. While winding our way up some three thousand feet to the crater we learnt the names of all the trees and flowers that we passed, as well as a number of interesting landmarks. Our driver kept our attention and shared his vast general knowledge of volcanos, in particular facts that related to the volcano where we would soon be arriving.

Mount Kilauea was amazing. We eventually looked down into a huge crater (and I mean huge) from its rim, and had a superb view of an area still active with steam and gasses billowing into the sky above us. The lava collects in a natural reservoir below the now solid base and eventually flows out of the side of the mountain into the sea.

To put the size of this spectacle into proportion, Mount Everest is the highest peak above sea level but Mount Kilauea is the highest mountain anywhere in the world measured from its base on the sea bed.

Suitably amazed by our first view of the volcano, we took a look at the nearby Thomas Jaggar Museum, an observatory, exhibition, and souvenir shop. There were several informative displays to look at including a number of seismology recorders for the volcanic sites on the island. Most of them were continually chattering away, showing just how much activity was going on. Earthquakes are common and the local papers report days when no quakes have been felt, in contrast to the rare headlines in Britain when we get a tremor.

From this first vantage point we drove around the crater edge for a few miles and then viewed the volcano again from a point almost opposite to where we had been at the museum. We were now seeing the crater where it had been inactive for some time, and visitors were allowed to descend into the caldera to walk on it. Down below we could see people appearing like ants walking across a now cooled and solidified lake of lava. Other tours from Aurora were in the same area as us, and one group was nearby preparing to cycle down a track for hundreds of feet to the crater. I later discovered they had a wonderful experience.

A short drive later we came to another volcanic spectacle

called a lava tunnel. This was created when a huge lava flow started to cool. The relatively cooler air makes the outside surfaces of the lava solidify whilst the still molten core continues to move beneath. Eventually the lava flow finishes and runs out of the middle leaving a tunnel. The phenomenon makes more sense when you see it, rather than my amateurish explanation. Anyway, it was spooky to walk through a few metres of tunnel knowing what it once was. This Thurston Lava Tube was formed during the 1974 eruption, and is in a rain forest, so at the far end we were surprised to emerge under a tree canopy to the sound of loud curious birds asking who we were.

The volcano aspect of the tour was now over and we headed down the mountain towards our lunch venue. On the way we made a quick stop to visit an orchid nursery, and this was another *"wow"* moment.

The colours, shapes and scents of row after row of these exotic flowers were a joy to our senses. It was quite spectacular yet relaxing to walk around the beautiful displays and I began to understand why gardeners can become so passionate about orchids. A crowd gathered by a large bowl of free blooms for the ladies to pop behind their ears, and the shop tempted people to bring out their wallets to purchase perfumed products and the usual selection of souvenirs. Our stop was only a few minutes but it was an absolute delight to see what is can be grown naturally in a place like Hawaii.

Time for lunch, and it was superb.

The venue was a Japanese Botanical Garden site that makes money to support itself by supplying lunch to visiting groups of tourists like ourselves. It was a buffet-style meal based on Oriental food, and was both delicious and generous. I didn't hear a word said against the lunch, and for a group of British cruise ship passengers that in itself was unusual.

After the meal we had a few minutes to walk around the gardens which were spectacular, with a wide variety of plants laid out to please both the eye and nose. We were given the chance to pick and eat any ripe fruit we desired, so I plucked a couple of fresh tangerines to give our taste buds another burst of pleasure.

Then it was back on the coach for the final couple of stops of our tour, starting with a visit to a macadamia nut processing factory. The large plantation acts as a vast factory to first grow the nuts before harvesting, processing, and packaging them. Several of us went to look at the processing factory but this turned out to be a waste of time as there was virtually nothing happening, so we quickly moved to the shop. We had all been given a sample of the nuts as we came off the coach, and suitably impressed, most people came out of the shop with bags full of nut products (mostly chocolate covered) to take home as presents...

... or (like us) as a late night treat during the evenings to come. Our last stop of the day was at the Rainbow Waterfalls that was very pretty, and probably impressive when the 'rainbow' is formed early in the morning. To us it was just a waterfall, and to be honest we have seen more spectacular examples in Norway. Perhaps a slightly disappointing end to the tour, but it was only a very minor negative to a day that had been a non-stop spectacular and fascinating experience.

Back on Aurora and after a long eight-hour day trip we were both tired. We had no time to do anything else on shore and that was sad as our dinner-table mates described it a lovely place to wander, look in the shops, or have a coffee or a beer. That is how it goes with tours – you take your chances making a choice from the best information you have beforehand. We had not been disappointed as our tour was a terrific day out, but it did stop us getting a flavour of the local culture. Based on what I saw and heard from others, the island of Hawaii is a little bit less 'American' than the *"in your face"* experience of Oahu and Honolulu the day before.

That was our last stop in the United States, so it was time to give back our immigration paperwork and become officially de-immigrated from the USA.

We decided to avoid the early evening entertainment as it was another female vocalist, and Deb took the opportunity to do some washing.

My only contribution was to make regular visits to the sauna-like laundrette to collect the freshly-ironed clothes and return them to where they belong.

Yes readers, I did feel guilty.

Laundry chores over, we went to another 'Tropical Night' party out on deck for a couple of drinks and a boogie under the stars. To round off the night we had a hot chocolate in Café Bordeaux, before going back to the cabin for a quick read and lights out.

The two days in the Hawaiian Islands had been wonderful, with a dual edged experience. Firstly there was a chance to appreciate the culture of the islands, and to see nature at its most beautiful, amazing and intriguing. But secondly we were reminded of its history and the man-made tragedies that have led to the creation of the inspirational Pearl Harbour memorial.

Aurora was steaming on to our next adventure and soon we would be crossing the equator into the southern hemisphere on our way to the Samoan Islands.

Sea Days to the Southern Hemisphere
2nd to 5th February 2012

It was our last few days in the northern hemisphere as we headed south towards the equator and life on board Aurora became relaxed again after the excitement of Hawaii. A handful of people had left the ship, mainly crew and cabaret artists, but there were also a few new faces on board to replace them and to brighten up our evenings in the theatre. The weather surprised us and the sea was on the rougher side of what we hoped for, but the temperature crept up again into the high 20°Cs. Sun worshipping became the most common activity for us, and in fact for most people. The swimming pool had also warmed up a little to tempt Deb back in again, and even I got in for a swim once. But as we enjoyed our tropical climate on board, we were aware of a cold spell back at home with widespread snow and frosts. At the dinner table, or during chats in the bars, winter in Britain regularly became a topic of discussion.

I'm sorry but we didn't have any guilt about laying in the sunshine.

A little treat for me was that a small theatre group, well two people actually, had arrived on board to present some Murder Mystery shows, of which one was going to be a play for a few of the passengers to take part in. I thoroughly enjoy amateur dramatics, and was given the all-clear by Deb to join in and desert her for rehearsals once a day until we got to Fiji. On that night there would be two performances of the play in the Curzon Theatre as the main entertainment for the ship.

Turning to the latest batch of professional entertainers, things had become a little more interesting. We had a pair of violinists who played both classical and modern music. They were perhaps appreciated by the men a little more than the women, as they were young females, but the music was also very good. Another act was a tribute to John Denver which was pleasantly enhanced by having videos to accompany the songs. The show included some lesser-known John Denver songs that really appealed to me.

We had another tropical evening on deck, but a Country and Western evening under the stars had to be postponed because of rain. That was a relief anyway – line dancing and *"Yeehah!"* are just not our cup of tea!

Daytime entertainment featured more talks, generally with three different ones each day. We didn't take advantage of many, but did remain faithful to Jo and her port talks on our upcoming stops. Every destination to come was an adventure into the unknown for us and these presentations were giving us a little help in deciding how to spend our time ashore. All the usual lessons and deck sports continued to be popular but our favourite activity was still soaking up the sunshine and feeling warm.

There were a couple of special moments and one of those was during the afternoon of Saturday 4th February when Deb and I became 'Shellbacks' as we crossed the equator. For those of you unfamiliar with this term, it means we have sailed across the equator for the first time. It was an amusing afternoon's entertainment with some of the ships' officers and entertainers playing various games in one of the swimming pools with plenty of different coloured gunk thrown about.

Apparently, King Neptune was content with the ceremonial fun, and happy for us to have crossed the equator. Hence we were able to proceed to our next destination with Neptune's blessing.

The other special moment was an invitation to a lunch for the passengers going all the way around the world. There were just over 600 of us completing the circumnavigation, requiring two sessions for this very special formal lunch.

Ours was on Sunday 5th February and our table was hosted by the Senior HR Officer whose job role includes 'hiring and firing'. "I bet she has a lot of friends!"

The lunch was superb with a wonderful menu and service by very attentive waiters, plus a generous supply of wine following a champagne welcome. As well as our host, our table had Mick, Brenda, Roger and Laura from our dinner table. There was also one final couple that we hadn't met before but they would become good friends for the rest of the cruise. They were Bob and Sandra (known as Sam) who had a wonderful story to tell. Both of them lost their partners at a similar time around two years before. Quite by accident they both took a cruise aboard Artemis in order to, as Sam described it, get away from friends and family trying too hard to be sympathetic. They ended up on the same dinner table and over those many meals a friendship formed. Bob said he would drop in on Sam for a cup of tea when they got home, and he kept to his word.

They eventually married and had their honeymoon aboard Artemis on its final voyage. Cruising was very close to their hearts, and on this one they would celebrate their wedding anniversary while we were in Istanbul. It is a lovely story and it was easy to see the deep friendship that they shared. We met up several times during the coming weeks, and regularly enjoyed a glass or two of champagne together at the 'Welcome on Board' parties at P&O's expense.

So with lunch over, and in a mildly hung-over state, I took the time to update my blog before we reached Samoa the following morning, for the next chapter of our adventure. I was sitting on the balcony with the laptop on my legs, searching for inspiration by looking out over the beautiful sea-filled garden. My peace was suddenly broken by the phone ringing, and it was the amateur dramatic group suggesting we had another rehearsal as time was getting short. I could hardly refuse so, still a little tipsy, I went off to practice 'Not the Butler Again' in which I was playing the seemingly sinister role of Doctor D'eath...

... Yes I know it's corny.

With the rehearsal over it was time to consider our evening, and more particularly food. It was formal dress code, but Deb and I weren't in the least bit hungry after our delicious lunch. So for the first time in 17 cruises, we did not adhere to the evening's dress code and just had a snack in the Orangery. That was not a problem as several people ate there on formal nights to avoid the dressing up, but when we left the Orangery and went to the theatre we felt so out of place that I wanted to slide under my seat to stop anyone seeing me. Of course we were not the only ones, and I eventually relaxed into the 'unclean' feeling and watched the female violinists again. The rest of the evening passed quietly in the bars where formal dress was not required, and then it was bedtime.

We had been at sea for a month and had sailed thousands of miles virtually half-way around the globe. The adventure would start to become even more exciting now as the stops became more frequent and of course Australia, and Sydney, was just a few days away.

Sumptuous Samoa
Monday 6th February 2012

We had arrived at the port of Apia on the island of Upolu in Samoa. It used to be referred to as Western Samoa but the 'western' has now been dropped. It is a beautiful island with typical South Pacific beaches and much lush vegetation everywhere, including rain forests. Now, I said rain forests and they were indeed being soaked by rain that day. In actual fact the whole island was being soaked from the moment we arrived until after we left.

Our arrival into the port coincided with what the captain described as a squall. That term does not adequately describe the weather that started with a sudden gale force wind, then rain so hard that we could hardly see the island. It was so bad that the ship had to wait offshore for an improvement, during which time the captain checked the forecast to see if it was even worth attempting to land. Luckily there was a small improvement, not that we noticed, and with a couple of tugs in assistance Aurora made its entry into the harbour. As we came through the breakwater, we could see that a number of marquees that had been erected to welcome us were strewn all over the dockside and frantic efforts were being made to stop them becoming fully airborne.

This was the fastest docking manoeuvre I have ever witnessed. The tugs worked their socks off to push us to the quay and then hold us steady while local stevedores grabbed our ropes and tied us up in the pouring rain and driving wind. We came through the breakwater in virtually zero visibility and five minutes later there were two ropes attached. Spectacular to say the least, and of course we were watching and got drenched for the first time.

There was no sign of the rain and wind easing, and it was

beginning to look as if the day might be a disappointment but no, this was the beginning of one of the most magical days we had ever had.

We went to the theatre to await our tour and an announcement was made that because of the continuing storm, the tours would be delayed a little. Our tour included a beach barbeque and we were given the option cancel the trip and get our money back if we wanted to. That was tempting, especially as we were already in our second set of clothes for the day, but after a lot of thought we decided to carry on with our plans and to hell with it.

The rain eased enough to leave the ship and we quickly got onto our small, but very pleasant bus with an extremely cheerful Samoan guide whose name was simplified to 'C-U Lee'. I dread to think what his name really was. The driver was simply called 'Bob'. They kept the day going when it could well have turned out a disaster.

After the usual *"here is a school etc."* we arrived at the first point of interest which was a waterfall. We stopped but no-one got out. It was chucking it down again, and we could see in the distance that the colour of the waterfall was a disgusting muddy brown from all the soil that had been washed into the river. C-U cheered us up by saying that there was a better one to look at later, and it had better parking. Strangely there were few protests, as we trusted his judgement, and our clothes remained dry.

We were now joking about the rain, which apparently, according to C-U, was very rare on the island. Bob fought his way along the flooded roads and avoided the potholes whenever he actually saw them. Onwards to our second stop at another waterfall, but this time we also had a demonstration of processing a coconut. Yes it was still raining, but we piled out of the bus, and quickly took photographs of the muddy waterfall before rushing under the cover of some beautiful traditional palm leaf-roofed huts. There were a number of these huts and each one had a demonstration of an aspect of traditional Samoan life. One of these was where the coconut demonstration was taking place and fortunately it was only brief as the hut could only accommodate a few of us in the dry. The process started with the husk being removed as if it was a mediaeval torture of a head being smashed onto a stake. The shell was then swiftly and expertly split into two equal parts with a single blow from a lethal looking knife. The contents were scraped out with a chisel-like object which produced what is referred to as the coconut meat. Samples were offered and greedily accepted, as fresh coconut is a delicious treat. Next the meat was squeezed in a furry material obtained from a banana tree, and this produced the thick coconut cream that is used in much of the local cooking. More samples offered and accepted.

And it was still raining!

We dripped back to the bus for the next part of the journey and saw our first example of what we all thought a slightly bizarre custom.

The Samoans are very family orientated and several generations often live together in a single house. When people die, they are buried in the front garden. Yes I did say the front garden, and in full view of everyone passing by. We thought that having this unusual rockery must make selling houses slightly difficult.

Onwards through the puddles we saw more schools, occasional shops, and various fruit trees that were pointed out and described by our guide. He also spent quite a lot of time running down Britain for pulling out of governing the islands, and then turned on New Zealand for not initially doing as well as Britain, and finally had a go at China for getting involved at all. Samoans are not the richest of people and they rely on overseas aid to enable their traditional way of life to continue. Eventually we arrived at the beach, and it had finally stopped raining!

With sighs of pleasure and amazement we stared at the beach and it was absolutely stunning with golden sand and even a washed-up tree in the distance. There were overhanging palm trees and a reef no more than 200 metres off shore making it a calm lagoon with a gentle slope out to coral patches about five or six metres from the shoreline. It was the type of beach you see on postcards, and the picture that is conjured up from descriptions of the South Seas in books. It was beautiful, and there were gasps of approval all around and the weather was forgotten because this made up for any discomfort we had suffered.

Within the first five minutes of the buses arriving, a handful of people had changed and were in the water. They shouted to the rest of us how warm the water was, and Deb only took a minute or two before she also shrieked her delight as she jumped around in the Southern Pacific Ocean. By the time I had got into my trunks, Deb had returned to get her goggles, saying that fish were visible. Soon we were both in the warm, clear water and having got myself wet, I looked down at a coral patch with its strange multi-coloured shapes, and sea anemones and other gently-moving vegetation, and yes, as promised there were the fish.

I am telling no lies here. In water only just up to my knees I could see small zebra fish, plus dazzling bright blue ones and some just a little less flamboyantly coloured. Other tiny fish of every colour of the rainbow darted in and out of the coral and sea anemones. From a little further away Deb shrieked with delight as the little creatures swam through her fingers. As I walked towards another clump of coral, I looked down into the water with my goggles and saw a good-sized fish just passing between my feet. Not knowing it was there, I could have easily trodden on it.

It had started to rain again but perhaps 20 of us in the water just jumped and frolicked like children, smiling and shouting our discoveries to each other and tempting others to come in and join us. The rain did not matter as our sheer pleasure made the weather irrelevant.

Drunk with pleasure it was eventually time to have our barbeque lunch. Many of us were still in our swimming kit but we draped ourselves with towels to satisfy Samoan modesty expectations as we queued in the rain to sample the local food cooked in the traditional manner. Sheltering under the shade of banana leaf-roofed beach huts we ate, and many people just sat silently contemplating the beauty of the setting. Only a handful of the stalwart British people were moaning about the rain......

... or the sand,

    ... or perhaps the food,

        ... or just about anything to be a pain!

The atmosphere of this place made me forget the rain, and forget that the weather was not as warm as perhaps I would have liked. This was a dream come true.

Books I had read, lessons that I had almost listened to in school, films and TV programmes, all came to life on this day. I may never get another chance to do this again, but at least I have tasted the sweetness of a South Pacific Island beach. Thank goodness we decided not to cancel the trip.

Our time on the beach was up and we got back on the buses to complete our trip with a scenic ride back to the ship. By the way, it was still raining as we splashed along the puddled roads as further landmarks were pointed out to us. Meanwhile our tour group was involved in a laughable round of banter with the guide and with each other.

Poor Bob (the driver) was really struggling to avoid the potholes and even to see the edges of the road as torrents of water were now surrounding and crossing the road. Our route was following some of the steepest roads on the island and Bob required all the bus's available power on the worst inclines, which meant that the air conditioning had to be switched off. This was having an effect as we grew hot and sticky in the humidity and the windows were misting over. Even that could not upset us today, well except for the usual few, and we laughed our way onwards.

There was one final stop at another waterfall, and for the moment it had stopped raining, so we started the mass exit from the bus with cameras ready.

Right on cue the heavens opened and the rain returned with its full force. Now as the first passengers started to leave the bus, a chain reaction became unstoppable and we all had to get off. By the time we completed the, at most, 20 paces to the photo point I was soaked to the skin even with my pakamac on. I was splattered in mud and my trousers were ready to be wrung out. Like a scene from an old comedy film, we all got off, ran to the viewing point, clicked our cameras, ran back and piled back into the bus. The whole event lasted maybe three minutes, but everyone giggled in delight and laughed at each other's drowned rat appearance.

Back on the ship we peeled off our sodden clothes, had a warm shower and finally got dry again. After dinner Deb and I relaxed in Carmen's with our e-readers, still chuckling in delight as we remembered this wonderful day.

Overnight we were sailing to our next stop at the American Samoan island of Pago Pago. Could it possibly get near to the delightful day that we had in Apia?

Pago Pago
Tuesday 7th February 2012

Before I describe the day, I feel I must explain the island's name. Pago Pago is pronounced Pango Pango. The reason for the apparently bad spelling is that the settlers who discovered and colonised the island did not have the letter 'N' in their printing set! Sounds an unlikely story but it was good enough to make us laugh.

As we woke and looked outside, the day looked like it would be another wet one, but our Captain told us otherwise, so we had to believe him.

Pago Pago is an American-controlled island and perhaps that was why there was some sort of bureaucratic problem that needed to be resolved before we could go ashore. Eventually the paperwork issue was sorted out and the tours were only about an hour late starting. By now we had become accustomed to Captain Neil Turnbull's little announcements before going ashore, but it always raised a smile around the ship as he bade us farewell as we left the ship *"at the speed of a thousand gazelles."* There were variations of animal species occasionally, and once he strayed away from the animal kingdom and we were likened to tuk-tuks, but gazelles remained his favourite.

Our tour today was one that went to a tribal village to look at how the local people lived, and to sample some of their food and traditional entertainment. We knew it would be fun today as we had been forewarned about the less-than-luxury coaches.

They are little more than small lorries fitted with a wooden box that has windows (actually just holes in the wall), and benches to sit on. They are usually brightly-coloured on the outside, and decorated inside to make them more comfortable. Ours had mock fur all over the insides with fairy lights and shiny dangling ornaments. Anyway, as I said, we had been warned about the slightly primitive buses, but of the 20 or so people on board there were still four or five people who had a shock and went into British 'whinge' mode.

Off we went and our guide, a young Samoan girl, helped us to gain our usual deep knowledge of the churches, schools, airport, golf course, petrol station as well as the location of the McDonalds and Kentucky Fried Chicken outlets.

We also stopped to look at a pair of tiny islands (large rocky outcrops, really) just a few metres offshore, one of which is known as 'Flowerpot Island' because of its shape and being topped with trees and other plants. There is a lover's tale associated with these islands which amused us, but it was difficult to give the story our full attention as our on-board port presenter had already recounted it. This stop was good as it gave a few people a chance to paddle in the sea while they took their photographs of a beautiful pair of tiny islands on an equally beautiful beach.

Onwards, no time to waste, accompanied by *"oos, aaahs, and wows"* we passed by more schools, churches and, oh yes, more family graves in peoples' front gardens. The stop at the island's golf course was probably one of the most bizarre ones we had on the cruise.

It was not spectacular, and there wasn't an opportunity for people to try a drive or even a simple putt. The stop just seemed to be a chance for us to buy refreshments in the club bar, where everything was $3. Surprisingly several people decided to take photographs of the course and its club house. Back on our charabancs we were off again and this time we were heading for the tribal village.

There were several buses on this tour, all following the same route, so our convoy arrived at the little village at the same time. We had a brief introduction from an elderly lady who seemed to be in charge, and a welcome to the villagers who could well have been her extended family. We were directed towards four very pretty huts where there were short demonstrations of how people slept, prepared coconuts and made a chocolate drink. The demonstrations were interesting, but perhaps a little brief, and lacking content.

The people in the final hut waited until everyone had assembled as we now had the finale. First we were shown how the village people made their ovens from stones, coconut tree wood, and banana leaves, and then various food stuffs were placed into the oven to cook. Just like a Blue Peter programme *("here's one we prepared earlier")* they then opened up a second oven where cooked food was ready for us to sample. This food – and all the watching visitors – was hurriedly moved to the large village assembly room. Every village has one, and they act as dining rooms, community centres and village council offices.

For those prepared to queue long enough, the food was wonderful, but our organiser was expecting rain and suggested we sat down by a large grassy area to watch a dancing demonstration. Once again this was a very pleasant few minutes with traditionally-dressed girls dancing to a Samoan tune, followed by a similar group of men, and finally a rather large gentleman in not-so-traditional costume (white shirt and tie plus a wraparound 'skirt') doing his version of local dancing. Now, whilst we were on the bus our guide had been trying to teach us a local chant, and now it was our chance to impress the said gentleman with what we had learnt. We did our best and our attempts caused a great deal of applause and laughter from the organising committee.

By now I had worked out quite a lot about this tour. Firstly, the drivers and guides were all part of the same community and also involved in the village demonstrations and dancing. Our guide performed the dance of the Princess and our driver was now in full local costume, and was dancing as well. Two younger men who had appeared at the golf course to answer any questions were now at the village and also getting involved. The village was a parking site for several buses like the ones we had arrived in. This was one very organised tour company, providing everything from the transport through to the end product at the village. It was certainly a very clever business venture.

Anyway, the dancing and singing continued to polite applause from the visitors until it was time to board the bus convoy again for the trip back home to Aurora. On the return journey we were told about more of the island's landmarks (churches, schools, graves in front gardens) and our guide entertained us with some more singing to listen to and chants to perform. Our enthusiasm for this was diminishing rapidly.

The journey took us past numerous beautiful trees and flowers, waterfalls, and other beaches, and I was slightly disappointed that nothing was being said about the obvious natural beauty of the island.

Back at the ship we made a decision not to look around the town anymore as there seemed to be very few shopping opportunities, and little else to encourage us. Perhaps if more of the people had followed the example of our tour hosts, and had seen the business possibilities available with cruise ships visiting, there might also have been a few more shopping outlets. The island has the same beauty as Apia and there are many reasons for ships to come and see it, but it needs to organise itself to welcome its visitors a little more, so as to make more from our bulging wallets.

Back on board we looked for mosquito bites (one each) and settled down to a day at sea before arriving in Fiji. I really felt I was becoming a traveller now, rather than just a holiday maker.

What Happened to Wednesday?
Thursday 9th February 2012

Last night when we went to bed it was Tuesday 7th February
but when we woke up in the morning it was Thursday 9th
February. So where on earth did Wednesday 8th February go?
With Samoa behind us we had continued sailing westwards
overnight and crossed the International Date Line. Rather than
putting the clocks back another hour during the night, we put
them forward a full day. Instead of being twelve hours behind
Britain we had suddenly become 12 hours ahead...
... very strange!
Another landmark for the cruise was that we also crossed the
180° line of longitude meaning we were half way around the
world from the Greenwich Meridian in London.
Although there were rain showers, we had a chance to worship
the sun again, and that was becoming expected each day now.
I began to feel a little bit like a reptile as I shed my skin for the
second time in a month. The sun was very hot and if you were
unprotected for even a short while, it physically chastised you.
For the last week or so I had been spending a considerable
amount of time getting ready for the Passengers' Murder
Mystery Play, and today it got serious with the dress rehearsal
before tomorrow's performances. The visiting professional
theatre group had given all the time they could to mould a
small group of us to provide a show in the Curzon Theatre as
the main entertainment for the following evening. Today was
the first time we had been allowed to go onto the stage, and
the reality of it was making one or two people slightly nervous.
The production was called 'Not the Butler Again' and was very
much along the lines of a farcical Agatha Christie play, but
certainly not close to Poirot or Miss Marple standards.
The dress rehearsal was a disaster with the need to use

microphones being a major stumbling block. With a cast of about ten people, who moved around the stage, it was difficult timing our arrival at a microphone to coincide with the moment that the lines had to be said. Several silent moments resulted, with people completely missing their cues and others reciting very good lines to the back of the stage. The professionals remained calm and considerate towards us, but they must have been slightly worried by what they were witnessing.

It would be alright on the night...

... maybe

Dinner time and it was Brenda's birthday. Well, it had actually been yesterday, but that day never happened of course. For the first time during this cruise our wine steward was asked to bring a bottle of wine to the table. Brenda's husband, Mick, proved to be a true romantic, and ordered roses for the cabin with petals spread over the bed.

... aaaah!

The evening was quiet and our highlight was the quiz in Masquerades with the birthday girl and her husband. We didn't win but passed away a pleasant hour before an early night in anticipation of our arrival in Fiji in the morning.

Fun in Fiji
Friday 10th February 2012

Aurora was at anchor in the bay off Port Denarau which was our calling point on the island of Fiji. This was the first of our tender ports.

For those not aware of the meaning of a tender port, it does not refer to its softness but to the fact that we cannot park the ship at the quay and so have to anchor, and hang around all day out in the bay. The ship's lifeboats, known as tenders, are then used to ferry the passengers back and forth to shore. This slows down the disembarkation process quite considerably as there only a limited number of the lifeboats that can be released for the role. Enough lifeboats have to be available at all times just in case there is a problem on the ship itself, when the lifeboats would be needed for their primary function.

Our plan today was to wait for the early rush to get ashore to die down, then make our way to the island, get a bus or a taxi to the local town and have a look around. So at about 10:00 we left the ship. P&O had organised a local pleasure cruise boat to help with the tendering, and luckily it was the one we caught. It carried twice as many passengers as our lifeboats, was much faster, and far more comfortable. Aurora had to anchor quite a way from the shore, meaning the trip took about 20 minutes.

We chose seats up on the top for a good view, but approaching Port Denarau we spotted the tell-tale mist rolling in across the water that announced rain was heading our way. Never mind, by now fully experienced in tropical showers, our pakamacs were always at the ready.

This was a true tropical shower being short and sharp and it had stopped by the time we got to the jetty. Everything was looking good for our visit. The port owners had invested a considerable sum of money to attract tourists with a marina for yachts as well as pleasure craft. For cruise ships it was ideal, with a small tourist-trap shopping centre immediately as you left the jetty. Main Street ran for perhaps 60 or 70 metres with shops, cafes, bars and restaurants on either side. Half way along there was a square with shorter streets at right angles to it. The pavements on either side of all the streets had permanent awnings above them to shelter visitors should one of the frequent showers came along.

Before we went to find a bus to the nearby larger town, we had a quick look around and caught a wonderful show with local traditional dancing by boys and girls in Fijian dress. There were plenty of seats surrounding the performance area that tried to resemble an amphitheatre but actually looked more like a large dry concrete pond. We photographed and applauded a superb few minutes of dancing but then, without warning, it started to rain again.

Unfortunately, this time it rained with real vengeance and came down as if there was a major leak in Heaven's plumbing system. The streets were instantly awash and the dancers ran for cover at the same time as Aurora's passengers scattered to shelter under the awnings. We felt sure it would stop soon so we decided to look around the shops. It was possible to stay relatively dry between shops by walking under the awnings, or under the stairways which crossed above the streets to shelter as we moved from one side of the street to the other.

There was a good selection of shops at reasonable prices. Having enjoyed an ice-cream, and with no sign of the rain stopping, we bought some souvenirs, plus one or two other bits and pieces, including more mosquito repellent.

Over an hour had passed and the rain never stopped or even got lighter. Hunger was setting in so we had a snack to keep us going, still hoping the rain would go away, but it continued to pour down.

We decided to give up.

At around 12:30 we joined the queue of partially-drowned P&O rats waiting for a trip back to the ship. One totally unprepared male passenger who had no coat with him had gone into a shop and begged for a large plastic bag in which he cut holes for his head and arms to keep himself dry.

The wait for the tender was another 30 minutes, and for most of the time we were under shelter but the last few metres to the jetty were open to the elements, leaving us standing in the rain for several minutes before eventually getting onto the boat.

The rain was so heavy that it was like fog, and the sea was getting pretty rough, but luckily we had the large pleasure craft again which had no trouble with the swell. We spotted one of the ship's own tenders waiting near the jetty and as we set off it followed us. We were standing at the stern of our boat and watched the tender as it struggled to maintain its dignity in the choppy water. Bobbing up and down rather wildly, the tender had no option but to slow down and eventually we lost sight of it as it disappeared into the rain and mist behind us.

Home again, we changed into dry clothes and got something more substantial to eat.

We heard later, via the rumours channel, that there had been one or two mishaps on the trips to and from Aurora and the port. One tender actually ran aground on a mud bank which should have been avoidable but the rain and visibility were pretty awful.

Another more substantiated account was about the tender that followed us back. It had already attempted a trip to the ship but gave up because they couldn't actually find Aurora!! It followed us back, using the local boat as a guide, but being less stable and slower it lost contact in the fog and got lost again. After some time, it did find our very large white ship, but had to wait for the pleasure boat that we were on to be unloaded. Unfortunately it had to bob up and down violently some distance away from the ship and this experience was too much for several passengers and their stomachs gave up the fight. I felt very sorry for those passengers, and was glad it was them and not me. The sea was extremely bouncy, and a tender boat is not very stable in those conditions even when it is moving, let alone when it's trying to sit still in the water.

I dread to think how many complaints were submitted to P&O for the mishaps in Fiji.

Oblivious to the carnage behind, we continued our day on Aurora slightly disappointed with the rain spoiling our day in Fiji, but there were plenty of other things to do.

Rather importantly I had the final rehearsal for the play at 6:00 before two performances at 8:30 and 10:30 to come. Rehearsals had taken up a lot of my time over the last few days, and I was glad that it would soon be over so that I could relax back into the holiday again. Of course I was also so very proud to be actually acting on the main stage, with professional lighting and sound systems. It transpired that this was the first time that the Aurora management had allowed passengers to do this. To make it possible, on the previous day we had all been given a safety show-around by the Stage Manager, and before going back on stage this time, we signed the register to officially become... **STARS!**

Oops, sorry I got carried away.

Despite the abysmal dress rehearsal, the shows went like a dream, except that I forgot my props in the second show and felt a complete prat. Deb and our friends came along to watch, and finally all was revealed. My part involved me being murdered, so it seemed, after about five minutes, but then I reappeared a little later, as I had just been stunned, but I definitely 'died' the second time round.

The play went on for 45 minutes of which I spent about 30 minutes either lying apparently dead on the stage, or slumped in a chair, definitely dead. The position I adopted in the chair was not the best decision and I ached by the end of the second show. I also had a series of bruises on my back from being dragged twice, whilst apparently dead, across the uneven joints of the stage.

The first house was about three quarters full with approaching 500 people watching, and the second show certainly had an audience of 100-plus.

It was never going to be easy for us to attract a huge audience as there was a popular comedian giving three performances in Carmen's at the same time as our play. There was also a 60s themed evening in Masquerades so there was a lot of choice for the passengers. I believe the Cruise Director, Christine Noble, was happy for us to be let us loose in her primary venue, and judging by the laughs we could hear, the passengers were pretty satisfied as well.

Of course Deb and friends all congratulated me on the performance, and I was oh so happy to have been involved. The only disappointment was that the photograph taken by the ship's photographer was lost so none of us have a reminder of what we did.

It had been a long incident-packed day. Aurora was now sailing towards New Zealand but the captain warned us that there was a tropical cyclone on our route. We hoped we'd be able to smile and laugh our way through that as well!

Sea Days to Auckland
11th and 12th February 2012

Saturday 11th February was a warm day and both of us were feeling lazy, so we spent long periods just sitting or sleeping in the sun on our balcony. Our old friends the flying fish put in an appearance again, and an occasional bird could be seen in the distance, but wildlife was generally scarce.

The only break from resting was the port talk on Yorkeys Knob, the port for Cairns, from where we were going on a full day's trip to the Great Barrier Reef with a chance to get up close and personal with the coral and the sea life.

That was a day that we were really looking forward to.

The New Zealand immigration authorities brought a representative on board, presumably while we were in Fiji. Just after lunch whilst dozing peacefully in the cabin, I had a telephone call to inform me that I had been randomly chosen to go and be inspected by this official. It turned out to be little more than a face-to-face passport check. I queued for about a quarter of an hour and the actual meeting took about two minutes consisting of me saying *"hello"* ....no response, followed by him looking at my passport, crossing my name off his list, and then asking me where I was getting off. It hardly seemed worth waking me up for, but at least the non-randomly selected passengers know that I did my duty for them.

Formal dress tonight, and the evening started with the second Portunas Club members party and a chance of a few free drinks, plus a raffle draw for a wine decanter that looked slightly like an up-market sample bottle.

Fortunately we did not win it, as we had very little room to store abstract objects, although the champagne to accompany it could have been dealt with satisfactorily! We joined a table with Bob and Sam, the couple who had sat at the Round the World lunch with us, and chatted with them for half an hour. We also managed to convince a friendly waiter to be generous and keep our table supplied with champagne.

Of course Captain Turnbull gave a little speech and explained that he hoped to miss the worst of Tropical Cyclone Jasmine but that it could result in a late arrival into Auckland. Instead of a direct route to Auckland he was going to set a southerly course initially, to go around Jasmine, before turning west again towards New Zealand. He warned that it was still going to be windy and lumpy during the night but hopefully not as bad as it could have been.

The excess of champagne resulted in a slightly drunken evening meal. Much of the time was spent explaining what the Portunas Club was to the two sober couples who hadn't completed enough nights yet to be invited to the party. We worked out that they would be getting invited to the party on the next sector.

For the evening's entertainment we went to a show by the Headliners troupe that we had not seen before, called 'Destination Dance'. It was really enjoyable, but we had come to expect that from these hard-working girls and boys. We rounded off the evening with some dancing of our own in Carmen's. Unfortunately, I couldn't dance too much as I was suffering the after-effects of playing dead in yesterday's Murder Mystery performances, with my head and neck at a ridiculous and uncomfortable angle.

The next morning (Sunday 12th February) we woke up knowing that the ship had been rocked around a bit during the night. While having breakfast the captain's morning message told us that we came as close as about 130 miles from the edge of the storm, and this produced force 9 to 10 conditions and a reasonably big swell. Things would be getting better during the day and there was not going to be a problem getting to Auckland on schedule. We were currently travelling at the rate of a thousand speeding Gazelles to get there on time, according to the captain.

The port talk today was on Darwin where we had nothing booked. After the presentation Deb and I discussed what we should do to occupy our time as the city seemed to be a quiet one. Most of the tours involved looking at wildlife so we trotted off to the tours desk and booked a trip to a wildlife park that should keep us amused.

There were suitcases in the corridor today as about 200 passengers were scheduled to disembark Aurora the next day. That would mean we had a slightly quieter ship, as not so many new arrivals were expected, apart from a stray cabaret artist perhaps.

There was a treat for some passengers in the afternoon with Chocoholics giving them a chance to wander through the galley and then pig out on a buffet where most things involve chocolate. We have joined in before and realise it is very nice but not something to go crazy for regularly.

I went to a presentation by Christine Noble on the heritage of P&O which was a very nostalgic talk with pictures and videos of the different ships. Christine was able to add a lot more information from her personal experiences during her long career with P&O cruising.

After dinner we had an invitation to visit the jewellery shop where we could have a glass of 'sparkling wine' while we looked at the Valentine's Day special offers. We had no plans to buy anything, but it would have been rude to turn down their invitation!

Semi-Formal tonight, meaning I had to wear a jacket, and the entertainment was a Scottish singer called Stuart Gillies. We did not recognise the name, but our Scottish friends had not been impressed with his first show. The alternative was to watch the last of the Murder Mystery plays being performed by the professional actors in Carmen's before they leave the ship in Auckland. We skipped both shows, and went to a quiz in Masquerades before an early night.

We were looking forward to a good time in one of the major cities of New Zealand the next day. Assuming the weather turned out to be dry; the plan was to have a long walk, do a bit of shopping, and to just be tourists. There was a new item on our shopping list now as we wanted diving masks and snorkels so we could practice for our trip to the Barrier Reef.

Amazing Auckland
Monday 13th February 2012

As we were having our breakfast the ship arrived in the busy and vibrant city of Auckland near the northern end of New Zealand's North Island. Like most of our arrivals, we were seeing Auckland coming to life before the local population were fully awake. First impressions of the scene around us reminded me a little of San Francisco. The ships and ferries used a series of berths just across the road from the end of a major street with its shops and offices. The skyline was dominated by skyscrapers displaying names of major international banks and companies. Of course Auckland is significantly smaller than San Francisco, and certainly less 'in your face' as we were to discover later.

Our plan for the day included a trip to a tourist spot called Kelly Tarlton's Undersea World and Antarctic Experience. Deb had found this in the cabin literature and it appeared to be perfect for us. After that we needed to shop again, as deodorant had joined the *"Oh dear we didn't bring enough"* list, and we also had to buy more postcards as well as birthday cards for our children. They understood that we would miss their birthdays but a card was the least we could do for their special days. Other than that we just looked forward to doing whatever took our fancy.

As the Captain and his little helpers gave us the all clear to go ashore, we galloped free, like his gazelles, to spend some currency that wasn't US Dollars that had been favoured up until now.

New Zealand proved a little trickier to enter than some countries, as they have serious restrictions on food and vegetation coming into their country. As we made our way through the terminal, sniffer dogs patrolled the line of passengers, not looking for drugs, but food. We had listened to the instructions and read the forms so we had no problems complying with their restrictions, but just behind us in the queue the little beagle went berserk. A young lady passenger was taken to the centre of the room to where the 'naughty table' was waiting. The dog was jumping and dancing in delight, and his handler rewarded him with praise and cuddles as a banana was extracted from the passenger's bag. We walked on smiling, but also amazed that grown 'intelligent' adults could not listen to, or read instructions, even after several announcements and reminders on board. I have no sympathy for the person concerned, and although I hope she was not punished with too much of a fine, I do hope she learnt her lesson.

Out in the street we were greeted almost immediately by the first of many friendly New Zealanders that we spoke to over the next two days. She welcomed us and asked if we had planned our day. I answered that we were off to the Kelly Tarlton Exhibition and considering walking to it. She advised that it was a fair distance to walk but there was a free shuttle bus going from just around the corner. When we asked how we would recognise the bus, she replied that *"It looks like a shark"*, which intrigued us somewhat. The bus left every hour, so after a little wander and a cup of coffee we took our place in a small queue.

Yes, we did recognise the bus as it did indeed look like a shark with a head appearing to come out of its roof. It only held 21 passengers so places were limited but the majority of those who got seats were from the ship. Just ten minutes later, after a helpful chat from the driver, we arrived at the 'Antarctic and Underwater' themed exhibition. Built underground, the site had two separate areas. The first dealt with the Antarctic and more especially the Captain Scott expedition. There was a replica of his hut with copies of the furniture, fittings, personal objects and details of how life would have been. It had been well planned and constructed, but I had been hoping for a little more written description on notice boards that I could read without having to resort to my glasses. The examples of letters and reproduced diaries were very special items, but the lighting had been made to match the period and I struggled to see things in the gloom. In the end I was more than happy to simply absorb the atmosphere and view the objects rather than trying to tie it all together. On the other hand, Deb has read much about Scott and she thoroughly enjoyed getting a little solid detail to enhance her knowledge.

In the second area we were greeted with a slight smell of fish which announced that we were moving towards living creatures. It started with peep holes in a wall revealing penguins in a snow-covered landscape. Apparently, they make three tonnes of artificial snow each day to keep these curious but beautiful creatures happy in their man-made home. As we meandered along the corridor, display boards of facts and figures about the Antarctic environment built up the anticipation before we arrived at the main exhibition hall. Here the hall was divided into two sections with a huge aquarium on one side and the penguin hall on the other. We quickly decided that the penguins would be first. There were small enclosed trucks carrying up to six people around the penguin enclosure on a track. The truck slowly made its way around the cold artificial landscape of snow-covered shapes representing an Antarctic scene. There were two types of penguins and they appeared quite happy with most just standing around, but to our delight several waddled about or swam in the water. The ten-minute circuit of the penguin hall was a lovely experience and I really hope those sweet distinctive animals are being treated correctly and not just as objects to make money from.

More thrills followed as we moved to the aquarium area. First there was the open-topped tank containing several types of large fish, most importantly stingrays moving around as if they were flying in the water. They were very impressive especially as the ends of their 'wings' came out of the water when they changed direction. Slightly disappointingly, there were no displays to help us identify the fish and rays that we were seeing.

Down another corridor were display boards and examples of sharks to prepare us for the walk along the aquarium tunnel. This was home to a multitude of fish of all sizes, but the most impressive and the stars of the show were the sharks! They swam freely all around and were awesome as they passed overhead. This area of the exhibition used a moving walkway to allow us to just stand and be taken along, but it was slow enough to jump off to take a more serious look if needed.

We next saw a series of smaller free-standing aquariums containing beautiful tropical fish of every colour with stripes, spots, and spines and different styles of fins and projections making them sometimes sweet and beautiful, but often curiously ugly. As well as the vibrant coloured tiny fish, there were piranhas, crayfish, lobsters, starfish and eels, together with coral and underwater vegetation to make it seem so natural. The finale was a favourite of many, the intriguing seahorses!

In just a few minutes I saw countless examples of living undersea creatures that up until now I had only seen in books or on TV programmes. This whole travel adventure continued to tick so many boxes in my head as the different parts of the world became real sights, sounds, and smells. I felt so happy at times and Deb often turned to me and gently told me off for grinning inanely or sighing for no apparent reason.

Souvenirs purchased, we made the return journey on the shark bus back to the city centre where we grabbed a ferry to cross the harbour to the village of Devonport. Seen by many as being a part of Auckland, it is a much quieter area with a few shops and several places for either a snack or more serious meals. We found a little café that was busy but still had tables available, and just ordered a simple light snack of chunky vegetable soup and garlic bread. Nothing turns out simple as we tour the world, and this soup arrived in what appeared to be small washing-up bowls, and was accompanied by half a loaf of garlic bread. It was as delicious as it was huge and Deb even had to resort to a knife and fork to cut the large chunks of vegetables in the soup.

I like New Zealand!

We completed our visit to Devonport by sampling the shops, but were not overly impressed. The prices were high and although many of the souvenirs reflected the Maori culture, we didn't find anything to tempt us.

We returned to Aurora for a quick freshen up and change of clothes. There was still time enough for another hour to investigate Auckland and soak up the atmosphere and culture of this vibrant and friendly city. As the afternoon drew to a close it was time to get back to the ship and prepare for dinner. By the time we had eaten, Aurora was ready to set-sail again and many of her passengers gathered to get their last look at Auckland. As we left our berth and turned seaward the captain blew the ship's horns to honk a fond farewell. The locals responded with shouts and waving arms as we moved northwards to the Bay of Islands.

There was just one last treat for the day when a group of Maoris in traditional costume and war paint gave a song and dance show in the theatre. This was colourful, emotive and spectacular with plenty of applause plus *"ooohs"* and *"aaahs"* as we were enchanted by their performance. Having shown us how to do it properly, the show turned to humour and laughter as some of the audience were given a chance to join in.

Several women passengers attempted to dance with 'poi', which are Maori throwing weapon that looks like pompoms on a length of string. That was amusing enough, but when a group of men then came onto the stage to attempt to perform the 'Hakka' the audience were rolling around in the seats with laughter.

This was one of the most enjoyable evening entertainment shows we saw throughout the cruise. Starting with the culture of the beautiful songs and dances from these proud people, it was made so funny with the clumsy attempts of the passengers.

With hindsight, we should have called it a day at that point while we were on such a high, but instead we went to Carmen's for another cabaret with a Charlie Chaplin look-alike and comedian. Here was an example of an artist dying professionally on stage in the worst way. His material was poor and the production let him down, all of which made the show a disaster. I am sure he will regret taking this booking.

Ignoring this final disastrous cabaret, our first day in New Zealand had been superb with charming friendly people, a wonderful visit to the exhibition, and the simple pleasures of lunch in Devonport.

Now millions of people around the globe could probably describe where Auckland was in the world, but we were now sailing further north to a place we had never heard of before, and would have been very lucky to even guess it was in New Zealand. The Bay of Islands is near the northern tip of the country and not so well known. We had little idea of what to expect, but it was going to turn out to be another stunning day.

Mind-Blowing Bay of Islands
Tuesday 14th February 2012 – Valentine's Day

This was our second day in New Zealand at a place called the Bay of Islands. It was also our second tender stop of the cruise, and we awoke to a tranquil scene with an almost flat calm sea surrounding islands of all shapes and sizes. It really did live up to its name.

We had no tour booked, and after breakfast just took it easy while we were waiting for tendering to start. There was time to look at the stunning views as we got our bearings for the little town of Paihia that was the planned landing site. After some moments we realised the boats were actually landing at a different point known as Waitangi Wharf a couple of miles outside of Paihia. This suited us perfectly as our plan was to visit the Treaty Grounds at Waitangi and this landing location meant just a short walk.

As with the visit to Fiji it took a long while to get the tendering under way, and we had to wait for the organised tours to go first. The journey to the shore was only about 15 minutes so waiting times were relatively short and nobody seemed impatient that morning. The lush scenery was the focal point for most passengers, and it certainly had a calming effect on us while we were waiting.

Soon we were bobbing gently up and down on the trip to shore in anticipation of another lovely day in New Zealand. As soon as we got off the boat a friendly local pointed us towards a sign-posted pathway that would take us to the Waitangi Treaty Grounds.

The path passed by the local yacht clubhouse and we were tempted in for a coffee and a cheesy fruit scone. We were asked if we wanted butter to which we nodded but then stared at each other in amazement to see a 250-gram pack of butter split into two with a slab placed on each of our plates. The generosity was so typical of this country, but we really couldn't use it all. A cheese scone with sultanas and cherries was slightly unusual but also absolutely delicious!

Suitably refreshed, we carried on along the pathway as it continued across a beach, and what a beach! It was another example of a postcard or film-set location, and Deb couldn't resist a paddle. She found it much colder than the water of wonderful Apia, so collected some sea shells as souvenirs instead. She planned to make them into a Christmas tree decoration to remind us of this beautiful place. Our peaceful walk took no more than half an hour before we arrived at the Waitangi Treaty Grounds entrance.

So, what is Waitangi and why is it such a tourist attraction? Put simply, it is the birthplace of New Zealand as a nation, and is where a treaty was signed way back in 1840 between the Maori population and the British. In the grounds there is a flagpole marking the spot where the actual treaty was signed. Close by a small building, known as the 'Treaty House' remains from that time and is situated just a short walk away from a traditional Maori meeting hut which is the only one in the country where visitors are allowed to enter and take photographs.

Finally, I was able to put significance to a place in the middle of nowhere on the coast of New Zealand.

Our short look around was both sweet and memorable. The meeting hut was stunning with each external roof support carved with heads showing facial expressions that we have become familiar with from seeing the Hakka on television. The hut is a sacred site but the only restriction for visitors is that they have to remove their shoes on entry. It was beautiful from the outside but inside the sights made my jaw drop with the simple yet colourful decorations plus more carvings bringing Maori history and culture to life. This must leave an unforgettably stunning impression on all but the most 'hot dog and candy floss' type of tourist.

Moving to the Treaty House, there is a typical English country garden surrounding a small building of little more than two rooms that has been restored as much as possible to its original condition. It was built in 1833 and was the family home of one James Busby from Britain. It is a simple property and certainly not luxurious even for that period in time, and gives visitors a small insight into what it must have been like for a British family in a country so far away from home. The house was later gifted to the nation by Lord Bledisloe, the Governor-General in 1932.

The peaceful grounds have walks with mouth-watering views out to sea as well as many unusual plants and specimen trees with plaques to show who planted them and when. Pathways meander between plants and bushes that sometimes had labels to help strangers identify unfamiliar vegetation. Every now and then we came across benches each perfectly situated to allow glorious views. At one of them we took a breather and sank into the peaceful tranquillity of this place.

We eventually arrived at the edge of the site and a boathouse containing canoe-like Maori longboats. One of them was attributed in the Guinness Book of Records as being the longest such vessel in the world. The boats are all painstakingly hand carved with Maori figures that stun welcomed visitors now but must have terrified unwanted visitors in the past.

We strolled away from this place of history and returned across the dreamy beach back to the yacht club where we stopped again for a cold drink while planning what to do next. We could either visit the nearby island of Russell or to get a tourist boat trip around the bay, so the first step was to get to Paihia on the bus to see what was on offer.

As it was Valentine's Day, the shuttle bus had been decorated by the driver who also gave out chocolates to the ladies.

... yet another old smoothie!

The men had to go without chocolate and Deb took great pleasure in devouring hers in front of me!

At the small town of Paihia we had a chat with the (once again) very friendly locals, and discovered that we didn't have enough time for a boat trip around the islands without the risk of being late back. We opted for the ferry to Russell instead.

This small island also has history, as it is the site of the first church in New Zealand. It also had the first pub, plus a reputation as being a riotous town in the historic past with the British sailors who visited. This reputation has now changed, and today the island offers the visitor a chance to look at small pastel painted houses in narrow streets that are full of cafes and, of course, souvenir shops.

Our first need was some lunch, and we found a little café where we had a very pleasant Panini and a cup of tea. Suitably refuelled, we took a look at the shops but decided we would be happier back at Paihia where there was an open-air market tempting us to spend our New Zealand dollars. So we jumped on the next little ferry back and sat out on the deck in the sunshine for the 20 minute ride.

With just a few minutes of the trip left, our luck ran out and it started to rain. As with our earlier experiences it really rained, and although we moved inside the ferry to shelter, I was already soaked. Back on shore the downpour continued and there was a mass gallop to the shuttle bus by those of us that were Aurora passengers. The day's visit for us was over and the comfortable and dry ship was the only attraction now.

As the shuttle dropped us off at the wharf, we were more than pleased to see the rain stop in time for us to join the queue for the tenders. Just across from the queue area we could see one of the ship's tour groups climbing into Maori longboats to start their paddle around the bay.

Then the rain returned!

We all had a little laugh at the sight of the paddlers braving the rain, but we were getting wet as well. We encouraged the queue to bunch up so that more of us could get under the limited shelter, but the paddlers had no such shelter. Undeterred, but needing some encouragement from their Maori guide, they pushed away from the beach. I am sure it was an experience they will laugh at and remember with pleasure in the future as they tell their friends back home. Now, Aurora had not had a good time with tendering so far and this was not going to be any better. One of the boats suffered an engine failure just as four more shuttle busloads of soaked passengers joined our lengthy queue. The tours would also start to return very soon with several hundred more tired (and probably wet) passengers all keen to return to the ship. Just a little bit of annoyance was creeping in as several people debated why there was such a delay.

The ship decided initially to try to handle the backlog with just three boats but then a second boat had an engine failure. We had a wait of just over an hour before we eventually got back to the ship but others were stranded for twice that long. Aurora's scheduled departure time went by and we were still watching tender boats running to and from the island to get everyone back on board. As the ship finally prepared to leave, the captain made an announcement to apologise and explain that a double failure of the tenders was very unusual. We now have concerns about future ports where the little tenders have to be used again.

As far as we were concerned, the day had been wonderful even if it had ended with a few problems. It was another memorable visit and many passengers remarked that *"we could live here"* as a reflection of how much the Bay of Islands had impressed.

There were now two days crossing the Tasman Sea before my long-standing dream would come true when we would arrive in Sydney.

Our Maori troupe remained on board as they were joining another ship in Sydney, and they inadvertently continued to keep us entertained. To see them in the Jacuzzi still wearing tribal face paint was somehow surreal. Even more confusing was when they were in formal evening wear (still painted), and apparently, they were taking on all comers at chess during the day. It really cheered us up to see these wonderful people whose roots go back to the original inhabitants of New Zealand, interfaced with modern clothing and customs yet maintaining their customs for future generations.

Sailing into Sydney
Friday 17th February 2012

It was 6:00 in the morning when I quietly shed a tear as the dream that I had had since my childhood finally came true. Despite being a prat in school, and despite my refusal to listen to the efforts made by my teachers, I managed to get a job with a company (the GPO) that gave me a *"job for life"*. Even here I was lucky as I failed the interview to be a telephone engineer one week, and then passed an interview seven days later to work at Goonhilly Satellite Earth Station. For the first time in my life I actually started to use the intelligence hidden deep inside my stubborn head, and made a success of my career.

Despite making some not-so-clever decisions, I did make a few good ones that furthered my career within the company to a point that my salary gave me and my family a comfortable life, and also eventually provided a reasonable pension.

Most of all, in spite of my phobia of flying seeming to make Australia an impossible destination, here I was sailing into Sydney harbour on a beautiful luxury cruise ship. The sun was just starting to rise and ahead of me was the bridge recognised virtually worldwide, and to my left was the iconic Opera House. I had no idea what the day would bring, but the anticipation was already producing a buzz of excitement in my head and through my whole body.

Whoever has been looking down on me, and giving me the breaks and the chances to bring me to this day...

... THANKS!

Simply Sensational and Stunning Sydney

By 7:00 we had docked at the Circular Quay, and we were 'parked' to allow a terrific view of the Opera House from our balcony. On our way to breakfast we passed numerous passengers who were just staring, or being photographed with the bridge or the Opera House in the background.

Obviously I was not the only one who had Sydney so near the top of the *"places to visit"* list.

We had an hour after breakfast before our tour of the city. That meant a chance for more photos to be taken and a complete stranger made my day by taking one of Deb and me with the bridge in the background. Sydney is not just a handful of landmarks, it is a beautiful city with a skyline to match anywhere we have seen.

... plus some very special bits of course.

Today's tour was a scenic drive around many of Sydney's historical places and top tourist spots. In that single day there was never going to be time enough to see everything, so this was a good way to sample as many delights as possible.

As we made our way through the modern cruise terminal building, we were greeted, and checked, by smiling customs officers, as well as sniffed by friendly dogs again. It was the end of the second sector of the world voyage with a lot of passengers leaving today, and we passed through the arrival lounge which would soon start to fill with hundreds of replacements.

Outside we quickly found and climbed onto our coach and discovered that we had a very knowledgeable guide. As we drove away she started by telling us about the harbour area where the city of Sydney began with just a few ships full of convicts oh-so-many years ago. We then travelled through the streets to see buildings and areas that the convicts created.

Thousands of visiting sailors would have frequented here, in streets with names that were so familiar but in the 'wrong' city, like Kings Cross, Paddington and Hyde Park.

One name being mentioned was that of Lachlan Macquarie, who was appointed as the Governor of New South Wales in 1810 and did much to turn the State, and more particularly Sydney, from a penal colony into the city that stood before us today. Anyway, before I get boring, my little story is not about telling you the history of the city, but it might help someone coming in the future with a few things to research.

As we left the harbour area and drove through the city we saw statues, museums, government buildings and some exclusive schools...

... yes schools again!

There were a couple of photo stops with magnificent views over the bay and the harbour. In the city's Botanical Gardens, we visited the site known as "Mrs Macquarie's Chair" where the Governor's wife is said to have regularly sat listening to the birds singing, and staring out over the sea watching the ships come and go. The view from there was stunning and I can understand why she enjoyed it so much.

Moving away from the city centre we arrived at Bondi Beach. I had been told by some who have been to Sydney that the beach is not that special. Well I assure you it was special enough for us to cast off our shoes and walk across the smooth golden sands and paddle in the water. Perhaps I have a bias towards this city but I thought the beach was as beautiful as the tourist guides make out. Bondi caters for all beach lovers with areas dedicated to swimmers and others for surfing. It also boasts the first ever Surf Life Saving Club who patrol the beach to keep an eye on swimmers as well as the young, and not so young, 'dudes' of Sydney riding the waves. Hundreds of surfers and bathers were in the water or simply enjoying the sun on the beach, and it was only just after 10:00 am.

Sadly the stop at Bondi was soon over and from the beach we began our return journey to the harbour area passing more buildings of historical or political importance, plus the naval dockyard, close to the infamous red-light area of the past. Major shopping streets were pointed out as well as smaller local spots that we might want to visit later. Eventually however we came to the major visit of the tour: the Sydney Opera House.

This was an outstanding moment for me, Deb, and virtually everybody on the tour. We now had the services of Alan, a guide from the Opera House itself, who showed his passion for the building as well as his knowledge about it.

After a quick introduction we put on our radio headsets that were tuned in to Alan's microphone and began with a walk through the area under the stages where sets, props, costumes and generally everything was stored. Walking awe-struck, we were receiving a history lesson that told the story of the Opera House from its conception to the present day. Seeing the physical aspects of the design and construction of this unbelievable building brought all that history to life.

The main concert auditorium was next, and we had a view of the stage set for a philharmonic concert that evening. The orchestra had just stopped their rehearsals for lunch, so although we missed hearing some of the music, we were able to have a rest in the posh seats. We had part two of the Opera House's history now, and it was very much about its architectural complexity, and especially the roof. Of course the construction went vastly over budget and took far longer than planned, just like most major 20th century construction projects. We heard about the designer (Jorn Utzon) who eventually resigned from the unfinished project in disgust. He never visited the site again, even after it was completed to worldwide acclaim. Hearing that, we felt a sense of injustice towards the man.

Before the final part of the story, we visited the Opera Auditorium where the blank stage would later be set for a performance of 'The Magic Flute'. Many of Aurora's passengers would be seeing the performance that evening. Once again Alan brought the place to life with a description of the adaptable stage and anecdotes about some of the famous performers who have graced this stage.

He continued our education with a description of the building's iconic roof, the construction problems it presented, and the solutions that allowed it to be finally completed. There was also some good news about the designer, who was eventually asked to help with a modernisation project and his son (Kim Utzon) was selected as the project architect. Jorn Utzon was finally recognised by the world as the genius behind the Opera House and his creation is now a World Heritage site.

Iconic is a term that can only be attributed to a few very special buildings around the world. The Sydney Opera House truly deserves that accolade. Show a picture of the building to virtually anybody, and they will to able to tell you what, and where, it is.

Finally I had a very special little moment of my own. We were all outside, and Alan was describing the construction of the sensational tiled roof. I went up to it, and as if I was just confirming his words, I touched it. Yes I am a soppy twit, but that meant so much to me and a shiver went through my body. Unfortunately, my moment was spoiled just a little as another passenger came up at the same time and also touched the roof. I momentarily felt hurt, as I wanted the roof to be mine, just for a split second.

... but perhaps so did she.

The visit to the Opera House and our morning tour were over

and Deb and I said farewell to the guides. We had decided not to return to the ship straight away but to do our own thing for a while. We had an ice-cream while we walked a short distance to the Sydney Police and Justice Museum that Deb wanted to visit.

We spent maybe an hour there but it was perhaps not what Deb expected as the majority of the exhibits are concerned with espionage, communist threats in the 1960s, and the surveillance tactics used by the police. It did still have some interesting displays, stories, and memorabilia of infamous criminals and their punishment as well as a mock-up of a courtroom and cells. Those aspects of the museum were far more interesting.

So far we had not found anywhere that took our fancy for lunch, so we returned to Aurora for a bite to eat and a change of clothes. It was after 2:00 and we had been up for 8½ hours and although quite tired, we quickly left the ship again. This time we concentrated our exploration on the area around the harbour known as 'The Rocks' to look for some souvenirs and somewhere to perhaps have a meal away from the ship that evening.

There were restaurants to suit the majority of peoples' tastes, and the prices varied from good value through to ridiculous. We had seen enough to feel quite confident of finding somewhere to eat later on.

Looking in the souvenir shops, I was pleasantly surprised to find that the standard was higher than some of the other places we had visited, and a lot of it showed up as being made in Australia. We made a few selections including the obvious boomerangs, plus a few cuddly kangaroos for our neighbours' children. Of course there was also another batch of postcards for the next round of *"we are here"* mail.

We ran into Jimmy and Isabel in the shops and exchanged

stories of our day so far, and although they had been to Sydney before, they were really enjoying the experience again.

When they heard our plans for the evening, they said they were going to Darling Harbour for a meal as there was a very good choice of restaurants there.

Going our own ways again, Deb and I chatted about what to do about an evening meal. The decision was that we would try Darling, but if it rained, we would just pop across from Aurora to the restaurants that we'd found earlier.

Yes I mentioned the word rain again. A customs officer warned us as we left the ship the second time, that it looked like it would pour with rain soon. Well that was an hour before, and it had stayed dry so far, but then our luck ran out. There was a heavy shower, though not as bad as our experiences on the Pacific islands, but it convinced us that it was time to get back to the ship.

We freshened up and changed into clothes a little more suitable for the evening. The rain had virtually stopped by the time we set off again but we armed ourselves with umbrellas anyway. Initially we considered getting a ferry to Darling Harbour, but the timetable was a mystery to us, and as the rain wasn't posing a problem anymore, we decided to walk.

Several people had told us that the walk to Darling was not very long, but we decided that they must have been having a laugh with us. It turned out to be much further than we expected and was made more difficult because we were going in the opposite direction to the majority of the workers making their way to the ferries, and home. We decided that whatever the weather later, we would not be making the return journey on foot.

When we finally arrived at the Darling Harbour area, we understood why so many people recommended it. It was busy with people, just like us, enjoying the now warm and sunny evening and listening to music while finding a place to eat or drink. After walking up and down looking at menus, as well as being told just how good the food was by enthusiastic waiters, we chose an Italian restaurant. We were missing a decent Spaghetti Bolognese! The food was ordered and as we were waiting for the meal to arrive, we saw Brenda and Mick also looking for a place to eat. After a short chat, our food arrived and our friends moved on to listen to another enthusiastic waiter trying to gain their custom.

It wasn't long before we had finished our very tasty meal and we were on our happy way to the ferry port. A couple of restaurants further along from where we had eaten, we passed Brenda and Mick tucking into their own dinner with their usual glasses of local beer. While searching for the correct ferry terminal we met up again with Jimmy, Isabel and their Scottish gang and exchanged progress reports once more. The harbour area was now getting much busier with hundreds of young people getting an early evening drink, before moving on to nightclubs or one of the fleet of small party boats that were encouraging them aboard. It was Friday evening and the social side of Sydney was coming alive.

Eventually we found the correct ferry terminal and, with the help of a friendly local, worked out how to get tickets. The ferry that we caught gave us a very pleasant half an hour trip as it zigzagged across the waterway, stopping at several places before eventually getting back to the Circular Quay.

By the time we passed under the Harbour Bridge it was just getting dark, and the Opera House and the Bridge were now being lit up in their evening finery giving us a different view to photograph. As we left the ferry terminal we walked along the harbour side and had another ice cream as we listened to the buskers singing to the crowds of people who were sitting on the grass watching the world go by.

It was mid-evening by now, and we were tired from our long day, but we had a final treat of a bottle of rather delicious champagne to drink on our cabin balcony while we watched and listened to a Friday evening in Sydney. The occasional snippet of music from the show in the Opera House could be heard but it was drowned out for most of the time by the live bands in the bars and restaurants around the harbour.

Eventually the opera finished and we saw hundreds of people leaving and walking towards the bars or the ferries that never seemed to stop. I hope the passengers from Aurora enjoyed the show and were as happy as I was.

What an absolutely fabulous day.

I think I smiled from the moment I woke up until I was too tired to stay awake any more. I find it difficult to think up a suitable appreciative adjective or superlative to sum up just how good it had been. The city was as beautiful as I imagined, the people were happy and friendly and the weather had been good virtually all day. I was so thrilled to have been there, and hope that others with similar seemingly impossible dreams, one day have the chance to make them come true as well.

With the champagne finished, and the air just beginning to chill, we took our last look at Sydney before coming in from the balcony. Aurora set sail from Sydney around midnight with a thunderstorm adding nature's own fireworks to wave us goodbye. We were fast asleep long before sail away, with smiles on our faces and heads full of dreams of a day we will never forget.

That was the end of the second sector of the world cruise and Aurora sailed on to explore more of Australia before moving to South East Asia and more exotic and mysterious countries.

Sector 3 – Sydney to Singapore

Sydney to Brisbane Sea Day
Saturday 18th February 2012

After leaving Sydney in New South Wales at the start of the
third sector of the world cruise, we had a sea day to recover
from our visit to the city. In effect it was the beginning of
another cruise with a lot of new passengers, and so many of
the daily games and classes started from scratch again. Deb
has always had a secret desire to be able to paint, and took the
opportunity to try out the art class. While she was busy, I tried
my hand at deck quoits and discovered that I need a lot of
practice before I can be more than a first-round loser. I
decided not to continue with that game, and to look for
something else. Slightly disappointed, I returned to the cabin
and not very long afterwards Deb came back proudly clutching
her new painting equipment and her first picture of a sky scene
with a stormy cloud. Unlike my deck quoits, she had enjoyed
the class and was rather proud of her effort. I congratulated
her on a very fine 'first ever' piece of art and it looks like she
was comfortable with the class, and keen to carry on.
The weather was rather hot and after lunch we had an hour in
the sun but Deb was beginning to struggle with the intense
heat and humidity and was keen to get back to the air-
conditioned cabin. I lasted a little longer but it wasn't long
before I gave in to a cool drink from the fridge.
I struggled to understand how some of the passengers could
lay down in the sunshine mid-morning, and still be there at the
end of the afternoon without any signs of melting.
This went on day after day with the same people lying in the
same spot on deck. Each to their own, but I think a home
tanning bed would be cheaper than a world cruise, if
sunbathing is all they want to do all day.
Aurora had now been joined by a large contingent of

Australians who were easy to identify. Firstly, they all seem to be wearing name badges hanging on a lanyard permanently strung around their necks. And secondly, the moment more than two of them got together they had a committee meeting to discuss world affairs very loudly. This was particularly noticeable at lunch and in the coffee bar, where they sought each other out (by the lanyards) before sitting at the largest tables to ensure that we could all hear their conversations about the ship, the entertainment, where they come from and where they are getting off. It appeared that some were going all the way to Britain but many were leaving in Singapore. A few had just taken a short break to Darwin, and one or two couples just having a day trip to Brisbane.

During dinner that evening, an unusual conversation started concerning a blotchy rash that I had on my legs, but strangely Mick and Jimmy both have what sounds like the same rash. When we left the dining room, we rolled up our trousers and compared blotches, and sure enough we had all caught 'Sydney Blotch-itis'. One suggestion was that it was a form of eczema and not serious, but I decided to keep a close eye on it in case it spread any more. If that was the case, it would mean a trip to the doctor and a significant bill for his time.

We had some new cabaret acts on board, and that evening we watched Ricky Zalez, a singer who performs Nat King Cole and Lionel Ritchie songs rather well.

Unfortunately he talked too much between songs like so many of the cruise vocal artists seemed to do. They are either very fond of the sound of their own voices, or have a very small repertoire and need to fill the time. At least the Australians enjoyed his show and they cheered, whistled, and *"whooped"* their appreciation just a little too much for the reserved British members of the audience.

After the show we rounded off the evening by coming second

in a Masquerades quiz and then winning another one in Champions. We now have a bottle of white wine to have at the dinner table tomorrow for Mick's birthday.

Brisbane
Sunday 19th February 2012

We arrived in Brisbane (Queensland) early in the morning, and it turned out to be very hot and exceedingly humid. We had left the tropics for a while but now, as we moved north again, the increasing humidity was sapping our energy. As per our usual morning routine we opened the balcony door to look at the view, with the bizarre effect of the mirrors in the cabin instantly steaming up. Now we knew it was humid.

There are around 250 passengers leaving the ship today, and some will be replaced by new ones. I hope the Australians who only had a day on board from Sydney enjoyed themselves, and hadn't worn out their talking muscles too much.

Today's tour was to a koala sanctuary that we are quite looking forward to, with a chance to see these cute creatures plus some other Australian animals as well. So with breakfast over we joined another customs queue to be frisked by dogs for food and drugs. At least the dogs don't argue about their jobs half as much as the passengers who continually moan about anything and everything. On the coach we sat back, relaxed in the air conditioning and listened to the commentary.

Minor pandemonium erupted as a couple who had just heard the itinerary for the tour realised they were not on the shuttle bus as they thought, and were heading away from where they wanted to be. After a few minutes of discussion, the unflustered guide and her driver made a detour to the city where the shocked couple were shown the shuttle meeting point and dropped off to do their own thing. The rest of the passengers laughed (some just a little angrily) as the couple strolled away with looking a bit sheepish. We returned to the commentary and scenery for the rest of the 30-minute trip to the Lone Pine Koala Sanctuary.

Within five minutes of entering the park we had bought tickets to have a cuddle with a koala, and have our photos taken as a memento. Somehow we just jumped at the opportunity to do such a stupid touristy thing. So Matt, a five-year-old koala was placed in Deb's outstretched hands, and his soft gentle arms wrapped around her neck. I filmed while the sanctuary photographer did his bit. Matt managed to scratch Deb a little, but the chances were that he wasn't awake enough to know what he was doing. Koalas sleep for about 14 hours a day, waking for periods of serious eating before returning to their slumbers.

It was my turn now to have this cuddly animal wrapped around my neck. I don't suppose I will ever have the chance to do it again so for anyone who thinks I'm daft...

... tough!

We moved on to look at other sleeping koalas plus one or two who were awake and eating. They really do appear very lazy, and I initially thought that this environment was harming them, but it seems they actually live longer in captivity than they do in the wild.

The sanctuary has more than koalas, and we were constantly seeing large lace lizards crawling wild around the site. One that was keeping a close eye on us appeared to like ice-cream after Deb dropped some, but not the chocolate which it ignored. I accidently dropped a small coin and almost lost it as our friendly lizard shot across the floor and picked it up in its mouth before spitting it out again in disgust. Mopping up any titbits that the lizards had left behind was a type of turkey that also had the freedom to wander around the park. They tolerate the lizards (and vice versa) but they seem to see each other as competition for the same food.

We next went to the kangaroo enclosure where these magnificent animals bounce freely around a large field amongst the visitors. Some dozed in the shade and were quite happy to be approached, stroked gently and fed from the hand......*amazing!* There is a roped off area where the visitors cannot go, which is for the kangaroos who want a rest from all the attention.

With koalas and kangaroos ticked off the list, what else was there to see?

Well, there were wild dingo dogs, beautiful rainbow lorikeets, emus, kookaburras and some other winged species that were totally new to me. There were a few crocodiles that were fortunately quite small and certainly not allowed to roam the site. We saw a duck-billed platypus swimming in its own tank but the Tasmanian devil and several other species decided it was too hot to come out and play. I understood their reluctance as the heat was really sapping our strength, too. The visit lasted just under two hours and was far better than I expected it to be, but by the end we were shattered. Our plan had been to stop on the return journey and spend some time in Brisbane city but it soon became apparent that we would be better off getting back to the ship's air conditioning to recover. Our guide gave us a running commentary about the city with a lot of interesting facts and stories concerning the catastrophic floods of the previous year. I had already looked at reports online from world cruise passengers from 2011 who had stopped in Brisbane and seen the devastation just after it had happened.

Unfortunately I was not taking too much in, as I dozed during most of the trip. One comment caught my ear, and attracted my full attention for a moment. The guide pointed out the Gabba cricket ground, and added that there was an international match being played. Before I slipped back into doze mode again, it occurred to me that sport is something that few of the cities we visit seem to consider worthy of a tour. Without any doubt, Australian cricket grounds would sit high on my wish-list, as well as Olympic stadiums. If they were on the tour lists I don't think I would be on my own.

My thoughts on Brisbane are that it is a beautiful city with lovely buildings and a great deal of green spaces for parks, plus the bonus of a major river running through it. The people who live there are very proud of it and have major stories to tell about the 2011 floods that did so much damage.

I don't want this to appear negative, but our visit was too short, and perhaps too hot, to make the most of it so I can't make much of a comment except to say there was a lot to see. It took nearly 20 minutes to get from the ship's berth to the city, and the traffic was bad enough on that Sunday, so weekdays must be horrific. Hence, as a guideline for others to come, a single day visit by a ship probably isn't long enough to investigate Brisbane properly.

Back on board, new passengers wandered around with confusion all over their faces, so we took pity on one couple and helped them work out which way was the 'pointy' end. We had a chat to give them a few tips about bars and theatres and they went on their way to first investigate the Crow's Nest. We also have new neighbours for the third time on one side of us, and they are staying on until Southampton.

After an air-conditioned rest we had recovered our strength again and enjoyed a wonderful evening show by David Copperfield (the comedian not the magician) that had the audience in stitches from his first joke until the end. Perhaps showing his age a little, but still a real professional as a comedian and also as an operatic singer with a tremendous rendition of Nessun Dorma that many thought he was miming to. We ended the evening in Carmen's watching the entertainment team performing their version of 'Call My Bluff' but it was almost certainly scripted (or at least well prepared) and did not come over as dynamic entertainment.

Oriana and Cricket
Monday 20th February 2012

I woke up early as it was getting light at just after 5:00 in the morning. By the time I eventually got up and opened the balcony door, the heat and humidity were already overpowering. It was still before 7:00 and the TV information channel said it was 27°C.

It was a sea day, and during breakfast the captain announced that Oriana (Aurora's sister ship) would be passing us during the morning as we crossed on our respective world cruises. After breakfast Deb had a swim for a cool down while I found a spot on deck with a light breeze to enjoy a few minutes in the sun. My leg rash was beginning to clear up, but I was being careful not to get my legs too hot or sunned too much. I assumed it was a heat reaction producing eczema symptoms while I was wearing trousers during the evening in Sydney. When Deb had finished her swim, we stayed a little while longer in the sunshine but all the vantage points on deck where we could watch Oriana passing by were grabbed. So, we went back to our cabin balcony instead and saw her power by with horns hooting on both ships. Lots of waving and cheering could be heard even when we were several hundred metres apart. She is still our favourite ship and we really must try to go back on her.

Deb was now having her art class in the afternoon and I was still determined to find something new to do. The memory of the cricket ground in Brisbane re-ignited my love of playing the game so the temptation of the afternoon cricket session in the nets was too much to ignore. I had played the game on board many times in the past but after wrenching an arthritic shoulder once too often I gave up for a couple of years. It was time to check out the body again so with Deb's permission to

risk worsening my ageing body I made my way to the nets.
The sessions had been going on since Southampton on each
sea day and there was a good-sized group of people already in
the court warming up. Looking at them many were of a
similarly stupid age to me to be playing this game, but a few
were less senior in years. I introduced myself and with ball in
hand I realised just how long it had been since I last launched a
ball towards batsman and stumps. The batsman flailed
valiantly to hit the ball it sailed by some two metres out of
reach. This was going to take a little bit of patience and
practice before my efforts were acceptable. Never mind, there
was a chance for a few more attempts at bowling, before the
game started but I never got my hands on the bat before the
organiser called us together.

It was like the days in school again as I waited to be chosen for
a team. Lined up with two nominated captains alternately
choosing a player, I realised that I was new, and based on my
efforts so far, I was going to be the last to be chosen. What I
didn't know was that I ended up in the team with a captain
who had played the game professionally.

Our team was to bat first and because I was the last to be
chosen, it was me to start the batting. Not to get too deeply
into the rules of the on-board game, a batsman has two or
three overs to show his (or sometimes her) ability to score runs
by hitting the ball beyond a series of lines or into the nets at
the other end of the court. The further the ball goes the more
runs he scores. If he is bowled or caught out, he loses five runs,
but continues to bat. Well I did alright and came off the court
at the end of my innings with a positive score. I was
congratulated for doing better than they perhaps expected.
Now I just had to sort out my bowling.

When it was our turn to field I quickly showed that at least I
could move quick enough to stop the ball and managed to

catch it regularly as well. My efforts at bowling improved but I think the batsmen rather enjoyed hitting me around the court with ease.

The professional cricketer who chose me had also chosen several good players and we won the game quite convincingly. After sweaty handshakes all round I returned to the cabin to announce that I thoroughly enjoyed it, and hoped to continue with the games. Deb laughed at me as I dripped with salty sweat rolling down my face, and my shirt stuck to my body but she was also pleased that I had a good time.

Before dinner we had the third 'Welcome on Board' party so it was a chance for the dinner table to get together in the Crow's Nest and enjoy several glasses of our favoured tipple.

We also had another photo taken with the captain.

The evening's entertainment was a disappointment. Billed as a 'Four Tops' tribute it turned out to be four singers who sang several Motown songs but very few that were actually by the Four Tops. I don't much like the music but Deb does and was seriously annoyed that the music was not what she had looked forward to. Several other passengers shared her views, but the Australians were very happy again with more loud whistles and whoops of appreciation. I wonder what they do if they don't like an act?

Deb and I went to Masquerades for another quiz and cheered ourselves up with a glass of wine as well as winning yet another bottle.

It was an early night for us, as tomorrow we had an early tour booked at a place called Yorkeys Knob where we would be travelling on a catamaran to go and swim around the Great Barrier Reef.

Just off the Port of Yorkeys Knob
Tuesday 21st February 2012

We were up early and having breakfast before our planned
thrill of a lifetime experience with a trip to the Great Barrier
Reef to look at the wildlife and coral and to go snorkelling.
Sadly, the day was just about to become a disaster.
Captain Turnbull interrupted breakfast and made an
announcement that we were not stopping and no-one would
be going on any tours.
The Australian authorities had refused to allow Aurora to
tender into Yorkeys Knob, and the ship was required to tender
into Cairns instead. This was to enable a full customs scan
because Aurora was unfortunately still suspected of being the
target of a drug smuggling attempt.
Aurora would have to anchor so far from the landing point in
Cairns, that there wouldn't physically be time to offload more
than a small number of people. On top of that, the length of
time the passengers would be in the tender boats was in
excess of the safety regulations. Hence the visit was cancelled.
Most passengers had been trying to find out what had
happened in San Francisco with rumours that further arrests
had been made in Sydney. There was also a suggestion that
other suspects were still on board. We wanted to know more,
but looking back it was probably impossible for the captain to
give many details while there was potentially still a crime being
committed.
Captain Turnbull's announcement was met with
disappointment by virtually everyone, anger by most
passengers, and tears from many who, like Deb, saw this as a
major reason for choosing this particular cruise. It is unlikely
that we will ever get another chance to get to the Great Barrier
Reef.

As we walked back to the cabin after breakfast, we met Jimmy and Isabel and our quick chat brought Deb's tears back again. Even David Copperfield (the comedian) came along and tried to comfort her, but the day was not going to be a happy one. Deb only needed the slightest trigger to bring the tears and hurt back again.

The ship slowed down and sailed along the coast with an extra day to get to Darwin. The views were spectacular with a beautiful and flat calm sea of a blueness to match anything we have seen before. On the shore side there were a string of islands of all sizes and shapes. Some were just a beach with a minimal piece of land, others were like small hills coming out of the sea with lush vegetation, and those that were larger could possibly have been inhabited. On the other side of the ship, looking out to sea there were vast numbers of reef outcrops and more islands.

It was such a pity that the spectacular views were tainted by the actions of a handful of drug smugglers. I hope they enjoy their up-coming enforced vacation with a considerable time looking at the view of their prison cell walls.

The day was very warm and extremely humid and time on deck was limited. Deb really struggled with the humid heat and even I could only last a few minutes. The open decks in the glare of the sun were almost empty today with most passengers preferring the shade.

I did venture out in the late afternoon to play cricket again, even though I was aching somewhat from yesterday. My clothes were totally soaked in sweat by the time I had finished, but I really enjoyed the exercise and competition encouraging my body to do something a little more athletic than usual.

Dinner was subdued with all of us a little upset and frustrated by the day. It was worse that the captain had not come clean with all the information, but deep down we all understood the difficult position he was in.

After dinner we went to the Curzon Theatre where the evening's entertainment was Ricky Zalez again with his Latin-style act. As with his first performance, the singing was good, but the constant chatter between songs was driving me and Deb insane. Tonight we were treated to the life story of Michael Bublé, and he also tried to get everyone to stand up and dance and sing along to 'La Bamba'. The Australian passengers still appeared to really like the man, did as they as they were told, and gave another round of whooping and clapping. A significant number of the British were finding it all just a little bit tiring and would have preferred to be entertained first and to applaud afterwards, if applause was deserved.

We rounded off the evening with an unsuccessful quiz and then an early night. We want to put this day behind us now and move on to better things.

Sea Days Towards Darwin
22nd and 23rd February 2012

Australia is a vast country, bigger than I ever realised. We were now sailing along the Great Barrier Reef coast with two more full days before we reach Darwin. I estimated that it took almost a week to maybe go a tenth of the way around the country from our first stop at Sydney.

This was the first of the (official) sea days to Darwin, the scenery continued to be spectacular, and the heat stayed at our limits of temperature and humidity. Like most of the passengers, we came in from the sunshine early in the morning and went to the port talk on Vietnam followed by a talk by another celebrity. This time it was the actor John Lyons who has been in many TV series but most recently was the police sergeant in 'A Touch of Frost' with David Jason. This was a very good talk about his life story up to the Frost era through 'Z Cars', 'Upstairs Downstairs', 'The Sweeney' and many other well-known programmes. He had a natural way of talking that seems to be just a chat, but we know the talk was scripted to match the content and time. He is a true professional at his job.

We had no internet or mobile phone coverage at this time, and a number of people were suspicious at the coincidence that it happened at virtually the same time as our aborted visit yesterday. The story from the IT Manager is that the satellite dish used for this service had become faulty and required an engineer with a spare part that will be waiting for Aurora in Darwin. One or two passengers suspected something more sinister, but we never had any proof.

Late in the morning, the captain made an announcement to clarify the situation. Three passengers had been arrested in San Francisco for trying to smuggle in a large quantity of drugs, and a further passenger was arrested in Sydney for the same thing. Investigations are still on-going and the Australian and American authorities are still very interested in this ship, and hence the problem we had at Yorkeys Knob.

This announcement improved the atmosphere on board now we had something to dispel the rumours, or in some cases to confirm them. We hoped we could put the bad things behind us now and start to look forward to more positive days to come.

The next morning, Thursday 23rd February, I joined Deb for an early swim hoping that it might help to ease the cricket pains. Neither of us had been in the pool for several days as it had been busy since the influx of Australians on board. They seem to enjoy just standing or walking around the pool having a loud chat, and they repeat this ritual several times during the day. The sea was virtually flat calm, and another hot day meant we could only last 40 minutes in the sunshine, even at 9:00 in the morning. We grabbed a mid-morning glass of orange juice and then went to the port talk on the first of the visits to Thailand. Deb left half way through to go to the morning art class as it is more to her liking than the afternoon sessions. At the moment she was learning how to paint sunsets to add to the other scenes being practiced. Combining everything she had been taught could result in a picture of a sunset behind Barrier Reef islands with storm clouds over a mountain partly obscured by mist.

I was still impressed with her progress.

Back in the cabin with some spare time, there was a chance for a little bit of housekeeping, Deb checked the on-board statement to ensure we had not spent too much. Actually, we had been quite economic. Perhaps we need to drink more! We noticed yesterday that the bottle of wine we took to the dinner table was not very cold, and it turned out that our fridge was not working properly. More seriously the bottle of coke, drinking water, and the chocolate are similarly not chilled enough, so the fault was reported to Reception. The engineer appeared late in the morning, poked and twiddled and reported that it should be alright very soon. Sure enough about two hours later the fridge actually felt cold again, so a 'warm coke and molten chocolate' crisis was averted.

It was another formal night and we had a pleasant dinner with just Jimmy and Isabel at the table. The others were having a change and eating in the Orangery. With four people missing, the service was extra quick, leaving little time to chat about our day. Soon we were on our way to the theatre for the second show by David Copperfield. He didn't let us down and it was a terrific 40 minutes of laughter and some very special singing. Without a doubt he had been one of the best artists we have seen on the cruise so far.

From the theatre Deb and I moved on to Carmen's for the formal evening ball. I could not get the same enthusiasm for the new dance teachers who took over from Alan and Ginny in Sydney. The newcomers (Avril and Terry) had a hard act to follow, and although I am sure their teaching is wonderful, their hosting skills at the balls were nowhere near the same standard, and the fun had gone.

We had a cup of hot chocolate to round off the evening and then an early night before our last stop in Australia tomorrow at Darwin. The clocks went back another 30 minutes meaning we'd be just 9½ hours ahead of home.

Darwin
Friday 24th February 2012

It was our final stop in a country I always dreamed I would like, and Australia lived up to my expectations. Today we were in the city of Darwin in the Northern Territories, which meant we had visited three of the seven states.

Early signs were that it was going to be another hot day as we had our breakfast and watched the arrival formalities on the dockside. The ship was still very much a drug-smuggling suspect, and there were numerous uniformed officers with sniffer dogs searching all over the quayside, presumably checking if anything had been thrown overboard as we arrived. When we eventually left the ship to go on our tour we had the now familiar Australian welcome with two separate dogs, one to check for food and one for drugs. The harbour area and terminal buildings were clean and modern, and it looked like there would be some stalls to investigate when we returned. Like Brisbane we had chosen a tour that would allow us to see some animals, this time at the Territory Wildlife Park situated a few miles outside of the city. The coach trip to the park was a typical drive-through, with descriptions of the city from our German guide, Greta. She knew her stuff about the city, and had an amazing knowledge with rather a lot to say about Darwin's railway system. Quirkily she was also very keen to see an Aldi store opened in the city. We quickly left Darwin and soon arrived at the park in a forest area with warning signs all around about taking care to avoid fires.

Oh, by the way our earlier suspicions were correct and it was really, **really**, hot here!!

When we got out of the cool coach, the heat literally smacked us in the face and the park staff immediately warned us to make sure we drank continually, and find shade whenever possible. That was not too difficult as the majority of the site was a rain forest environment with lots of trees to protect us from the direct sunlight. To help hot and weary travellers, there was a series of little land trains to take us around the park. We could get off at any of the special areas that were dedicated to a particular species of animals or type of environment. Some of these were inside a building, but they have also included more natural outdoor habitats for some of the animals.

There was a series of aviaries for smaller birds in one spot, and then a little further on a building full of aquariums for fish and small reptiles. Far more spectacular was a billabong area with a pond surrounded by trees where larger birds and crocodiles lived reasonably naturally while still being visible to the visitors. Our favourite was a vast caged monsoon forest environment that had been created with a pathway to walk along that meandered past large aviaries where birds live and fly around, alongside reptiles in their ponds and small rivers. The pathway then went up into the tree line, as if a bridge, to look down upon larger birds and mammals truly living free, either in the trees or below in the bushes and man-made rivers.

One very special exhibition in this forest area was a glass fronted area (inside a large shed) that continually changed from one weather condition to another.

Initially it was a hot dry environment with little sign or sound of life but then it changed to a cooler tropical storm with torrential rain and thunderstorms.

As the rain stopped the forest area started to come alive with the sounds of animals coming out to enjoy the cool temperature and the waterways that had been created by the storm. I know it was artificial, but the demonstration reminded me of Curacao where it rained while we were in the Hato Caves and as we emerged the birds were singing and iguanas appeared.

That was the last area we looked at, and as we set off down the road we were very happy to accept a lift on the train back to the main building as the sun was beating down on us with such strength that I was almost wilting. Never mind, an ice cream helped to bring our body temperature down a little, before we returned to the air-conditioned coach. This had been another wonderful trip even if the heat had made it a bit uncomfortable. The only real problem was that the visit was too short to really appreciate the place. We had just two hours there, and I don't think we would have got bored if it had been twice that duration.

It was early afternoon, and rather than go straight back to the ship we got off the coach for a walk around the city shopping area with the intention of getting rid of our excess Australian Dollars. We each bought some casual clothes, more postcards, and a new mouse for the laptop, some Coca Cola and a few small items as souvenirs. Oh, we also had an Australian pie and a drink. We had heard many good reports about the pies, and yes, they were good and filled the small gaps in our tums. Back at the terminal we had a final chance to shop at the stalls we had seen being set up as we left. We still had a few dollars left but managed to spend the lot on a new shirt for me, plus some more small souvenirs. Then it was back onto the ship to unload our spoils, write postcards, and relax for a while. Looking out at the harbour from the balcony we could see divers checking the water around the ship in one last drug search. This was now some six hours since our arrival so the Australian Authorities were doing everything possible to find more drugs.

Australia has always been somewhere that stirred feelings inside me and this visit left me wanting more. I don't suppose that will ever happen, hence my sadness as we sailed away from this vast, beautiful, friendly, land of surprises and thrills. Perhaps the customs teams from the other countries we were to visit would be a little less enthusiastic, give us the benefit of the doubt, and trust that we were not all drug smugglers. In Australia and America we were treated as guilty, before we even arrived. The sad thing was that we never knew why until several days after the events. Even some family and friends back home had read about the drug problems, but we had been kept carefully in the dark.

There were two days at sea again now before we arrived in Indonesia at the island of Bali. This would be a significant culture change from the previous couple of weeks, and I had no idea of what to expect.

The End of the Drug Story

After we left Australia there were no more reports of any passengers being arrested for smuggling drugs, and no more drugs were found. If there were any more on Aurora then I assume the culprits either got away with it, or somewhere on board there were some little bags tucked away behind a bulkhead where they had been abandoned.

It was time to bring the saga to an end and get on with our holiday. The damage had been done and the name of our beautiful ship had been tarnished by a small number of crooks. To set the record straight I have included some information from US and Australian News reports describing what had apparently happened in San Francisco and Sydney.

On the 25th January in San Francisco an Australian was arrested while attempting to smuggle around 7kg of cocaine. The news report stated that while the Australian was being interviewed by immigration personnel, an anomaly in his story was noticed resulting in his cabin being searched. This was where the investigators discovered the cocaine.

Presumably the smuggler now started to come clean leading the investigators to pay a visit to the cabin of a New Zealand couple. Here they eventually got in and found a further 5kg of cocaine plus evidence that the occupants had been trying to flush items down the toilet before the door was opened. It seems they were planning to take the drugs to New Zealand, but fortunately for the young people of that country, the crooks' holiday was cut short.

The street value of the cocaine found in San Francisco was well in excess of $1,000,000.

Moving on to Sydney, an even bigger plot was uncovered. This time a British man was arrested after a sniffer dog called Sherlock (yes, really!) alerted customs officials. The report says that when he was searched a number of silver packets were discovered hidden inside a wetsuit that the man was wearing under his normal clothes. A search of his cabin then uncovered a further 25kg of cocaine.

The total haul was 30kg, this time with a street value of in excess of $3,000,000.

Nowhere in the different articles I had seen about these cases had there been any suggestion that the two incidents were related. These are not the first reported attempts of smuggling drugs on a cruise ship, so it is quite possible that there were other passengers on board who took a similar chance and got away with it.

These finds were probably the tiniest tip of an iceberg, but hopefully a few people will have had to look elsewhere or looked for longer, for their cocaine buzz, and perhaps just one person might have decided not to bother at all. Unfortunately I suspect I am naively wrong.

From a personal point of view, Deb and I lost the opportunity to visit the Great Barrier Reef which should have been to be a highlight of our cruise. Because I am now retired without an income to fund another world cruise and because of my fear of flying, there is possibly no way we will ever get another chance.

Sea Days to Bali
25th and 26th February 2012

Our two days at sea heralded the final move away from the Pacific and into the Indian Ocean, involving crossing the Timor Sea before getting to the South East Asian countries of Indonesia, Vietnam, Cambodia, Thailand, and finishing the sector in Singapore. Although there'd been so many differences between the places we had visited so far, going into less highly-developed countries was likely to be a real culture shock. There would be a lot of very ancient history associated with these countries, and my first real contact with active Islam and Buddhist religious beliefs and practices.

My knowledge of these countries was virtually zero except for the history associated with the Vietnam conflict, and a little about Cambodia's sad past. Thailand conjured up a more modern tourist-based image, and Singapore was perhaps a little more familiar from my work in satellite communications when I had regular dealings with the Sentosa earth station in that country.

We were also moving back towards the northern hemisphere with the equator due soon after Bali. The majority of us enjoyed the sunshine and its heat, but constantly sweating meant we had to do some serious rehydration, and I don't mean alcohol. We had become used to heavy showers drenching us on a regular basis and once again the rain put an end to a deck party, this time one planned for our departure from Darwin.

With the temperature remaining rather high, the open decks were not as busy as usual and a lot of people went to the theatre to listen to the talks. John Lyons returned to give an amusing talk about his time with David Jason in the 'Touch of Frost' series. As well as recounting his stories there were film clips, many of which were to do with an on-going desire by David Jason to play tricks on John. The session was amusing and enjoyed by most. John stayed on board for much of the remainder of the cruise and we often sat next to him during the daily individual quiz.

Oh yes and Deb finally managed to win one of those quizzes, and I was very proud.

Another popular guest speaker was an ex-policeman who gave several talks on London gangsters and famous robberies that he had been involved with. Not my cup of tea, but several passengers raved about the detail and fun he brought into his subjects.

Several port talks were given, and they were very important to us as they included the Vietnam and Thailand stops. It looked like our choice of tours would be ideal for us to get an overview of the countries.

On one of these sea days everyone was tasked to complete the entry and exit cards for our visit to Indonesia. Rather similar to Australia and New Zealand it is an immigration requirement that the ship gathers names and passport numbers for all the passengers and crew.

An announcement was made as a reminder that just in case anyone else was planning on smuggling drugs, Indonesia has the death penalty for such crimes.

Deb's art class continued, and I also carried on with the cricket. There were one or two Australians taking part at this point and they were making fools out of some of us arthritic Brits. I was struggling because I stupidly took part in a dance called 'Oops Upside Your Head' one evening. For those who have never heard of it, the idea is to sit on the floor in a line with your legs outside of the person in front. Then, to the music, you rock back and forth or side to side with arms waving. Only when it was over did I realise my body was no longer really capable of doing this, and I had to wait for everyone else to get up so I could roll over onto my front before standing up again. I appeared to have strained something in my thigh or groin, and moving quickly in cricket had become too painful to enjoy. I knew I would have to give in eventually, but I hate the consequences of growing older.

In addition to the cricket, I was also taking some slightly less energetic exercise, by walking around the Promenade deck for a mile each day. Although the walk was still possible, the thigh or groin strain was worse than I first thought, and I had to give the cricket a miss on the Sunday.

The sun still shone on us, and on one of the days we lay out on deck after lunch with resident band Caravan playing some wonderful music for an hour to relax the passengers. They really are a good band, but rarely get a chance to play anything other than strict tempo dance music. That day's music was a mixture of rock and pop from the 60s through to the present day, and the applause confirmed their popularity.

No doubt because of the recent bad experiences with tender boats, the captain made an announcement to say that everything was looking good for our visit to Bali. The original anchorage point had to be changed but this should not impact on our stay.

Our evenings were quiet and we missed both of the theatre shows. On the Saturday it was because the Motown band, that had disappointed us earlier, was performing again, and on the Sunday we decided to treat ourselves to a meal in Café Bordeaux. It was as superb as we expected with mouth-watering food, and was well worth the cover charge. Marco Pierre White should have been very proud of how his menu was prepared and served on Aurora. The waiters were attentive, good with the food and talked with the customers with politeness but also some humour.

After being careful not to overindulge, (yes, I am lying) we went to see the Headliners perform their Abba tribute show in Carmen's. The singing and dancing were really good and the girls and boys always looked as though they were enjoying it, even if they were bored and hated every minute of it.

The two days at sea gave everyone a chance to catch up on routine things before we had several busy days of port visits. The laundrettes were constantly busy, and the Reception desk was rarely without a queue of people sorting out niggles. At the Future Cruises desk people were regularly scanning the brochures and queuing to see how good a deal they could get, but we managed to stay away from there.

The water leaks around the ship continued, but most of us were used to them by now and we were no longer shocked by the sight of green and red buckets in the middle of the corridors. I had serious concerns that a ship just twelve years old was suffering so badly from presumably worn out pipework.

Our holiday continued and we remained as excited and enthusiastic as the day we started. It was time to move on to South East Asia and visit Bali.

Bali
Monday 27th February 2012

We had an early night to be ready for Bali but on the way back from a small-hours trip to the bathroom I noticed the phone had a tiny red light flashing, which meant we had a message waiting. Immediately I was horrified that the message might be bad news from home, but at 4:30 in the morning I knew not much could be done. Deb was still fast asleep so I decided not to investigate. I lay there for nearly three hours until Deb stirred and then I listened to the message. It was one that we had missed from 11:00 the previous morning confirming Deb's appointment in the spa for a treatment. It was a relief to know it was nothing to worry about, but also annoying that I had lost so much sleep over it. The early night had failed to give me any rest, so from then on I always checked the message light before going to bed.

We got up and spent a few minutes staring at the island of Bali over an early morning cup of tea before setting off for breakfast. The island looked to be a beautiful place dominated by an imposing volcano above green hills with waves breaking over a sandy shoreline set amongst the palm trees. In the bay were lots of little coloured boats that we described as 'spider boats' as they have projections that from a distance look like multiple legs. In reality they are nothing more than canoes with a motor and a sail if needed, but to give them stability they have two outriggers attached by arms to the sides. The Balinese fishermen work as teams using nets and the little boats are a joy to watch flitting around the sea.

Everything seemed to suggest we would be enjoying a few hours here.

This was a tender port and we were at anchor in Labuan Amuk Bay. Our plans for the day were to have a late morning trip to shore, catch the shuttle bus to the nearby town and have a look around. We hoped to find a beautiful beach and dip our toes in the water, but we decided not to make any solid plans of places to visit, but to just chill out. There was an initial delay until all the organised tours had been safely delivered to shore, and this gave us a chance to absorb the tranquillity of the setting as the ship gently turned on its anchors, allowing us a wider view of the bay.

Finally at around 11:00 we got on the tender and had a smooth journey to shore, landing at the little seaside village of Tanah Ampu. It had a newly-built terminal to attract cruise ships and was extremely pretty. We landed at the pontoon and strolled down the jetty in the blazing sun. There was a suggestion that it was 35°C today, or 100° F in old money. Our route took us through an ornate gateway built as if it was the entrance to a temple...

... stunning!

Beyond the entrance was a building with marble floors giving a cool escape from the heat outside, and we quickly spotted signs directing us to the shuttle bus. The short walk was unfortunately through a crowd of taxi drivers, and they were really persistent, to the point where I was struggling to stay polite.

The bus was not there and we were getting strange messages from disgruntled passengers that the service had been stopped. That couldn't be right, so rather than joining the queue we had a stroll around some stalls, in an attempt to put off the taxi drivers, until a bus arrived. Eventually we spotted a bus approaching, and although it struggled to get through the crowd of taxi drivers, it stopped and dropped off its passengers. Now there was chaos. Instead of more people being allowed to get on, the driver closed the bus door. From what we could make out, the taxi drivers, upset with the lack of business, had used their influence to force the bus driver to stop. After a moment or two of mutterings and moans, a good number of us decided that taxi drivers would not dictate how we spent our day and we returned to the tender boat jetty to take our dollars elsewhere.

By now the tide had turned, and quite suddenly the sea became a little less tranquil. In fact it became difficult and quite dangerous getting passengers onto the pontoon from the recently arrived tender boat. The movement of the sea, and the worryingly unstable pontoon, caused some passengers to resort to jumping ashore, and one or two others ended up crawling on all fours across the pontoon. After quite a delay, the tender was emptied, and we got on it for the trip back to Aurora with no further problems. There was also a fair bit of bounce at the ship, and just as we got on board the captain announced that the tender service was being suspended due to the sea conditions, until the shore pontoon could be made more secure.

This was just after midday.

We had a quiet lunch and on our return to the cabin noticed a lack of activity below our balcony where the tender boats were just bobbing up and down. At 2:30 the captain came back on the air and, with noticeable frustration in his voice, announced that there was still no resolution to the pontoon problem, and the water was still rough, so he had arranged for the 1500 people on shore to have lunch at local hotels.

We were now rather pleased that we had returned when we did. Looking out towards the island, it all seemed quiet and tranquil but we were confused and concerned that there were several plumes of smoke rising from the trees. Later we discovered that Mondays are the favoured days for cremations, and the smoke was from the funeral pyres.

Untroubled by any of the chaos on shore, Deb and I relaxed in the cabin for a while, and then spent half an hour in the swimming pool to cool off. Deb even tried out her mask and snorkel in readiness for another attempt at swimming on a coral reef when we arrived in Sharm El Sheik.

To put the problems of the day into context, many of the passengers had a wonderful day on this beautiful island. They went on their tours before the trouble started and enjoyed a thoroughly pleasant day. Many others arrived before we did and successfully caught a shuttle bus to the town and also had a good time. It was only when they came to the end of tours, or became bored with the town, that they discovered that something was going very wrong. Information was limited and there was confusion when the passengers were invited to go to a café or bar and have something to eat and drink.

Brenda and Mick later told us that they suspected they were being taken hostage, as they were continually being told to sit and drink with no explanation. As passengers arrived back at the port and joined the group of really unfortunate ones who never made it away from the village, the picture became clearer. They were stuck on shore with limited shade on a very hot day.

On the ship the captain made several further announcements, and his voice betrayed his attempts to stay calm as his frustration and annoyance increased. It appeared that the local authorities were unable, or unwilling, to fix the pontoon, so Captain Turnbull had sent a working party ashore to make temporary repairs.

As we wandered around the ship it felt a little like the Marie Celeste with practically empty rooms and deserted decks. The two or three hundred of us passengers were outnumbered by the crew, and groups of bored waiters twiddled their thumbs whilst cleaning anything they saw.

Mid-afternoon, and the passengers were still effectively

stranded on the island but at least they were about to get cooler as it started to rain. At 3:00 a tender left the ship full of various officers and crew, with water, plastic macs and other supplies. The tender delivered crew members with different skills and responsibilities to help with the situation. Some distributed water, others handed out plastic macs. There were a number of the medical team for those who needed attention, and the entertainment staff did their best to keep morale up. At last, the stranded passengers were getting some information, and plans to bring them home were being implemented. Queues were arranged to enable those who were unwell or disabled to get an early return when the tenders could start a service again, and just after 4:00 we saw the first of them heading back to Aurora with passengers. There had been moments during the afternoon when we thought it might become a lonely ship that night, but now we knew that all would be well, if just a little later than planned. A further announcement was made to inform us that times for dinner and the evening's entertainments were being put back by 30 minutes, and that Aurora would be leaving Bali much later than scheduled. The restaurant was still very quiet when we eventually ate, and the atmosphere was strangely subdued. Deb and I were joined at the dinner table by Brenda, Mick and Isobel. Jimmy was safely back but not feeling like eating. We chatted about the adventures of the day and realised that we had missed out on a beautiful island, but we certainly didn't mind missing the confusion and queues they experienced at the jetty.

From various announcements made during the early evening we learnt that everyone was back on board by about 8:00, and we finally lifted the anchors and set off again just before 9:00. Because of the chaotic and disappointing day, the captain apologised and advised that everyone on board would be receiving £50 on board credit as compensation. It had not been P&O's fault, but the day had been ruined and this gesture was appreciated.

This had been the third tender port, and each one had been just a little bit of a disaster. It was starting to look like Aurora had a bit of a jinx.

After dinner Deb and I went to the theatre to watch a comedy vocalist by the name of Jay McGee who had also been caught up in the Bali queues as he arrived today for his cabaret stint. Back home he was still touring with a group called the Rocking Berries but this was his solo act. His jokes were just about funny and the songs were sung well. He was however, by his own admission, still jet-lagged and the act did not flow too well, but he promised his second show would be much better. Show over, we went to a Masquerades quiz along with Brenda and Mick who gave a longer account of the day's farce. We lost the quiz (just) and that was enough for us, and for most people on the ship, to call it a night.

Our visit to Bali had been a disappointment but I have to congratulate Captain Turnbull and his crew for the incredible job they did in a ridiculously stupid situation, and their actions possibly averted a more serious outcome.

This had been a very strange day!

Sea Days Towards Vietnam
28th February to 1st March 2012

Tuesday 28th February was a quiet day with many people discussing their adventures in Bali and comparing stories with each other. Our small tale of woe was insignificant set against the hardships endured by some others.

Indonesian disappointment was quickly put behind us we started the day with an hour in the sun. Then it was off to the theatre for a port talk followed by another hour with John Lyons. He brought his acting career up to the present day, followed by a question and answer session. He had been an interesting speaker with a real freshness to his story.

During the afternoon Deb went to art class and then relaxed with a pampering session in the Spa where she had a special sample of six different treatments. She enjoyed it very much, and I just wish they would offer something similar for male passengers. Her treatments continued until quite late in the afternoon so I went to the individual quiz by myself for once. Later on our way to dinner we met Jay McGee, the comedian from the Bali evening. We thanked him for his show and he recounted the story of his day as an apology for what he saw as a bad act. Jay had travelled for 30 hours to get to that jetty in Bali, and while waiting in line to go aboard, was grabbed by the powers-that-be to get an early tender. He was wanted on board by the orchestra to rehearse his music for the evening. He was very jet lagged and had no idea his first performance was to be that night.

He was never properly introduced to anyone nor had the theatre protocols explained to him, and when I noticed him before his act, he appeared to be a bit like a lost child in a busy shopping centre. His performance was a little awkward as I said before, but perhaps there were some excuses. Since then,

Jay had spent virtually all day in bed and had just got up to start finding his way around the ship, as well as getting something to eat. He had spoken to Christine Noble, the Cruise Director, and apologised for his performance but apparently, she had just replied *"oh that's all right"*.

As a passenger I would like to say that what might be *"alright"* for Christine was an evening's entertainment for us.

Is this typical of the way that P&O treat their artists?

Jay was a nice friendly character with undoubted talents, but he was now relying on his second performance to give a true taste of his act before flying back to Britain from Ho Chi Minh City. We'd been entertained by several singers, but Jay was the first young comedian on the cruise and perhaps we were not seeing the best of him.

The entertainment on Tuesday evening was a double bill with a magician (Michael John) who did a basic set of tricks, and his partner (Emily Reed) who was a very good singer. The evening ended with a video quiz accompanied by Brenda and Mick. We lost again. All four of us were really tired and an early night was in order.

On Wednesday 29th February the sun welcomed us again. The morning port talk was on Cambodia and we were really looking forward to seeing a country still trying to recover from a decade of war and oppression. There were only two official trips at this destination and they both visited the same temple and school before spending some time on a beach. We chose the longer tour with lunch included at the hotel that owns the beach. Seasoned travellers had warned us about the visit to the school where many visitors give small gifts to the children. For nearly two months we have been storing our pillow chocolates to have something to give them. Other people had the same idea, so these children could end up with very bad teeth!

Later in the morning we went up on deck and enjoyed the sun, but Deb struggled with the heat again, and could only toast one side. I sweated it out for a 'both sides' roast, but even I struggled to stay out for more than an hour.

Just after lunch we crossed back over the equator and returned to the northern hemisphere. There was a tiny feeling of *"we are on the way home",* but there was still a lot to see and do over the remaining six weeks.

That evening began with a special 'Round the World' party featuring chats with officers, canapés, and free drinks for the 600 or so passengers like ourselves. Six of us from the dinner table sat together plus Sam and Bob who had become friends with us. It was an enjoyable half an hour and the captain made an amusing update speech about the places to come before we get back to Southampton.

That evening's entertainment featured Benjamin Makisi, yet another singer. His profile described his act as containing both popular and classical songs. We did not watch him but reports were that he was very good. We had drunk quite a bit at the party, so after dinner went back to the cabin and read for a while and both of us fell asleep. Carmen's was hosting the 'Black and White' ball so having woken up a little refreshed we spent an hour there. Dancing was avoided because of my dodgy leg. And as I said earlier, I couldn't get on with the dancing instructors, and they were putting me off getting up and joining in. Considering that we had made a point of dancing at every formal ball up until Sydney, it was very strange that we had hardly been on the dance floor since this couple had come on board.

Thursday 1st March was our final day at sea before arriving in Vietnam, and we woke up to find that it was a little windy but still hot and humid. It was the Portunas Gold Lunch today so Deb decided against a swim because it would mean having to wash her hair again, and instead we both had a brisk walk to get some exercise. This was meant to be around the Promenade Deck but that was closed off for maintenance so we had to go around Sun Deck instead. Still very pleasant and we got a good sweat on but it does not give the same satisfaction as walking on the Promenade Deck where we know that 3.2 times around is the equivalent of a mile.

After mid-morning coffee we trotted off to the port talk to learn about our first stop in Malaysia. We had a tour already booked and the description we heard confirmed that it is the one for us. We would have lots of walking, with lunch included, during a full day highlights trip around Kuala Lumpur. It was time to get ready for our lunch now, and this would be quite a landmark as it would be the last Gold lunch we would ever have. We only had one on this cruise and the Portunas Loyalty Club would cease to exist on the day we arrived back in Southampton when it would be replaced by the Peninsular Club.

The meal was delightful and with the other passengers on the table we soon succumbed to the alcohol and had a good laugh about all kinds of subjects, from pets to the entertainment staff and their possible facial enhancements.

There were five other guests: Terry (who was on his own), Sheila and Alistair, and Margaret and Nigel. An empty space stayed unused. It turned out we should have been joined by the captain, but sadly he was busy elsewhere. Had he been there it would have been an honour for us, but it would probably have changed the conversation a little, and possibly not been quite such a laugh.

With the meal finished, we returned to sleep off a little of the generous helpings of champagne and wine as we both had things to do later. Deb went to her art class with plans for paintings of pelicans and the Sydney Opera House. I returned to cricket, and played quite well considering I was not totally sober. The team I played for lost again, but the results tended to depend on who had the professional player on their team. Although rather full, we still went to dinner to be sociable and the pair of us just had a bowl of soup plus another starter for the main course. We had really eaten too much that day.

We went to the theatre for a show from the Headliners troupe where they performed 'I Write the Songs', and although we had seen it once on the cruise already it was worth seeing again. Another quiz failure in Masquerades completed our day before we took to our beds to dream about our arrival in Vietnam the next day.

Nha Trang (Vietnam)
Friday 2nd March 2012

Our initial view of Nha Trang was very promising with a calm sun-drenched bay dotted with small fishing boats and ferries. One small vessel near the ship had a coracle strapped to it, and later I spotted someone in a coracle fishing all alone and looking like a dot in the vast expanse of sea. In the background there were a few golden beaches overlooked by mist-covered hills, and in the distance huge mountains. It was yet another tranquil early morning setting with just the sound of the small vessels passing by in the deep blue sea.

As we sat with our breakfast the captain came on with his usual arrival announcement and he was able to fulfil an ambition of his own by loudly saying *"Goooood morning Vietnam"!* It was before 8:00, we were already at anchor, and the ship was just about ready to let the passengers loose on the tenders for an early start ashore. He changed his little sign-off today and described our departure as being at the speed of a thousand tuk-tuks rather than his customary gazelles...
... very topical.

Our trip did not require us to be ready until well after 9:00 so we could relax and take in some more of the views and watch the tenders starting their journeys. All seemed to be going well, and Aurora was using two of her pontoons to speed up the tendering process, so this suggested the shore-side facilities could cope with multiple vessels loading and unloading at once.

Until recently the port of Nha Trang could have allowed us to berth alongside, but a local Russian-owned luxury hotel complex had installed a cable-car system across the bay between its island and the mainland. The cable-car system now prevents ships of Aurora's size from passing underneath.

It looked like money talked louder than sense sometimes in a developing country like this.

We were soon away on the tender, and after a successful trip to shore we boarded our coach for a 'highlights' trip of the city. Contrary to the warnings from our port presenter, the coach was pleasantly air conditioned, and this was a very positive feature with the heat and humidity we faced during the morning. Our guide was a girl called Thanth who might have still been a teenager or maybe just into her twenties. She was slim and dressed in the national dress known as an 'Ao Dai' which is a pair of trousers and a full length fitted top split from the waist to the hem. It was perhaps cream or ivory in colour with the top embroidered with intricate designs. Similar traditional clothing was worn by a high percentage of the younger ladies we saw during the day. Western style clothing was also worn, but it was unusual rather than the norm. Thanth's mastery of English was not brilliant, but perfectly adequate to explain things and she had an obvious enthusiasm for her role.

We relaxed into our seats and listened to the usual introductions as we passed through the harbour gates towards our first stop at a maritime university that also housed a public aquarium. As we settled down for a ride through the streets, we were totally surprised as the coach immediately turned right and stopped.

We had arrived!

There were giggles from all around the coach which worried Thanth who thought something was seriously wrong, until she realised that our mirth was for the short ride and nothing to do with her commentary.

The aquarium was crowded with students and visitors like us. It was rather good with huge tanks showing examples of all kinds of sea creatures and corals. Most of the fish were alive but the exhibition was also backed up with mummified creatures and skeletons of others. Although the water was not as clear as the aquarium in Auckland, it was fascinating to see the variety of sea life found off the coast of Vietnam.

Unfortunately, the tour was very rapid with far too much to see as we were almost marched from tank to tank in room after room for the 30 minutes allowed.

Back on the coach we had a much longer ride through the city. Unfortunately, we had to disappoint our Captain, as we never saw a single tuk-tuk, let alone a thousand of them.

We were amazed by two things however.

Firstly was the number of small motorbikes that went wherever they wanted to, and with as many people on board as could fit. Examples of the driver plus three or four passengers was quite common. The driver's view was often obscured by all kinds of objects being carried, such as incredibly large boxes and even a settee was spotted once with a small head peering around the side. It was a crazy way of commuting but obviously worked.

Secondly the size of the Vietnamese people was confusing us. They were all generally shorter than us, and almost everyone was slim. I don't mean they were thin in a starved or unhealthy way with gaunt faces, they were simply naturally slim. I can only put their stature down to a healthy diet, but also perhaps the country has not yet caught the pariah disease known as 'greed' that afflicts so many nations.

Thanth proudly described the views as our journey showed us the downtown area of the city before we arrived for a brief stop at the city's Catholic Church. As was to be expected, the church was a beautiful landmark with plenty of photo opportunities. Our arrival attracted the first of the street hawkers trying to sell their postcards, coolie hats, jewellery boxes and 'Ralph Lauren Polo' shirts. None of us really took any interest at that stage as we all knew the shirts were fakes, but curiosity was getting the better of some of us. Back on the coach our guide responded to a question by telling us that we should not pay more than $2 for a coolie hat. I then noticed through the window a salesmen using hand signs to offer the shirts at two for $5, while nearby one was spotted offering three for $10 to another coach. We had been told to haggle over prices and this was our first chance to judge what we might get away with.

We moved on again to the Long Son Pagoda for another 30-minute stop. This amazing complex is situated through some gates just far enough back from the street to be almost invisible to passers-by.

We climbed the 100 or so steps of this amazing building to see the 'Reclining Buddha' about half way up, and then the 'Big Sitting Buddha' near the top. Both were pure white and huge, with the first being long, and the second being tall. The complex was full of sculptures of dragons and other mythical animals, plus pagoda-styles temples and shrines. There were incredible views of the city from the top of the site, and the street noise had almost disappeared even though we were just a few tens of feet above it.

Street sellers had become more numerous and were tempting us at every corner. As we returned to the coach the first of the coolie hats and polo shirts were appearing in the hands of the passengers.

 Prices were discussed between us and noted for later opportunities.

Our next trip was across Nha Trang's waterway on the Xom Bong Bridge to see the Po Nagar Cham Tower...

... and no, I am not making these names up.

The Po Nagar Cham Tower is an older complex of towers and temples at the top of a little hill (more steps) with a long historical past. It was an oasis of peace in this mad city and the buildings were magnificent with totally beautiful altars within the numerous temples. Inside these temples the air was heavy with the smell of incense and this added to the visual beauty to tickle the senses of visitors. The grounds were peaceful and stunning with various little statues or monuments to catch our gaze and occasionally make us sigh with pleasure.

We spent the remaining time at this spot wandering around the grounds, constantly finding more things to photograph and more perfect vantage spots to capture the buildings and views over the city. It was as if the architect had planned his dream to give visitors a different visual thrill at every turn. Our 30 minutes were soon up, and Thanth called our group back together for the next little journey.

A few minutes later we were walking around the 'Dam Market' where hundreds of stalls were selling all manner of foodstuffs, clothing, jewellery, boxes, beads, watches (genuine fakes of course!) and in fact anything you can imagine to satisfy the needs of the local people as well as tourists with bulging wallets.

Now the serious buying began and we came away with several items that attracted our interest, either as fun items (coolie hats) or souvenirs as a reminder of this wonderful city.

The prices were ridiculous and I felt guilty haggling over figures that were already perhaps a tenth of what they would be at home, but haggling is expected of everyone.

Thirty minutes later we were on the coach again for the final stop at a silk embroidery factory. I have run out of adjectives to describe the stunning artistic work and handicrafts here. The stitching is amazingly intricate, beautiful, and all hand created by ladies who start work at the age of 18 but then require two years training before becoming sufficiently skilled to undertake the delicate work. The designs portray images of flowers, fish, or landscapes on all kinds of backgrounds with some being semi-transparent whilst others looked like paintings. Like many of the other passengers we could not turn down the opportunity to buy something.

We climbed on board the coach for the last time, on our return trip to the port. It had been a really lovely tour and a memorable four hours, for all the right reasons, as a change to some of our recent experiences. I think every passenger genuinely thanked Thanth for her knowledge and her wonderful part in making the day in Nha Trang so good.

On our way along the harbour side to the tender jetty, there was another market for final temptations, and yes we were tempted. Many of the passengers' bags became a little fuller with beautiful souvenirs, and of course, more Ralph Lauren Polo shirts.

As an estimate, we spent about $100 that day for which we have clothes, keepsakes, and presents that would have been closer to £200 at home. Compared to the physical objects however, our memories of Nha Trang were worth far more.

After a faultless tender trip we were soon back on-board Aurora again. The tenders had behaved themselves perfectly that day, so the jinx had been laid to rest.

Our first priority was to change our clothes before we had a quick snack and a relaxed afternoon.

That evening it was just Jimmy and Isabel at dinner with us, so the meal was quite rapid again. As we were not going to the theatre show we went back to the cabin and read our books for a while, before going to Carmen's to watch the comic Jay McGee perform his second show. There was time for a couple of dances before his cabaret and later in the evening as we drank a hot chocolate, we even had a *"well done"* from a couple who had seen us do a rumba.

Jay came on and gave a very amusing and musical

performance. He had got over his knock-down from the first show. There were a handful of songs that received good applause and his comedy act was finally given the laughter he so wanted. Some of the jokes were perhaps a little old, but he has marvellous facial dexterity to put life into his act. There was a twist to the act at the end that I won't describe as some of you might go and see him one day and it would be best to keep it a surprise.

He actually thanked people for the support that had been shown to him after the first show and gave the two of us a personal thank you afterwards. Jay flew home the next day via Istanbul, so he had another couple of long flights before he got into his own bed again.

It had been a lovely day with and I understand Vietnam just a little now. Tomorrow is Vietnam part two, with a trip to Ho Chi Minh City, or Saigon as we used to refer to it. If the experience turned out to be anything like as good as today, we would have to think up some more adjectives of praise for this intriguing country.

Ho Chi Minh City (Vietnam)
Saturday 3rd March 2012

"Good Morning Vietnam!"
... sorry, but Deb and I are a little excited about today!
Another lovely morning greeted us as we woke up and looked
out from the balcony. We were passing mangrove swamps as
we made our way up the Nhà Bè river to the port of Phu My
from where we would later be taken to Ho Chi Minh City. As
we glided almost silently along, we saw small sampans
chugging their way along the river with Vietnamese men
wearing coolie hats and long smocks. Sometimes near the
bank I spotted houseboats, or more accurately house 'things'
made from boats with various other structures attached to
them. It was impossible to know how many people lived on
them but we knew that these must have been some of the less
well-off families to be making their home in such lonely
inhospitable places.
We had our breakfast and by the time we got back to the cabin
Aurora was tied up and ready to start offloading passengers for
their tours. The ship was going to be virtually deserted today
judging by the number of coaches waiting below. Our tour was
an all-day outing to Ho Chi Minh City that was some two hours'
drive from the port.
Early as usual, we made our way down to the theatre to get
our tour tickers and within five minutes we had been directed
to the coach for an early start.
The port we docked at was nothing more than a terminal with
factories, warehouses, huge container cranes and storage
areas. There were no shops or houses in sight except for a
handful of marquees on the quay tempting us with souvenirs.
Our guide was a young man whose English was superb and he
even joined in with our humour.

It was probably a couple of miles to the main road and we realised that access to this dock was not yet completed and we were driving over pot-holed dirt tracks for most of this journey. It was not long however before we were on the main highway which was perfectly fine. Both sides of the road were lined with small shops or factories that doubled up as family homes. There were hundreds of people out doing their Saturday morning business, plus thousands of small motorbikes. I really am not exaggerating, and on the journey to Ho Chi Minh City yesterday's astonishment at these scooters turned into utter disbelief. Even the guide said that there is an art to driving here, and it may seem dangerous (no, really?) but the people know how to drive in the difficult mixture of lorries, buses, cars and bikes. Another *"I don't believe it"* sight today was a scooter on which the driver had two items of metalwork that looked like roller shutters maybe six metres long strapped to either side.

As we got nearer to the city there were special lanes just for the motorbikes and in some places this lane was solid with the bikes chugging along.

Traffic lights were just about obeyed, with the bikes all going to the front of the queue, and sometimes there was around 100 bikes that swarmed away in all directions as the lights turned green. Lane discipline did not exist, and just because you wanted to turn left, it didn't necessarily mean you had to start the turn in the left-hand lane...

... just close your eyes and forget it George.

By now the buildings we were passing were changing from ramshackle structures to office blocks, apartments, and skyscrapers, and the traffic was increasing to levels typical of any major city. The simplicity of the city had changed but the poverty was still visible with beautiful expensive apartments on one side of the Saigon River and tin huts dating back decades on the other side. Our guide said that the huts will all eventually be torn down as the area is developed. The poverty-stricken people can either find new places to live, or the government will rehouse them. I doubt they will be rehoused in the beautiful and expensive apartments that will replace their homes.

Our first stop was at a small factory unit used by a company that produces lacquer ware items, with mother-of-pearl or eggshell designs lacquered onto wood. These products were truly beautiful and totally unlike the plastic versions that can be found in the typical souvenir shops. We bought a small piece as a keepsake of this country, but would have loved other larger items if we could have justified the cost and found a way of getting them home.

From the factory we had more of the city's landmarks pointed out to us before entering Chinatown and arriving at the Thien Hau Temple. This temple is dedicated to sailors and is more commonly known as the Sea Goddess temple. The smell of incense was overpowering but it added to the serenity of the temple with its golden altars, statues, pictures and wooden carvings. Our guide was very knowledgeable about Buddhism as his grandmother was (as he put it) a believer.

He recounted stories, including the importance of the temple and its items of religious significance. Inside, people can purchase simple tokens of remembrance such as sheets of paper with a message, or a small basket with the same paper message, or a long paper candle dedicated to the deceased. These are then burnt alongside altar candles and the incense. There were a considerable number of tokens and candles being burnt while we were there, and the air hung with paper soot as well as the smell of smoke and incense.

There was no opportunity to get seriously committed to

Buddhism as it was time to move on again.

The coach did its work again for a few minutes and took us through more of the Chinatown area, and then back into a more central area of the city. We passed by the Rex Hotel that even I remember from the war period, plus the amazing Post Office building and several other major landmarks. Our target destination was now a hotel where we were to have a buffet lunch. At the mention of food, some of the passengers who had slowly meandered off the coach at previous stops were now forcing their way through to the coach steps taking no prisoners in their attempts to get to the front of the meal queue.

This eagerness to eat never ceased to amaze me but thankfully not as much, and not in the same way, as the architecture and history that surrounded me. Once more this experience was bringing a chapter in history to life.

The buffet lunch was superb, with a selection of traditional Vietnamese as well as more western food. It was enhanced by local music on some very simple, but unusual drums and stringed instruments. The instruments were mainly made from bamboo which gave an unmistakeable and almost eerie oriental sound. Young dancers in traditional costumes also entertained us with graceful hand movements and waving of fans, hats and silk ribbons.

Once the short break for lunch was over, we took to the streets on foot to visit the Rex Hotel and its famous bar where the wartime journalists met and created their reports. Just across the road was a park with a gigantic statue of Ho Chi Minh standing just a little way from the People's Committee Building that was formerly known as the City Hall. This was where much of the rebuilding of the United Vietnam was planned and governed after the American forces had left the country.

We returned to the coach again for a short journey to the Post

Office building that stands opposite the Notre Dame Cathedral (a smaller version of the one in Paris). On the way our guide gave us stories of the Post Office including one about an employee who worked there for so long that when he retired, they gave him an alcove where he could continue to sit daily to help and chat to people. It's a splendid architectural building and was full of tourists as well as the local people who continue to write and post letters despite the changing email culture all around them.

The photo opportunity for the cathedral was short because it closes from late morning until mid-afternoon, so only external views were possible. We had seen couples being photographed in their wedding clothes as we passed here earlier, and apparently this was not necessarily after the wedding service. Weddings are so expensive that couples often have the photos taken long before the actual day to avoid spending too long in the heat on their magic day.

By now most of us were not too concerned about looking at the cathedral for too long, as the heat was really getting to us and a drink seemed more important than getting across the busy roads again. For those who did want to make the effort to get closer, they could use the help of 'Tourist Assistants'. The city employs these young people, mostly college students, who dress in green just like our paramedics at home. When they spot tourists trying to cross roads, they leap into the traffic with a sharp blast on a whistle, and the bikes and cars stop to allow a safe crossing. They must be totally mad, as many of the bike riders appear deaf and partially sighted when it comes to stopping unless they have arrived at their destination. These angels of assistance also give advice to tourists when they see people staring at maps or generally looking bemused and confused…

… a little like us for most of the time I suppose.

A short ride in air-conditioned comfort took us to another major landmark – the Reunification Hall, or what was once the Presidential Palace.

This was where two North Vietnamese tanks smashed through the gates to symbolise the defeat of the South and the start of the reunification of the nation. It is open to the public but we were not allowed to enter through the gates (I don't know why) so we only had a chance to photograph the imposing building and replica tanks.

Our visit was nearing its end now, but not before we went to the National History Museum. This is another huge complex taking the visitor through the formation and history of Vietnam and its dynasties and rulers. There were serious numbers of statues and remnants of temples as well as the mummified corpse of an old lady referred to as the Grandmother of the Nation.

I am sorry to say that by now we had reached a point of exhaustion and disinterest.

It was sad that this part of our tour came at the end of the day, as we would probably have appreciated it more if it been in the morning when we weren't so hot and drained. We did wake again for a final treat however, which was a water puppetry show in a small theatre created in a pond within the museum. This was entertaining as well as being a chance to sit down to watch the different puppets apparently swimming around, in a show which included underwater fireworks and traditional music.

Our guide had realised that further ancient history would be wasted on us, and gave us a chance to buy a cold drink before we got back on the coach for the final time before starting the two-hour journey back to the ship. Some people slept on the journey, but most relaxed and just looked at the never-ending traffic, including another factory full of motorbikes buzzing around us like bees.

On the way the guide answered questions from the passengers, and several people wanted to know about what happened to the babies of the Americans or French troops after the war, as well as the sympathisers of the South's resistance. The answers were too complex to discuss here, but it was obvious that they did not receive the fairest of treatment by the authorities.

This visit has certainly reinforced my desire to read more about the modern history of Vietnam since 1975.

He also answered one question about the Vietnam Boat people with a surprising story, as he himself was one as a young boy. His parents had sufficient money to help pay for a boat and all the supplies that would be needed during an attempt to escape abroad. The boat was hidden until the time was right to leave, as there were heavy penalties for anyone caught attempting to escape. Eventually they set off and for several days chugged their way to a better life. They didn't find their goal and eventually got to the point where fuel, water, and food were running out, and they needed to be rescued before they died. Fortunately a boat spotted them and came to their rescue. Sadly for the escapees, the rescue boat was a Vietnamese Coastguard vessel, but at least they did not become another statistic with the thousands of other people who drowned while attempting to escape.

After capture, our guide went to prison with his mother for a short time but his father was more harshly treated. The details of the punishments were not fully explained to us except to say that the family was no longer financially comfortable, and any professional status they had previously was taken away from them.

For the few minutes that he talked about his past, I sat fascinated as his story unfolded. Like millions of people, I had listened to or watched reports of the thousands of Vietnamese trying to escape an unwanted regime. It was horrifying to know what people were willing to do to find a better life. Now to have actually listened to one of those people (even if he was just a child at the time) speaking about his own experience was just mind-numbing.

By the time we got back on-board Aurora it was almost dark and there was just time to unpack our purchases, cool down and have a drink before we had to say goodbye to this amazing, beautiful, mysterious, country. Once again, I have to say *"thanks"* to whoever is looking after my life, for this opportunity to visit yet another unforgettable place.

We had a very quiet and informal evening. Dinner was just a snack in the Orangery and without a cabaret capable of matching this amazing day, Deb did some washing and I took the opportunity to catch up with my blog. After that we had a quiet drink in the Crow's Nest followed by an early night.

Simply Sensational Sihanoukville (Cambodia)
Monday 5th March 2012

Leaving Vietnam behind us we had a quiet Sunday (4th March) at sea while we sailed towards Cambodia. This was yet another country where my knowledge was restricted to books and news reports.

I woke early on the Monday morning, and before I grabbed the kettle to make our first cup of tea for the day, I opened the curtains. The scene before me was an armada of small motorised sampans all going alongside Aurora as though they were escorting her into port. When I had put some clothes on, I opened the balcony door and now the *"putt putt"* sounds of the boats' engines could be heard.

Over our tea we sat and watched the Cambodian scenery pass by, wondering what surprises and excitement the day would bring. We only knew a tiny amount of the country's history that featured in news reports of the leader of the Khmer Rouge, Pol Pot, who took control of the country in 1975. The KR attempted to rid the country of their political opposition and academics over a four-year period. During that time (a time known to us as the Killing Fields) upwards of 2,000,000 of the country's citizens were murdered by the state. Eventually in 1979 Vietnamese forces ousted Pol Pot and started the long drawn out process of giving Cambodia back to its own people. We knew we were about to see a country that had been through a nightmare, but which had woken up again and was now trying to establish itself once more. Tourism was still in its infancy and so there were only had a limited number of attractions to show visitors, and the industry also had to make use of a fleet of quite outdated coaches. The country was investing huge sums of money in its attempt to modernise, and while we knew we would see poverty, we were also aware of many luxury resorts being built.

The tour started with the usual introductions from our guide, a young man, who struggled with English but smiled with delight to be showing us his country. We passed a huge pair of imposing but stunning golden lions in the middle of a roundabout, before stopping at the nearby Independence Memorial. It resembled a tall temple with a large golden urn in the middle. Any pre-conceptions that we wouldn't be seeing anything beautiful in Cambodia were quickly dispelled. From the memorial we drove along various standards of roads with excited descriptions of new industrial parks, as well as the reopened Angkor beer breweries that had been forced by the Khmer Rouge to close in 1975. We could still see the older aspects of the country such as buffalo in the paddy fields, but our guide was making sure that we concentrated our attention on the newer things. He proudly announced that American investment was just about to make Cambodia an oil producer with the first production to start at the end of 2012.

Eventually the coach turned into a clearing in the forest area where we could see a pagoda, temples and Buddhas, but more importantly a small village. This was where we would be meeting the local people, and visiting their school.

Now please believe me when I say that the pagodas and statues and temples and Buddhas are amazing, beautiful, ornate, awe-inspiring, and so on, but we had already seen a great number of them during our recent stops, and they were beginning to blur into each other. I would recommend that anyone planning to come to this part of the world for the first time should seriously consider making such visits sparingly to maintain their magnificence.

On the other hand, if you get a chance to visit a village then jump at the opportunity.

This turned out to be a heart-searching, tear-jerking morning.

As well as the temple, the little village had maybe a couple of dozen dwellings that housed a number of extended families, plus a busy school that had been set up and funded by donations.

As we arrived and parked the coach, the children of the village came running out to greet us and they stayed with us for every second of our visit. The children we saw ranged from tiny boys and girls just able to walk, through to others perhaps six or seven years old.

We soon realised that, just like in Vietnam, these people are smaller than we expect, and their ages are difficult to estimate sometimes.

Many of the children were in school uniform and we asked our guide why they were not in school. It seemed there were so many young children in the village that some go to school in the morning and the others go in the afternoon. They are so proud of their school that they all put on the uniforms as soon as they get up.

Parents were rarely seen as the fathers were at work and the mothers stayed in their homes looking after even younger children. One or two older women were seen, but grandfathers didn't exist as most had been victims of Pol Pot. As we gathered in front of the traditional bamboo-roofed huts on stilts, we found ourselves surrounded by children whose eyes darted between their guests with expectation.

We had been warned of what we would be seeing and most of us had either brought tiny gifts of pencils, and notebooks, or had been squirreling away the pillow chocolates and cabin biscuits. The children knew it would happen and eventually one by one we gave them our little treats. They squealed with delight and crowded even closer to us. As a bag or pocket was opened their hands cupped to accept the gifts, and although they had little English to thank us the smiles and gestures said it all. Blonde women were especially popular and the children grabbed and held on to their hands throughout the visit.

We had a look inside a typical home. Built on stilts above the ground it allowed the family's animals to be kept safe under the living accommodation.

The elderly owner smiled as we climbed up the ladder and surveyed inside her modest house of two rooms. I was quite fearful that the floor would collapse under our weight as the thin planks sagged and twisted as we walked on them. The rooms were sparsely furnished but the old lady beamed in pride. We took photographs of her, and to say thanks we practiced what we had been told and placed our hands together, as if in prayer, and bowed our heads. This made her smile even more and she returned the gesture.

As another coachload of Aurora's passengers took our place at the village huts, we moved on to visit the school where we found more children hard at work. There were several classrooms that were busy for six days a week. We started by seeing the younger children in their schoolroom, where the morning class sang their hearts out to us. As we surveyed their classroom and its stark essentials, it made us realise how little there was to aid their education. We clapped at the end of their songs which made them sing some more so we clapped again to their delight and that of their teacher. Many wallets and purses were opened to give financial gifts to the teacher as well as some pens, pencils, and other teaching aids for her to share out amongst the children. This is when I thought back to just how lazy I had been in school. I took school for granted, never considering that some people were crying out for the opportunities I had. Yes, there were silent tears from myself and no doubt from others too, and consciences pricked with guilt.

We moved on to the more senior school where the nine and

ten year olds were slightly better provided for with a few old tattered textbooks.

Their teacher turned out to be the enthusiastic director who had set up the school, and who continued to maintain it by begging for help from anywhere and anyone who will listen. Charity boxes were again fed by people who have had more education than these children and teachers could imagine. When we left the school for the next coach party to see, there was another humbling moment as we went to the Buddhist temple building. We stepped forward in turn to be blessed by the monks who sprinkled us with water and flowers as they quietly chanted. Although I didn't understand their words, I hoped and assumed that it was a symbol of thanks for the very little help we had provided during our fleeting visit.

The vision of that school and the children of the village has remained with me ever since.

Cambodia had more to show us, and unlike the people of the village, we were going to have our lunch in a 5-star luxury hotel complex before relaxing for the afternoon on a beautiful beach.

On the way we had another stop at a place called Wat Krom which I can only describe as a Buddhist university. It was situated in an amazing complex with the usual temples and shrines, but also had training buildings where perhaps a hundred trainee monks in orange robes sat in prayer or listened to the wisdom of their elders. All around us were statues of people and animals with an abundance of gold evident. Buddhas were depicted sitting, reclining, or standing and other figures rode horses or sat on most of the astrological symbols of the Chinese years. It was stunning, and cameras were working overtime to capture the almost magical things we were seeing.

The historical and cultural side of our tour was now complete, and we arrived at the Sokha Beach Resort where we sat and ate a wonderful lunch of both local and western food. Once that was over we strolled onto the beach of soft golden sand with palm trees for shade. We quickly changed and commandeered a couple of sun beds for the afternoon before splashing into the warm water. Deb and I had maybe half an hour in the sea before relaxing in the sun.

Becoming a bit bored with sunbathing, we had a walk along the beach and came across a group of local girls providing traditional Khmer massages. Several of the passengers, including me and Deb, paid the equivalent of £6-£7 for a delightful twenty-minute massage on a bed beside a beautiful beach. The Cambodian girls were small but incredibly strong and there were moments when I thought they must be walking on my back rather than using their hands and arms to roll away the fatigue from my tight and stressed-out muscles.

This had been a terrific day with *ying and yang* experiences of the village and then the 5-star hotel, lunch, and beach complex.

What did I enjoy most?

Obviously the afternoon on the beach was a luxurious treat that I enjoyed, and I can still remember the feeling of the sand between my toes, the warmth of the water, and the relaxation from the massage. On the other hand, I can still see the smiles of the village children, and their shrieks of joy at receiving small pieces of chocolate or a simple toy.

I still remember the tear in my eye as the children sang their songs in the classroom and I looked at their drawings around the walls. The image remains of a small boy sitting cross-legged in the school library reading a tattered magazine that was his reference for learning more about the world.

To be honest I loved it all, and Cambodia (like Vietnam) had become a country that I would visit again if I ever had the chance. It is a country that has started to grow from the ruins of war and murder, and is now just beginning to find its feet amongst the rest of the world. It has beauty, history, luxury and yes it still has poverty. I hope that the money it gets from its oil reserves is used wisely to give its children a chance of better schooling, better housing, and jobs. The luxury hotel complexes are a means of attracting tourists who, like us, have had their eyes opened to see Cambodia as something other than a Killing Field. I am sure thousands of tourists will visit here in future years and perhaps lie on the beaches for two weeks without going beyond the gates of their hotel. They will enjoy themselves, but they won't get the thrill of seeing the smiles of those children.

If you are going to visit a country where there are similar village school schemes that give you the opportunity to pay a visit, please think ahead before you go. They will be over the moon if you can spend maybe just £10 to buy pencils, notebooks, simple toys or anything that a child would enjoy. I wished I had known this before leaving home so that I could have given more to ease the ache (and a little guilt) in my heart at the visions I'd seen.

Bangkok
Tuesday 6th March 2012

Overnight we had sailed west towards to Thailand where we would be visiting two ports in two days. On the Tuesday morning we arrived at our first port, Laem Chabang, where we had an all-day tour to the capital city of Bangkok. Our trip would involve a two-hour journey there and back, and with another hour taken out for lunch we would have no more than four hours to see the major attractions of the city.

Today would not turn out to be the best of experiences, and things started to go wrong from the moment we arrived on the coach.

Now I am neither short nor excessively tall, but when I got on the coach and took my seat, I discovered that I couldn't sit with my legs in front of me without pushing them against the seat in front. I looked around for an alternative seat but it was obvious that the only ones with greater legroom were already taken. So, for two hours I sat in various positions with my legs splayed out for a while, sometimes turning to the right where Deb had to make some room, or twisting out into the walkway to my left. It was noticeable that several of the men were struggling in the same way, with several pairs of legs blocking the gangway.

I was in physical pain for long periods of the journey, and certainly uncomfortable for all of it.

There was no alternative, so I resigned myself to the situation in the knowledge that there would soon be the excitement of exploring a new city.

We eventually got through the initial traffic jams and joined the main highway. Near the start of the journey I had a moment that really cheered me up. My career had been quite varied but for a number of years in the late 1970s and early

1980s I was involved for a very rewarding period of time, bringing new satellite earth stations into service, remotely from the UK. One of those stations was in Thailand. I had always hoped that one day I could put a picture to the name, and this was to be that day. At the side of the road I spotted a cluster of satellite communication dishes in a clearing beyond some trees. They certainly looked the right size, and the site had all the other sorts of buildings and masts required. My memory told me what the name of the station ought to be and I scanned signposts for a few minutes until I was rewarded and saw one showing the area to be that of Siracha. I excitedly told Deb, who could see the pleasure in my eyes.

My excitement passed and my knees started to ache again, so I sat back in the seat, found a less painful position for my legs and wished away the time.

Eventually we arrived in Bangkok city where our first stop was at the Wat Trimitr building that houses the huge Golden Buddha. It was a beautiful and impressive temple and the description of the statue was correct. It was certainly very big standing (well actually sitting) just short of four metres high, and yes it was made of solid gold, weighing five tonnes. Unfortunately, there was the tiniest thought in my mind that it was just another Buddha, and its impact was sadly less than it should have been.

Once again for those who are new to these Buddhist symbols, and excited about seeing them soon, please do not be alarmed by my comments. They are magnificent and a joy to behold but be careful not to try and see all the major Buddhas in Indochina in the space of ten days!

Having stretched our legs for a while as we looked around the temple, Deb and I had felt a bit more positive as we squeezed back into our seats.

Sadly it all started to go wrong again as the next part of the tour was a scenic drive through Chinatown and we instantly became stuck in a traffic jam. I think this was the fourth Chinatown we had seen so far, and it was not to be the most inspiring.

The guide did her best to hold our interest by explaining what some of the shops sold and directing our gaze towards statues or buildings of interest, but even that was difficult. She was at the front, while we were near the back. As she pointed something out it was perhaps ten minutes later before we arrived at that spot due to the traffic. Quite often the object or person she had pointed out had actually gone by the time we got there.

After failing to find anything of interest in Chinatown, we arrived at the next landmark building. This was the Grand Palace where the Thai royal family has their historical home. They have now moved to a newer palace but this one is still used for ceremonial meetings, coronations and royal cremations. At the time of our visit the King of Thailand (King Bhumibol Adulyadej) was seriously ill, and one of the princesses had recently died and was awaiting cremation. Our guide made it quite clear that the nation had a great love and respect for their royal family so were quite upset at that particular time.

The Grand Palace and its grounds were truly wonderful with temples, statues, and buildings that cannot fail to delight. The mix of bright colours and the abundance of gold leaf and paint makes it glow and shimmer in the bright sunlight. There are dragons and lions and all kinds of mythical creatures guarding the buildings to confirm the importance of the palace.

It also housed two major exhibits.

The first one was the only Emerald Buddha in the world. Actually, it is jade, but still very beautiful and loved by the people. This was in the Wat Pra Keo temple where photography was banned and we had to remove our shoes and cover virtually all of our bodies. Fortunately the guide provided baggy trousers for those of us who were unprepared. This really is a seriously revered icon, and the temple was crowded with people from all over the world kneeling silently in awe and many praying.

The second major exhibit was the ceremonial coronation room with the thrones of the kings. Once again it was a room of great reverence where we couldn't take photographs or wear shoes. The room housed two thrones, both golden, with gems galore adorning them. The older one was in the shape of a ship, but that had now been superseded by a more traditional chair-style throne. The older one is now just used as an altar. These two buildings had been very pleasant to visit, but now we were rushed around the rest of the palace site from temple to statue to picture to icon, and it was all far too fast to really appreciate what we were being shown

By the way I forgot to tell you that it was also really hot and humid!

Just minutes later we were back on the coach again and totally exhausted. We resumed our drive through Chinatown and became bored to tears once more, as well as getting rather hungry.

Eventually at 2:30 we arrived at the hotel to have our lunch. It was a beautiful luxury hotel and we enjoyed a delicious selection of Thai food. We had been treated to a lot of this style of food recently, and maybe, just maybe, my taste buds were looking forward to some basic British food as a change. Anyway, because we had arrived over an hour late, most of the other tour coach parties had finished and were leaving. This meant that as we ate, the staff were clearing away the tables and chairs making the atmosphere less than special.

Onwards again at 3:30 and I was thinking we would be on our

way back to the ship but no, there was another visit to make first. We went to a Gem Factory, where they prepared, but more importantly tried to sell us, all kinds of jewellery and their precious stones.

This was a total waste of our time, and I have to ask why anyone would want to spend a lot of money on jewellery, from an unknown factory, when the ship sells its own expensive jewellery at tax-free prices and usually with a good discount? Deb and I were hot, tired, and totally fed up so we sat outside waiting for our uncomfortable coach to return so that we could at least get back to its air conditioning.

That was our final stop in Bangkok and we finally started our two-hour journey back to Aurora. It was about 6:15 when we arrived back at the dock. With only 15 minutes to go until dinner, and with an aching back and knees, we opted for a leisurely snack in the Orangery.

Surprise, surprise, the night's speciality menu was Thai food! This had not been a good day.

Splendid Koh Samui (Thailand)
Wednesday 7th March 2012

It was our second day in Thailand and we were visiting the gorgeous island of Koh Samui. This was to be so different from Bangkok, and would restore our faith in Thailand.
We awoke to almost total silence outside our balcony. The sea in the bay was so calm that the surface was merely dimpled with the spent force of a million waves. Even the bow wave from Aurora was just a gentle rise and fall of water that dissipated almost immediately. This was another tender port, and I heard the splash, and the rattle of the chain as the anchor was dropped. Because there was only about 12 feet of water below the keel, the anchor stirred up the mud and turned the surface an unsightly brown. This attracted small hungry fish to find their breakfast from the disturbed mud and unexpectedly a whirlpool formed in the water. I decided this was caused by larger fish herding the smaller fish into a circle to allow themselves to gorge on them as their own breakfast. It seemed like a good theory to me anyway!
As usual our breakfast was quickly over and we had plenty of time before getting ready for the day's tour. In the back of our minds there was just a little concern after yesterday's experience of Bangkok.
It was time to go, and we caught a local pleasure boat that was helping with the tendering process. It gave us a smooth ride to the shore where we were politely greeted by tour guides and drivers with a far higher-standard of coaches than yesterday. Ours was cool and had plenty of leg room and Deb and I felt oh so much more positive as we drove away with our guide (Nom) giving us the details of the trip.
The plan was to firstly visit Kunaram Temple (the Temple of the Dead Monk), followed by a demonstration by monkeys at a

coconut plantation. After that would be The Temple of the Big Buddha before having lunch at a luxury hotel, and the final stop was to be at the Chaweng Beach for an hour.

It all sounded so much more interesting than the day in Bangkok's Chinatown area.

During the first part of the drive, we relaxed and had a chance to see the lush vegetation around us. We also watched the people of the island going about their daily business while Nom described the scene and gave us the usual facts and figures. As with nearly all the places we had visited, tourism played a major role in the economy of Koh Samui, but the island was also a leading producer of coconuts with more than 100,000 palm trees.

The island authorities were in the process of improving drainage and water supplies after some recent floods, and this disrupted our first stop at the Kunaram Temple. Our coach had to stop on the opposite side of the road from the temple because of the road works. Nom was very apologetic about us having to cross the road, but we all managed the little bit of exercise without accidents. So there we were at the site of the temple where a dead monk is preserved in a glass case. It sounds morbid and to be honest it is, but who are we to dispute their faith? Nom gave us the story of the monk who predicted the day he would die and asked that he be put on show for eternity. His small body sits (cross legged) inside a glass box wearing his robes and a pair of sunglasses, surrounded by the normal finery of gold and jewels adorning his resting place.

As well as the temple, the site was busy with a number of traders at stalls selling souvenirs and drinks. It was hot and humid once more and the drinks were very popular even at *"good grief"* prices. The souvenirs were much better value, so once we had taken some photos of the mummified monk, we had plenty to look at and buy.

We were treated to some more of the island's beauty as we drove on to a small coconut plantation. Here we saw a demonstration of how the locals use monkeys to climb up the trees, who then select the ripe fruit, twisting it until it breaks off and falls to the ground. The two monkeys on view were very efficient and having shown their skills sat looking confused by the round of applause we gave them.

Nom explained to us that the male monkeys are taken to a training school where it takes about three to five months to train them to select the correct fruit and the harvesting method. This costs upwards of $8000, but pays for itself as one monkey can pick up to 500 coconuts a day with a sale price that can make the farmers quite wealthy. There is of course the questionable issue of animal welfare, but we can only trust what we were told, that the monkeys become pets after working for about fifteen years.

Although we'd seen it done before, we now had a chance to watch the farmer take a ripe coconut, remove it from its husk and prepare it for use. Just as in Apia (so many weeks earlier!) the spike used to remove the husk was a health-and-safety nightmare, and the rest of the process would similarly fall foul of our laws. A single blow of an axe is used to crack the nut which allows the milk to drain into a collection bowl. Then with a second blow the nut is split into two equal halves. Next a tool similar to a cheese grater was now gripped between the operator's thighs and used to scrape out the fruit from the nut. Samples were offered and quickly devoured as fresh coconut is a delight to taste. Finally the farmer took a handful of the grated fruit plus a little of the almost colourless milk, and after rinsing and squeezing it, produced the white coconut milk used in cooking.

Those who hadn't seen this demonstration before were now

amazed to learn that every part of the coconut is used, either as food, fuel (the husks), or building material (leaves for roofs), and of course the empty nut shells are turned into bowls and other small items for sale as souvenirs.

Suitably educated we returned to the coach for the trip to the Temple of the Big Buddha. The ride was really pleasant and allowed us to see the coastal beauty of Koh Samui with its golden sandy beaches. Inland we saw more of the luscious green vegetation, and occasionally a glimpse of buffalos in the fields. Everywhere we went, the local people smiled and waved at us as we passed by. Of course the island is a tourist trap, but it has tried to hold on to the traditional elements in contrast to Bangkok that has moved almost totally towards commercialism. Bangkok seems to have forgotten to look after the poorer elements of society, who hide behind the main streets of that glitzy city. Koh Samui was more rural, with its narrow dusty roads, the working countryside, and its temples in the middle of nowhere, but it was also developing the beaches and unworkable land for hotel resorts of the highest quality.

The Temple of the Big Buddha was what it said on the packet. Wat Phra Yai is a temple erected on a small headland at the end of a narrow causeway just wide enough for a single vehicle. The site was packed with tourists, cars, jeeps, and coaches. The Buddha is depicted sitting cross legged and certainly is big at about twelve metres high. Golden in colour, it is flanked by buildings, other statues, and smaller temples all beautifully constructed and coloured with the artwork that we had grown familiar with in our visits to South East Asia. There were also scores of market stalls selling food, souvenirs, and clothing, to tempt the hundreds of tourists to spend some money. This was not difficult with the prices so low as to be embarrassing, even if most of the brand names were fake, and the goods perhaps of low quality. I found some wonderful shirts, Deb was seriously tempted by the Asian dresses, and we were quite taken by various elephant objects. Well, we did buy one or two items of clothing, but it was very busy so we decided to wait until later to buy souvenirs...

... bad mistake!

The only drawback to the island trying to remain unspoilt was that the single-carriage road to and from the headland became a nightmare with the number of coaches and other vehicles using it. It took perhaps ten minutes for us to get back onto the main road again, but we learned later that other groups had seriously longer delays.

In terms of major attractions that was the end of the tour, but we now had the luxury of a buffet lunch in one of the superb hotel resorts.

The one we visited was typical of what is available, and absolutely stunning with a main hotel building, flanked by villas all within a stroll from the beautiful beach and an even more spectacular swimming pool. The food was delicious and served in a restaurant area so close to the beach that you could go and paddle between courses. A musical duo played for us as we sat under a parasol eating delicious food with the sea lapping onto an almost deserted beach to our side.

Time was limited, so after the meal we explored the hotel grounds a little before leaving. Built on a side of a hill, there were small streams supplying rock pools created beside pathways with fish swimming in them. All around it was peaceful and there were trees to give shade plus flowers making it so beautiful. For the less able there were even golf buggies to bring you from the car park to the complex if needed.

This was truly absolute total luxury.

Back at the coach Nom and the driver gave the traditional

greeting with heads bowed, and hands in the prayer position, and now familiar with this we returned the gesture to their obvious amusement.

Our last destination was Chaweng Beach where we had an hour to take a swim or to visit the little town for a spot of shopping. At the beach we met Jimmy and Isabel with a group of their friends so we had a chat until they jumped into a taxi to continue their privately-organised tour of the island. We took a look at the beach but it was very busy and most people were just a little young with the occasional overly browned poser in a thong showing off his muscles and...

... well virtually everything.

We agreed to forget the swim and go and do some shopping for more treats. In the end we bought nothing but a drink in MacDonald's, of all places, plus a couple of bottles of cola and some chocolate in a local shop. We really regretted not buying souvenirs at the Big Buddha headland, as the town of Chewang had virtually nothing to offer.

We were hot and tired by now and relieved to get back on the coach to relax in the air conditioning. All that was left was a 20-minute drive back towards Aurora.

With everyone back, Nom explained that our return trip would be around the coast of the island so that we could see all of it before returning to Aurora's tender jetty. We drove slowly, allowing us to look at the scenery for the last time, including climbing up a hill to give a different view out to sea. Many dozed off during the journey, but everyone was relaxed and probably thinking about their wonderful day. There were still things to see and I occasionally received a gentle poke in the side to wake me up as we passed a more interesting view, or a group of locals doing something unusual, or maybe just to make sure I saw as much as possible of the island. Koh Samui is definitely a place to return to if at all possible.

Back at the jetty after farewells to Nom and his driver we faced the dreaded queue for the tender. But today it wasn't too bad as we were the first coach of many to arrive back. Our ride to the ship was without problems and soon we were back in the cabin unloading our shopping and returning the remainder of our dollars to the safe. We had not spent much but we seemed to have bought a lot over the last week.

We were too tired to change into formal wear for the evening, so after a shower and freshen up, we went casual (yes, we were rebels again) and first watched Roger and Laura performing in the Aurora choir before having yet another snack in the Orangery.

There was a superb evening cabaret in the theatre with Tom O'Connor giving us an hour of jokes and stories that had the audience laughing and applauding throughout. His show managed to wake us up from our earlier exhaustion, so afterwards we went for a drink in Champions. Mick and Brenda came along and we spent an amusing hour and half with a 'Guess the Tune' quiz accompanied by several glasses of red wine.

It had been a lovely day, and one that sits in the 'special' area of my Round the World memories. The disappointment of Bangkok was not forgotten, but Thailand had been forgiven. There was one more sea day now before reaching Singapore where we are busy with two tours so probably another exhausting day. That would signal the end of the third sector of the cruise with a lot of passengers, plus several of the entertainment officers due to leave.

It had been nine weeks since we left Britain and we had sailed nearly three quarters of the way around the world, covering well in excess of 20,000 miles. The dream still had a while to go, and although it may be the only time we experience these places, I am sure the memories will last forever.

Spectacular Singapore
Thursday 9th March 2012

After a day's rest at day at sea, we arrived at the port of
Singapore on the island of the same name.

One of the problems with cruising is that larger passenger ships
are not always catered for by many of the locations, and we
end up moored alongside some ugly container dock. Singapore
was no exception and our home for the day was huge, and is
apparently the second busiest commercial port in the world. It
was like a small city of containers either coming or going
through this gateway between east and west. Very close to
Aurora, a car transporter was putting down its ramp as we
arrived and cars, vans, lorries and diggers were being moved
on or off constantly until it got dark in the evening, and even
then, I don't think they had finished. In front of us was a
parking lot with in the region of 10,000 new vehicles awaiting
transfer to their new owners somewhere in the west.

Enough of that, we were here to have both a cultural day and
some fun. The culture aspect was something many people
might find unusual, but we had opted to do a morning tour
called 'Battlefields'. We would be looking at sites connected
with the Japanese invasion, and the British surrender of
Singapore. A major consequence of that surrender was the
resulting period of confinement for some 3,000 prisoners in
the infamous camp of Changi. This was another period of
history that I was aware of but not knowledgeable about.

After lunch, our second tour was the fun thing as we were
going to look around the city as a tourist, including the 'must
do' – having a Singapore Sling in Raffles Hotel.

With breakfast over we were quickly onto our coach and away
to the first stop at the Old Ford Factory Museum. I was puzzled
to start with, but our enthusiastic guide enlightened us with a

wonderful history lesson. This was the location where the British officially surrendered to the Japanese on 15th February 1942 after deciding that continuing the battle to hold on to Singapore was impossible.

Against all the planning proposals of a modern city intent on expanding, the Old Ford Motor plant had been retained and converted into a museum to keep the history available to the next generation. The exhibition was quite small but had a fascinating range of displays and memorabilia to tell the story of the period leading up to the surrender. There were letters and audio recordings giving accounts by local people and soldiers relating to that day and the period until the Japanese eventually returned the island to its people at the end of their war.

As we left the museum, a coach load of youngsters was arriving but our guide sadly told us that the children do not understand the war. She blamed gaming machines as a catalyst to desensitising the next generation to the horror of war and death....*and I quite agree!*

Our next stop was at Kranji and the Commonwealth War Cemetery and Memorial. I have been fortunate that no-one from my family was ever killed or injured in the wars, but these graveyards never cease to bring the hairs up on the back of my neck, and sometimes even a tear to my eyes.

Kranji's layout is simple, and our tour party spent some 30 minutes just walking around, looking at row after row of gravestones and the memorial walls. Some 4,500 casualties are buried or commemorated there, with about 850 of them unidentified. The soldiers, sailors, airman, medical and other military personnel commemorated are not just British, and there are many ANZAC troops together with Chinese, Indians and local forces. The headstones all face the same direction except for a special area for the Islamic faith soldiers who lie facing towards Mecca.

The most painful headstones to read are those of unknown young men, and as I described for the Pearl Harbour trip, I just hurt inside thinking that they never knew if their sacrifice was justified. Deb pointed out a pair of stones she had spotted, with one showing it as the resting place of a 19-year-old private, but almost directly behind it was another for a 58-year-old officer. Death came to everyone no matter what their age or rank. Another grave that caught our eye was that of a young airman with the inscription that described him as 'one of the few'. He had survived as a hero of the Battle of Britain only to be sent to die here in Malaya or Singapore.

Thank you, and may all of you brave people rest in peace. Feeling deeply moved, we returned to the coach for the journey to our final stop of the morning at the museum for Chanji prison. This small peaceful site is close to the original prison, which was rebuilt after the war and is now a women's prison.

The museum contains reconstructions of two chapels that the prisoners themselves built and used, and also has a huge display of objects and stories of life in that hell-hole of a prison. Most come from those who suffered, and some are accompanied by photographs or pictures created at the time. There are books written by the prisoners and gifts made and swapped between the male and female sections to let each other know that they were still alive. Some of the books have since been rewritten and published for a wider audience to relive those years of imprisonment.

One of the reconstructed chapels had paintings of biblical scenes on the wall that were created by a patient in the prison hospital. He had subsequently been asked to come back to the museum to reproduce those pictures for the display.

There is so much squeezed into this building and it does its best to describe the atmosphere and conditions that the prisoners had to contend with. While we visited the museum there was a steady stream of other visitors and very few of them were of the older generation. So, it looked like the memories were being kept alive, and passed onto another generation.

The Singapore people have a saying *"forgive, but don't forget"*, but this city wants to move on, and I cannot see this expensive piece of land remaining for too long.

You may detect from this entry that I was deeply affected by the morning and I have another 'must do' added to my list, which is to learn some more about the conflict in Singapore. That is my way of remembering and honouring the sacrifice of so many people during the conflict, and the subsequent horrendous conditions in Changi prison for those who survived the fighting.

Our return to the ship included a tour around the city and a chance to look at its highlights. It is a new city of beautiful high-rise buildings with imaginative architecture. The people are polite and the city is clean with on-the-spot fines or penalties if you drop litter. They are quite a wealthy nation but have very little land or roads. Prospective car owners have to buy an expensive permit before they are allowed to purchase one, and these permits are restricted to a small number each year.

I almost had a private treat when I spotted many signs for an area called Sentosa. That was the name of another of the satellite earth stations that I dealt with years ago. I spoke to our guide and explained my interest, but she told me that Sentosa Island had been completely redeveloped and the satellite station no longer exists. Never mind, I did at least see where it had been.

So far I was impressed with Singapore and looked forward to

the more touristy experience coming up later.

After a quick snack and freshen up on board Aurora, we were on the quay again and boarding another coach to go back into the city.

Our first stop was at the famous Raffles Hotel where we were taken to the Long Bar and enjoyed a Singapore Sling cocktail like the tens of thousands of others who visit Singapore each year. It was a wonderful experience with a drink that has a hidden kick to it. There was also the chance to eat peanuts at the tables and be allowed (in fact encouraged) to just throw the shells on the floor...

... what a strange, but interesting tradition

Our drink was provided as a part of the tour and was probably a mass-produced cheaper version of the original. To actually buy one of these cocktails was costing people nearly £20 each, yet there was no shortage of punters to fulfil this very British tourist experience.

Oh, by the way, the hotel is also beautiful with splendid rooms where you can have afternoon tea, plus dreamy courtyards with fountains making unforgettable settings to get married just as one couple we saw were about to do. Outside there was a uniformed concierge to meet and greet the well-to-do in their Rolls Royces, Ferraris etc. I somehow doubt I will ever have the opportunity, or the money, to sample this magnificent hotel as a guest.

From Raffles we had a short coach ride before changing transport to a trishaw (a three-wheeled bike carriage) for a quaint and quirky ride around some of Chinatown and Little India. It was pleasant and gave us a chance to look up at the skyline of the city while being able to see and smell the city at ground level as well. I wasn't impressed with the area we were being shown however. Just as with Buddhas and temples, we had seen a lot of Chinatowns over the last couple of months!

To round off our tour we then had 45 minutes to shop in Chinatown. To be frank I would have preferred to have returned to the ship as there was little we wanted to buy. The market was full of stalls selling a lot of the same items we had seen throughout our far eastern locations, but there was a major emphasis on clothes for young women to wear. I can only leave the style of the clothes to your imagination but the vast amount of them would be like those found on a busy street in British cities on a drunken Saturday night. Perhaps this was the wrong market for British pensioners! Back on the ship it was obvious that there were new passengers on board, as people came out of lifts and looked both ways as if checking for traffic before moving off down corridors with just a hint of *"where the heck are we"* on their faces. Sail-away was seriously delayed as we waited for all the passports to be sorted out and cleared by the Singapore authorities and then made ready for Malaysian immigration. As well as hundreds of new passengers, we knew that several of the entertainment team had changed, including the Cruise Director. Christine Noble had left and was replaced by Natalie Milverton who we had known for several years since we first saw her as a young entertainment team member. We thought there would be some changes during the coming days, and Deb and I both hoped they would be for the better.

As expected, we were back too late for our evening meal in the restaurant but we had a table booked in Café Bordeaux instead. For an hour or so we savoured a delicious, relaxed meal with friendly attentive, and slightly cheeky, waiters rounding off a wonderful day. Full up and slightly tipsy we dropped in on a quiz in Champions and spent half an hour chatting to a couple about the cruise before having an early night.

Our stop in Singapore marked the end of the third segment of our trip around the world. Segment four would take us westwards now, with the first stop being Malaysia the next morning...
... what a life!

Sector 4 - Singapore to Dubai

Kuala Lumpur, Capital of Malaysia
Saturday 10th March 2012 – Our daughter Lynsey's birthday

From our balcony we could see a mangrove swamp as we sailed into the terminal of Port Kelang from where we would travel by road to Kuala Lumpur. As we went to breakfast the port area could be seen and it was just an isolated cruise terminal no more than a couple of hundred metres from a major container port. There was no dockside associated with the terminal but it did have a building so it was already better than some we had seen.

Our trip today was an all-day tour called 'The Best of Kuala Lumpur'. Because such long trips were planned, Aurora docked unusually early, before it was fully daylight, but passengers still had to rush a little to be on time for tours. Almost as soon as breakfast was over, we heard the *"You may proceed to shore"* announcement so quickly grabbed our bits and lined up in the queue to get off. Unfortunately, there was then a thirty-minute delay while minor gangway problems were sorted out. This caused some moaning of course, but the alternative was to jump, and very few of the moaners looked capable of doing that! One very vocal lady just behind me in the queue complained about the fact that it was still dark when she got up and it really wasn't good enough!

I'll leave you to decide what my thoughts were!

We were soon on our way to Malaysia's capital city and just over an hour later entering another skyscraper-dominated scene typical of the major cities of this area. Our guide, who was originally from India, had told us that being Saturday it would be quiet, but the traffic looked pretty busy to us as we weaved through the congestion to our first stop at the National Museum.

As we drove into the relatively small car park we were greeted by the unusual sight of trains. There were steam ones and diesel ones, and it made a pleasant change from the usual religious statues and icons. In we trouped and the guide pointed out the toilets but told us to wait a moment while he arranged the entry fees. That is the first time we have been faced with toilet charges but everything was soon organised for us to have free access...

... very efficient!

Deb and I looked at more of the transport exhibition that was on display in an area just outside of the main museum building. This ranged from a bullock-drawn wagon, through canoes, rickshaws, bicycles and tricycles, plus an old Austin 7 and eventually the Malaysian Proton car. Our guide was very proud of the Proton brand but it was difficult for us to show the same enthusiasm for it. Eventually we were given our tickets and entered the huge museum building via an impressive flight of steps.

Inside there was a large square foyer with entrances to four major exhibition halls, two on the ground floor and the other two on the first floor at the top of an ornate staircase. The different exhibitions covered periods of Malaysian history from ancient times through to the present. It was really well displayed and presented but we only had a 45-minute stop. This was not nearly long enough, so I gave Deb the choice as to which ones we looked at. We managed rather quick looks at three of the display rooms and the quality of what we saw a tremendous mix of original objects, reproductions backed up by pictures, models, and audio and video presentations.

This was somewhere I would recommend visiting if you are interested in history, but allow yourself plenty of time, and don't expect children to be over-excited once the trains have been seen.

From the museum our coach took less than five minutes to

arrive at the Malaysian National Mosque where we simply stopped to take photographs. It was a beautiful and architecturally dominating building befitting its name. Unlike some that we had seen recently, it made a change to have a religious building without excessive gold and ornate decorations.

Our guide now pointed across the road from the mosque to where we could see the old Railway Station. This was another treasured attraction in Kuala Lumpur with an imposing colonial-style façade, now used as a hotel. Mr Efficient Guide had managed to organise a single stop where we could see, and photograph, two attractions without having to move. "Everybody back on the coach!"

This was becoming a bit of a whistle-stop tour, and having meandered for a few more minutes through the now very busy traffic we came to an oasis in the middle of the congested city at Independence Square. Referred to in Malaysian as the 'Merdeka Square' it was formerly known as the 'Selangor Club Padang' or putting it simply the Selangor Cricket Club green. This was the site used to celebrate the independence of Malaysia from British governance. Parades are held there annually to remember the historic date of the 31st August 1957.

Befitting its original use, the square is a vast central grass area dominated by what looks like a huge pavilion along one side. This is the Royal Selangor Club where many of Kuala Lumpur's colonial elite used to come together socially. The green is still used for cricket matches, and I presume the old pavilion still plays its part. Across from the green stands the stunning Sultan Abdul Samad Building that was used by the British for various purposes, from 1897 until the country's independence. It was now a wonderful setting for the Ministry of Heritage, Culture and Arts. At one end of the cricket pitch we saw a huge flagpole that our guide described as the tallest in the world and while we couldn't confirm that, it certainly stretched the wide angle lenses of peoples' cameras.

Time here was up, so we drank a bottle of chilled water, given to us by the guide, and then it was....

..."back on the coach!"

The last stop of the morning was at the City Market, described by our guide as being somewhere to buy handicraft items. It was a huge covered market that sold all the usual stuff that we had been tempted with in Vietnam, Cambodia, Thailand and Singapore, except that the fridge magnets now said Malaysia. No matter how cynical I might sound, most people still found things to buy, especially at the prices they were asking. We came away with a number of souvenirs to remind us of Kuala Lumpur as well as some presents for friends and family.

At midday, the exact time shown on the itinerary, we arrived at a luxury hotel for our lunch. Yes, it was another sumptuous buffet meal, but I was really getting bored with Asian food and had a real yearning for steak and kidney pie, chips and peas. Precisely an hour later we were being encouraged back onto the coach to continue our tour.

There were two more stops to make, and the first was a photo opportunity to add pictures of the Petronus Twin Towers to our collection. Until recently they had been the tallest buildings in the world, and at nearly 400 metres tall they were certainly impressive. Along with several other coach parties we stood and stared at these imposing towers. They loom over most of the other sky-hugging buildings of the city, but an optical illusion makes them appear lower than some that are built on higher ground. They are magnificent examples of modern architecture, and I could understand the pride of the Malaysian people for them.

One building that did appear taller than the Twin Towers was to be our final stop.

Known as the KL Tower, this was a telecommunications hub built on the highest point in the city. We were whisked to the top of the 250-metre tower by high-speed lift to view the city from its observation platform. Yes, it was impressive, and for the numerous 'tower junkies' on the tour it was another tick in the box, but to me it was so overcrowded that it made me feel distinctly uncomfortable. From our window above the city, we looked down at the Petronus Towers and the beauty of Kuala Lumpur with its imaginative architecture all around us. Rather strangely, scores of apparently sound buildings were being demolished all over the city, presumably to make way for more eye-catching structures, and probably even taller ones. There must be a lot of money washing around this city compared to those closer to home in Europe, where such developments are struggling to get finance.

The clock told our guide that it was time to go but he was delayed for a while trying to round up the last of his passengers. The tower's lifts could only hold small numbers of people, so our group became split up. Being British we did as we were told and made our own way back to the coach park, but in a slightly less organised manner, as we took different routes to stop for ice cream, toilets, shopping and generally looking around at the views. Our guide had been unable to deal with a group that had briefly decided to do their own thing. Slightly chastised and a few minutes later than planned we were on our way back to the ship.

It had been a very long day and several passengers had a little sleep and having finished reading his newspaper, so did our guide. He had been very good but a little regimented, and not as enthusiastic as some of the guides we had been entertained by in previous cities in south-east Asia.

Back on Aurora we had time to shower and change before our

first visit to the Medina restaurant for several days.
Unfortunately, I was not feeling overly hungry and was quite
exhausted after a combination of long days, extreme heat and
unfamiliar food. I knew I should eat something so after much
consideration I chose a simple gammon, egg and chips option...
... but without the gammon
          ... absolutely delicious!
Deb and I were both very tired so the sum total of our
evening's activities consisted of a rest in the cabin before going
to a quiz just to stretch our legs before bedtime.
Tomorrow would be another Malaysian stop in Penang where
we had no tours booked and so it would be a chance to relax a
little, and do just a little less, for a change.

Georgetown, Penang
Sunday 11th March 2012

It was dark again as we started the final manoeuvre into the port of Georgetown in the province of Penang in the North West region of Malaysia.

Our terminal was on the mainland but a lot of the tours were going to the nearby island, also called Penang, and apparently very beautiful. This was a day off from touring for us, and we just planned to go for a walk, at our pace, and when we felt ready. After breakfast we looked towards the shore area to get first impressions. The terminal was in a poorer part of the city with older buildings compared to the skyscraper vista in the distance. The most noticeable thing was that the water, for as far as we could see, was filthy. It wasn't just sludge stirred up after the ship's docking movements; it was mud plus man-made rubbish floating along on the tide all around the ship and the nearby water. This was the worst example I'd seen anywhere on our journey, and as the day progressed it became even worse.

Anyway, I was still feeling quite exhausted from the busy schedule of the last few days, so we didn't rush into anything. With the launderette practically empty, Deb took the chance to do some washing while I caught up with my blog. By mid-morning the itch to get off was growing so we had a cup of coffee in Raffles and after a chat with the new Cruise Director, Natalie, to catch up since we last saw each other, we strolled off the ship and towards the city.

Getting away from the port area we came across a park that was peaceful with some shading from the trees. This was originally part of what's called Fort Cornwallis, named after a famous Governor of India. There were some statues and cannons plus a large gathering of locals with their motorbikes.

We didn't hang around there too long, but moved on to see what else Penang had to offer. The heat and humidity were overpowering, and within a few minutes and with nothing to grab our attention, we decided to abandon exploring Penang in favour of a cool air-conditioned ship. We'd been out for no more than three quarters of an hour but rather than possibly getting dehydrated we returned to Aurora.

This was the first day when we relaxed on board (other than sea days) since that strange day in Bali. Unlike that day, there were a few more people with us on board relaxing or lazing on deck.

During the afternoon while staring out from our balcony we had some entertainment watching a small fishing boat slowly passing Aurora and dragging a large net behind it. After a while the crew of the boat pulled the net back in to inspect their catch. They had caught absolutely nothing suggesting that the filth and pollution in the water may be affecting the life of the local people who depend on the river. Malaysia is a rich country but as it moves into the same league as the established Western world, it might discover the downside of ignoring the effect of their actions upon nature.

Approaching our own departure time, we watched another cruise ship leave as we leant on the balcony rail and chatted with the people in the cabin next door about our adventures so far.

Being a port day, the dress code for the evening was casual so it was a chance to wear the new shirt I had bought in Koh Samui. Deb offered to iron out the packaging creases but I said no, it would be fine. Isabel saw me on the way into the restaurant and after remarking how nice the shirt was, she said that I should have ironed out the creases before I wore it. I felt the daggers from Deb's stare and I was the butt of 'creases' jokes throughout a lovely meal. Afterwards I was whisked away to have my shirt stripped from by body and ironed before being allowed out in public again.

We didn't do much more that evening except venturing out for a soft drink in Masquerades while a competition ('Family Fortunes') went on between a team of passengers and a team from the Headliners theatre troupe. That passed half an hour and afterwards we moved on to check out Carmen's where Caravan were playing dance music. I was not interested in exerting energy, especially as tomorrow is a formal evening with dancing at the Ball.

We had a reasonably early night made even earlier by putting the clocks back another hour, making us just seven hours ahead of Britain.

There were another couple of sea days to come now before the next port in Sri Lanka where we had booked onto an expedition to see an elephant orphanage. This was to be a real adventure as we would have to leave Aurora at 6:30 in the morning to enable us to get there and back in the day. We had a police escort arranged for the journey to the orphanage and back to clear the traffic so we don't get held up and make the ship's departure late.

Sea Days to Sri Lanka
12th and 13th March 2012

It was just a month to go before we would wake up in Southampton, but today we were crossing the Indian Ocean towards Sri Lanka and then travelling onwards to India. The sun was shining and as we opened the balcony door the dressing table mirror instantly steamed up, and the heat took our breath away just for a moment. We were back in the tropics, where this was a common morning occurrence as we looked out over our ever changing back garden.

So, what had changed since leaving Singapore?

Well, there'd been a significant changeover of passengers, but more noticeable was the change of some of the entertainment team, waiters, room stewards, and one or two of the officers. We had a new cabin steward, Phillip, and he appeared just as efficient as Savio had been. The only drawback was that he was not quite so quick in pouncing on our cabin as we left for breakfast. We regularly came back to find that he had not yet been in to do his jobs. We presumed he was still learning our daily pattern and would notice that we breakfasted early and our cabin was ready to be serviced before many others.

The Entertainment team had certainly changed, with most of the previous more senior members leaving in Singapore. Natalie, the Cruise Director, had brought a new top team with her and we thought there might be some changes. Obviously we had not noticed any difference with the cabaret acts yet as they would have been booked months in advance, but we were looking forward to see what new ideas and activities might come along.

The first noticeable addition were Zumba fitness sessions, which began that first morning after Penang, and presented by Natalie. This was a reasonably high-energy exercise class with a lot of Latin dance movements to loud music. Deb went along to try it out, and no, I did not join her. I admit to watching it for a while and it involved coordinating arms and legs to do different moves at the same time. A bit like patting your head with one hand while rubbing your tummy with the other, only very fast.

... most definitely not for aging men!

While Deb was 'Zumbing' I had my own bit of exercise with a brisk walk of just over a mile around the Promenade Deck. After breaking slightly into a sweat, I went to the theatre to watch the port presentation on Mumbai, where I was almost immediately joined by Mick (Brenda was in the laundrette), while Roger and Laura appeared soon after. Deb came in as the lights were just going down but did not spot us so she sat elsewhere. While she was not there to keep an eye on me, I thought I might possibly have a nap if I wanted to. As it turned out, the information on the city of Mumbai actually interested me so I stayed awake.

... well, for most of the time.

Checking with Deb afterwards, we were already booked on the tour that had sounded the most ideal. It was to be another full day's trip in just four days' time.

We were on our way for a coffee but stopped and chatted to Neil, our friend with an artificial leg, about the tale of woe concerning his cabin. Neil and his wife Christine found themselves in a balcony cabin surrounded by chain-smokers, and had pleaded for a change of cabin virtually from day one. Since then, they had moved from cabin to cabin as they became available. Unfortunately as each new sector started the replacement cabin was needed again. So they kept ending up back where they came from or, as was the current situation, in a lower grade cabin. I was amazed that knowing their request existed; P&O were still selling empty cabins, at probably ridiculous prices, for each upcoming segment, without considering a solution for Neil and Chris.

With the current UK laws on smoking, I believe there should be a tightening of cruise ship rules to somehow segregate the smokers into certain cabins of the ship. To allow smoking on any cabin balcony seems to favour the smokers and hence the minority. When in port, and with no wind, the smoke goes in all directions, up, down, left and right, so one cabin with smokers can annoy several cabins around them......sorry for the rant!

Lunchtime again, and we were being really quite good most days, with usually just a bowl of soup and a ham or cheese roll. ... oh, plus a bit of salad,

      ... plus a pudding sometimes,

             ... oops!

Once we'd eaten our fill, we had a post-lunch snooze on our shady balcony, cooled by the breeze. When we woke up it was time for me to have a haircut while Deb had half an hour in the sunshine on deck. We met up again just before Deb grabbed her painting kit and trotted off to the art class (pagodas and temples today). That was my cue to go and get very hot playing cricket where there were new players. One was Maurice Grumbleweed, a cabaret singer and comedian whose first show we had missed, and the other was Pete Matthews who turned out to be a juggler who had not had his show yet. Being a juggler, he was very good with the ball but he never played again for fear of doing some damage to his hands.

Back in the cabin I peeled off my shirt and poured a glass of coke for me and Deb as she returned from art. While we were talking, I glanced over her shoulder out to sea and spotted two or three whales swimming by with a performance of spouting fountains and graceful dives...

... wonderful!

The evening was formal dress code, and started with the 'Welcome on board' drink and speech party for the fourth segment. As usual we arrived at the Crow's Nest bar well before it got started so that we were to the front of the queue. This allowed us to have a quick photo with the captain (again), without missing too much of the serious drinking business. For half an hour we enjoyed a number of drinks and a pleasant chat with friends. Oh, of course there was also a repeat of the captain's welcome speech. We really just made up the numbers as the occasion was primarily for new passengers, so we sat and laughed politely at the now familiar jokes, and grabbed another drink.

The entertainment later that evening was exceptional. Chris Watkins is an incredibly talented violinist and gave us a performance that was a mixture of classical and more popular pieces of music. His act went under the title of 'Fireworks on Four Strings' and this reflected his skilful, enthusiastic, and also imaginative playing with unusual 'twists' to the original. We both looked forward to his second show.

As it turned out, we were lucky to have gone to his first performance of the evening, as about half an hour before the second was due to start an area at the rear of theatre was flooded by a burst pipe. This also caused a part the ceiling to collapse. It was fortunate that few people were in the theatre at the time or there could have been some serious injuries. Yes the ship was still plagued by burst pipes and buckets, but the pipe that burst in the theatre was a high pressure one connected to the fire sprinkler system, and required more than a bucket. The outcome was that the theatre was closed for several days until it could be repaired and made safe again. A knock-on effect was that daytime presentations and talks had to be moved from the theatre, and several had to be cancelled altogether as there was now only one venue available. All the evening cabaret acts, destined for the theatre, had to be moved to Carmen's lounge bar, but being smaller it meant that the entertainers had to give three shows a night to allow everyone a chance to see them. As well as restricting talks, the lack of a venue also meant that some alternative entertainment shows were cancelled.

Elsewhere around the ship the water leaks were still happening but we had become used to the sight of a plumber with his head in the ceiling, blowers in the middle of soggy carpets, and new carpets being laid when the plumbers and blowers had done their job.

On the Tuesday morning we had some excitement. Captain Turnbull announced that everyone on board had to take part in an exercise to simulate an attack by pirates, and explained the actions we needed to take. In a few days' time we would be sailing into potential pirate areas, and like all shipping, we had to take precautions and be prepared in case any unwanted guests tried to board Aurora. The exercise involved us being told about the warning alerts that would be used, and how we should respond by sitting in the corridors outside our cabins while the threat persisted. This was presumably a way to protect us from any gunfire.

I suppose we'd all heard about pirates and the threat to shipping, but this made us think about it a little more. For the moment that was all that we did, but there would be several other things going on around the ship as we got closer to pirate waters.

The day now resumed its normal lazy sunny state but just before I was leaving to go to cricket, the captain made another announcement.

He had received information that the authorities in Mumbai had made a change to the time we had to dock and it was going to have to be much earlier than originally planned. To make this arrival slot on time we would have to leave Sri Lanka just after lunch rather than the scheduled evening departure. Unfortunately the end result was that our stay in Sri Lanka would not be long enough for our planned trip to the elephant orphanage.

Would this cruise ever have an announcement with some good news!?

OK, we had become conditioned to hearing and accepting bad news and the loss of one more very special tour was just another kick up the backside. Deb and I sulked for a moment or two but we realised that Mumbai was a priority port and nothing would change this decision. Our trip to see the elephants was gone, but we didn't bother booking another tour. Tomorrow would be another restful morning while we were docked in Colombo.

Anyway, the cricket went well and there was much amusement as an American joined in. Having quickly explained the basics to him (well actually explained them to a very blank and confused face) he was soon standing with the bat to face his first ever cricket ball. His stance was that of a baseball player swinging the bat around and staring menacingly at an aging British gentleman about to propel a ball at him. He faced his obligatory 18 balls, completely missed over half of them, was caught out twice, but eventually did score a few runs.

Still very confused he walked out of the court asking:
"Why are they called runs?"

He apologised for his performance (we loved it) and then took a great deal of advice and instruction from a few of us explaining more of the finer points of cricket such as the batting crease, stumps, wides, no-balls, being in or out, plus the business of scoring runs.

After that we instructed him in the rudimentary aspects of

bowling before he had a go at it. His attempts at bowling were much better than had been expected. He was able to stop and catch the ball as well as many of us aging British.

When the game was over he thanked us and left still looking rather confused, but with just a little knowledge and experience of the game of cricket.

In the evening we watched Pete Matthews, the juggler, and had an absolutely brilliant hour of comedy and skill. We weren't totally convinced about watching him but it turned out to be really good. If you ever get a chance to watch his act, go along and enjoy yourselves.

It had been a strange day of fun plus bad news, and it left me wondering what else could go wrong. The experience of cruising the world was amazing and I had to pinch myself sometimes as we sailed into port after port in country after country. There had been such wildly swinging moods with thrills one day, followed by disappointments of missing once-in-a-lifetime opportunities the next.

Whatever problems we had endured, this cruise was still the right thing to have done.

Colombo, Sri Lanka
Wednesday 14th March 2012

Since leaving Malaysia we had crossed the Andaman Sea, skirted around the southern end of the Bay of Bengal, and were now in the port of Colombo on the south-eastern tip of Sri Lanka. Although not the island's capital, it is the largest city and is around 250 kilometres across the Park Strait from India. Our longitude was 90° east, which meant we had travelled three-quarters of the way around the world.

Today we should have been at an elephant orphanage but instead we were to be found relaxing on board Aurora with no plans to go anywhere beyond the dockside. Although we had a short lie-in this morning, our instincts were still to get up and have breakfast before the rush, allowing plenty of time to see the port wake up below us. Those who still had tours to go on had bounced down the gangway and boarded their coaches, whilst others were walking to the dock gates to find a taxi to take them to the attractions of Colombo. There were still a lot of passengers left on the ship who had no interest in haggling with taxi drivers, and like us would do little more that morning than go for a walk to look at the line of stalls that had been set up on the quayside.

By mid-morning we had joined the crowd on the quayside looking at the clothes, souvenirs, and of course, various packages of tea. I think almost everyone on Aurora must have bought some sort of tea product, but a lot of the other items being sold were quite attractive as well.

Deb took a fancy to a tan-coloured leather footstool like some giant deflated football with elephants embossed on each of its numerous panels. It was rather appealing but we were concerned that it was very large and there might be a problem packing it away. The stallholder showed us how it could be compressed down to quite a manageable size and then informed us that it was superb quality and made of giraffe skin. Now I am no expert on sources of different leather, but I seriously doubted if this was made from a giraffe. We bought it anyway.

There was also the tea of course and one or two smaller items but as we haggled for a bargain, the stallholder asked if we had any chocolate as his younger assistant had a sister who adored it. He said he would give us another small souvenir if we had any to give away. Without committing ourselves we took our leave and returned to the ship to offload our purchases, before considering our remaining pillow chocolates. Deb put them into a bag, went back ashore, and made the young lad smile in delight, before she came back with a key ring. We had been talking about buying one anyway, so the chocolates had saved us a few pence.

Very few people had tales of foul play during their three months at sea, but our visit to Colombo resulted in two alleged criminal acts.

The first affected a couple of our friends from the dancing. They finished their walk around the shops, and were just deciding on their best way back when they were stopped by someone saying he was a waiter on the ship. He suggested they share a taxi back to the port. Now we British find it very difficult to tell the difference between an Indian and a Sri Lankan, and the local low-life seemed to know that. Having accepted the offer, they arrived at the port gate where the driver demanded $50 which was three times the going price. Our friend refused to pay and gave the driver $20 saying that was all he was getting. When the supposed 'waiter' popped up and asked where his share was, our friend told him he was a liar and was getting nothing. The argument now drew the attention of the port security guard who said that a passenger couldn't be allowed to leave the country without paying a debt. It appears the guard's English was good enough to understand our friend's version of the scam, and he and his wife were eventually waved on towards the ship.

Story two is more horrifying, and involved an older woman who had just become widowed and was a little confused by the value of the local currency. Having been offered a taxi she said she only had US dollars but the driver refused them, suggesting she withdrew some local cash from a machine. Being too trustful she allowed the driver to enter the required amount but he omitted to tell the lady about the extra zero he put on the end of the amount. The outcome was that she paid in the region of $400 plus a $50 tip for the $20 journey.

Please understand that these are just two stories from almost 2,000 passengers' experiences and in reality, it is a very small percentage of criminal activity. For those coming out to this area of the world just be aware that the local crooks are just as intelligent as some of the hardened criminals of our own country, so be careful.

Anyway, that summed up the story of our short visit to Colombo, so I will move on to the rest of the day. Aurora left the port just after lunch and while Deb was at her art class, I went for a Swedish massage. Now call me naïve but I did not identify any 'Swedish' element. The masseuse was from Eastern Europe and there wasn't the slightest hint of Abba music, but it was a good massage... I think.

For a reasonably small young lady she was able to put some real pressure on my muscles, and as she manipulated my neck there were times when my face was severely squashed into the table. The other slight problem I had was being told to relax as she worked in the area of my armpit, severely triggering my 'tickle' reflex. Similar problems were had when she turned to the soles of my feet but she was squeezing them so hard that it felt more like pain than tickle.

The after-effects were that the next day I was bruised from my neck to the middle of my back and muscles were aching that had not ached for many years. I assumed it had been a worthwhile exercise, and I was still able to move sufficiently for a hard swim in the pool as she recommended.

Maurice Grumbleweed provided that evening's entertainment and was very good. Perhaps he pushed the level of his humour to the limit of the acceptable, but nobody complained.

In addition to his comedy, he sang some show songs as well as one or two musical ditties based on his experiences on board Aurora. A real bonus was the appearance of the magnificent violinist, Chris Watkins, to accompany Maurice as he sang the Irish ballad, 'When I was sweet sixteen'. The resulting applause, cheers, and whistles of approval were the loudest I had heard in Carmen's, and yes, they were deserved.

On the way out of show lounge we met the captain and had a long chat about our day, our cruise, the problems of being a Captain in a world of turmoil, and generally had a laugh with him about the 'moaners'. I don't envy his period of command during this cruise as he has had an excess of problems to deal with. When I expressed my sadness about missing some of the ports, and the drugs issues, he replied that in six months' time we would reflect on an experience that few people have ever had, and laugh about it.

… He was very definitely right.

Deb and I finished the evening in the Crow's Nest listening to The Miles Foreman Orchestra over a glass of wine. Although Swing and Trad Jazz music may not be our favoured genres, the sound was magnificent. You don't have many opportunities to listen to a seven-piece band of true musicians in such an intimate venue very often.

The day had not been what we expected it to be, but it had still been enjoyable. We now had a further day at sea before the highlight port of Mumbai in India.

Magical Mystical Mumbai

Friday 16th March 2012

It was early morning when we arrived in India at the port of Mumbai, and what a busy port this is.

There were so many ships and boats in the bay that it was difficult to see how we found our way in to the berth. Our cabin faced out to sea today so after breakfast we spent a few minutes watching the quayside scene from the starboard side of Prom Deck.

Several hundred of the waiters and stewards from Goa were getting time off Aurora today to meet their families who had travelled for up to ten hours to get to Mumbai. This resulted in two queues to get through the passport and customs control, one for the passengers and one specifically for the crew. The home-sick crew were like a bunch of excited school children, with bags of gifts for their waiting families, and one group even had a trolley that appeared to be carrying three wide-screen televisions. The boys and girls of the crew had little more than two or three hours to meet friends and relations today, but they've been singing, whistling, and smiling continually for the last few days.

We all felt very happy for them.

It was going to be a long day for us, and just after 9:00 we were climbing aboard our coach for a day out in this city. We had arrived with very little knowledge of Mumbai and perhaps what we did know may have reflected some of the more negative aspects.

Once out of the port area it was soon obvious that the city was full of historical buildings mostly with a huge British architectural influence. They were impressive and summed up the opulence that we introduced to lands that we controlled in the past.

I am not an expert in architecture so will not even attempt to describe the buildings we saw but they make you look, firstly to capture their magnificence, and then look again as the incredible detail draws your eye to seek out further magical features. Most were now government buildings, police stations or hotels, and were separated by modern buildings which stretched towards the sky, reminding visitors that this was a busy commercial city as well as a living museum of its British colonial past. Some buildings are past their best, and will no doubt soon be replaced by more modern structures. It seemed clear that the government wants to wipe away evidence of a past that is perhaps not looked on favourably by modern India. The new buildings however were still magnificent, showing that planners and architects were replacing the opulent past with a shiny and iconic present. Undoubtedly, vast amounts of money were being spent in this thriving city.

Having talked about the buildings, what else did Mumbai have to offer the curious tourist?

Well firstly we quickly experienced a 'holy cow' moment with two or three of these revered animals on a street corner being fed grass by the passing locals. This resulted in the cows doing what the cows do best...

... all over the pavement.

An old woman had the honour of picking up this holy treat (not the most solid holy treat either) and then wiping the pavement clean with old newspaper. The unsuspecting passer-by would hardly notice what had been there except for perhaps a slight lingering *odour de cow*.

... nice!

We walked on and came across more beautiful buildings but then a surprise to remind us (well most of the men anyway) of India's love of cricket. In the centre of this vibrant city we came to a park where the locals were playing cricket. Not just one game, as this park, known as the Oval, was big enough for at least four full-sized cricket pitches...

... yes, I did say full sized pitches.

Some had high standard games with teams in matching strips and umpires in full white dress. Next to them were two teams of youngsters without matching strips, but equally committed to their sport. All these young men were serious, with leather being propelled at high speed toward willow with equally expert responses from the targeted batsmen. I was amazed and, like several of the other men, tried to get some video footage through the metal railings while Deb was telling me to get a move on.

Eventually our guide relented and let us go into the park and look at this magical scene for a moment or two. It was a mixture of young and mature, amateur and expert, first class kit and rufty-tufty hand-me-downs. It was sport in the raw where everybody could play and live out their dreams of being the Indian equivalent of a Boycott or a Botham without having to be a member of an exclusive club or earning a banker's salary.

Later we passed another field of a similar size that was also hosting several cricket matches, plus of course the Test match ground and a further three pitches. How many more are there?

Mumbai's diverse architecture and culture was confusing to the mind yet intriguing as we almost rushed to each corner to see what was coming next. Preconceptions had gone and Mumbai was proving to be absolutely sensational.

Without a doubt our tour was protecting us from the poverty we knew existed, but there were some negative aspects we could not avoid. India, and certainly Mumbai, has a history of terrorist attacks and on a number of street corners we came across members of the army crouched behind sandbag barriers with rifles ready.

Being tourists, we were quite used to street sellers and whenever we stopped there were beggars thrusting peacock fans and postcards at us. Several of these people were without a leg or had deformed limbs enticing us to be charitable, but they were not very successful.

Unlike other cities we had been to, many of the roads were in need of repair, and the pavements often became difficult to walk on as their surfaces either needed work, or were in the process of being renovated.

Something else we all remarked on, though perhaps not a negative feature, was the traffic.

Now traffic in Mumbai rates amongst the worst I have witnessed. Roads, and their junctions, were treated as open pieces of land with no rules except anarchy. Obeying traffic lights seemed to be a game for the weak, with the general rule being no matter what colour lamp is showing, drive on until all available space is full, and then find someone less assertive to eventually let you through. If there were no traffic lights, such as at a roundabout, then it was similarly straightforward – just drive into any available space until someone less assertive eventually lets you through.

... I think you have the idea.

There was one other thing: every driver must use their horn whenever another vehicle gets into the space that they intended to occupy, no matter who had the priority. The same horn is required if a light inexplicably turns red, or a pedestrian attempts to cross. These rules applied even if there was a policeman stupidly trying to give some semblance of order.

Our guide fortunately always tried to get our coach as close as possible to the sights, and then used her knowledge and experience of crossing the roads to ease our passage through the chaos. Oh, she also had the authority provided by an extremely threatening umbrella.

There was no way of visiting Mumbai without a stop at one of the incredible railway stations to witness the main alternative transport system to the car. The experience lived up to the stories I had heard, and we witnessed thousands of people either arriving or departing the stations.

Mumbai's railway system handles millions of commuters daily. With the permission of the officials we were allowed to look inside a train which appeared wider than in those in Britain, and being a local slow commuter train, its carriages were stark with simple wooden benches and wide door-less gaps to allow more people to get in and out at a time. Of course, India had one further twist, with some carriages being reserved for women.

Another piece of Indian magic that we had heard about was witnessed at the stations. Mumbai has a unique industry where the wife (typically) prepares a hot packed lunch in a flask or tin for their husbands, which is then handed to a courier along with the address of the eventual eater's office or shop. The couriers give the lunch box a code and then take it with other similar lunch packages to a central collection point. Either by handcart or train they get moved on and distributed eventually by another courier at the far end. There is no computer system used and the price is very low and yet failure to deliver the correct lunch to the correct person is virtually unknown. While at the station we saw three or four handcarts piled high with flasks and cardboard boxes being pushed at high speed to or from a train to allow the consumer to get his lunch before it went cold.

Imagine the complexity that this would require in Britain for perhaps a small town, let alone a city of millions!

It was time now for our lunch and we were treated to another wonderful meal in a top-of-the-range hotel. Initially there was a slight panic as we arrived at the hotel to see a crowd of armed guards and press photographers outside the entrance. We did wonder if Aurora was back in the news again, but it turned out that a delegation from Pakistan was also due at the hotel, so we were just getting in the way.

Full of predominantly Asian food once more, we moved on to the Ghandi Museum to gain a little insight into this iconic hero of India. It showed the simplicity of this great man with virtually his only remaining possessions being a library of books that are still being sorted decades after his assassination. There is a mock-up of his bedroom with a simple bed plus a number of spinning wheels for which he seems to have had a fascination. Elsewhere in the museum Ghandi is remembered in photographs, letters, and historical reports.

As with so many wonderful places we saw around the world, we were only given 30 minutes for this visit and almost all of us said it needed significantly longer.

Sadly, it turned out that we could have stayed longer.

After a panoramic drive past some more amazing buildings, including the stunning Gateway to India monument, we were presented with nearly two hours to go shopping. There was a general revolt amongst our group about the excessive time given to shopping at the expense of other experiences. We even made it quite clear that we preferred to go back to the ship but our guide was insistent that the programme said 'shopping time' and we were not going early.

As is usual with these shopping stops, we passengers were initially shown into a highly respected department store. I believe most of our group boycotted this department store and quickly went their own way. Certainly eight people were disgusted enough to say goodbye and make their own way back to the ship.

Deb and I teamed up with another couple and we walked back to the Gateway to India monument for a real look and to take photographs. This was a superb few minutes.

The monument stands on the edge of the harbour and at the end of a huge square. It is obviously a tourist trap, but is also somewhere the local people go to for an afternoon out. Hundreds of families sat with picnics and children ran in all directions shrieking with excitement. Chai-tea sellers tempted visitors and locals alike and although we never tried the drink it was very popular. I know the square was bombed in the recent past, but this has got to be a must for any visitor to Mumbai. After that the four of us crossed the road to the six-star Taj Mahal Palace Hotel for a bottle of beer in its Harbour View bar. This was probably the most luxurious hotel in the city and we paid a lot of money for the drinks, but the experience was worth it, and somehow infinitely more rewarding than the planned shopping spree.

We returned to very sombre coach for the short journey back to the ship. It had been a wonderful day, and the tour (except for the shopping stop) had left us with so many memories of beautiful, crazy, mystical Mumbai and India. All the passengers, and perhaps more surprisingly all the crew, were back on time and we sailed away towards our next destination in Oman.

Our evening started with an enjoyable buffet snack in the Orangery. With the theatre still under repair from its water leak, the cabaret show was in Carmen's with the Headliners troupe performing their 'Queen' tribute show. We'd seen it on many occasions before, and it was a tremendous tribute to one of my favourite groups.The night was completed with a quiet drink in Champions where we chatted to a very happy waiter who had spent the afternoon with his friends and family. What a lovely day!

A Day in The Arabian Sea
Saturday 17th March 2012 – St Patrick's Day

As we moved towards our next stop in Muscat, we crossed the
Arabian Sea before entering the Gulf of Oman. This had put us
into an area of the world that was subject to pirate activity.We
knew it was coming and we had already seen some of the
precautions that were being put into practice to keep us safe.
During the daytime there were security guards all around the
Prom Deck watching the sea for any signs of suspicious boats
taking a more than healthy interest in Aurora. The guards used
high-powered binoculars, and there were additional electronic
devices that checked for less visible craft. If something had
been seen that posed a threat, we'd have been sent to our
cabin corridors to keep out of the way while the ship did its
best to discourage the unwanted Johnny Depps.
The only obvious deterrents were water cannons around the
deck, but we had suspicions that Aurora had recently gained
some passengers who looked as though they had handled guns
for a living. They'd only appeared at breakfast so far and were
perhaps more active at night. We also knew that naval vessels
from various countries were patrolling nearby and were ready
to come and help if necessary. There was a consultant on
board to give advice to the crew and to oversee what was
happening, and he probably had the authority to request
assistance from those friendly vessels if needed.
We did our best to ignore the hosepipes and guards and
carried on as normal. In the morning it was Zumba and the art
class for Deb (working on a picture of the Sydney Opera House)
while I updated my blog and then sat in the sunshine for a
while. After lunch we both enjoyed the sun for about an hour
before retreating to the cool cabin for a read, and yes, I did
doze as well. There was some good news with an

announcement that the Curzon Theatre had been repaired and would be back in full use from tomorrow.

Being a sea day, I had another chance to play cricket. On the way to the nets I looked at the sea and there were ugly stretches of something green in the water. Initially I thought (like several others) that it was an oil slick but apparently it was algae. Whatever its cause, the sea became similar to a green pea soup as the ship churned it up.

... yuk!

The evening was a full formal evening so out came the white tuxedo for its airing plus a green bowtie to match Deb's dress for St Patricks Day. Our colour scheme was a complete coincidence actually. We had a good meal with plenty of chat and laughs with our table-mates as we caught up after Mumbai. It was thumbs up all around the table for the city even though most of us initially had concerns that it was not going to be good. Part way through our meal we had the announcement that we were moving into night time piracy precautions and the restaurant's curtains were drawn.

During the hours of darkness every possible attempt was made to make Aurora look uninteresting to potential pirates. This meant making it as dark as possible except for the standard deck and navigation lights. Cabin windows were kept covered to avoid obvious clues to it being a cruise ship, as they do make good targets with significant amounts of money and jewellery to be liberated from its passengers. The Prom Deck was also off-limits after dusk to stop us getting in the way of the guards, and possibly also to stop us seeing what they were carrying. Even restricted to the inside areas of the ship we still didn't go to the evening show as it was another singer. Instead we joined Mick and Brenda in Masquerades for a St Patrick's Day quiz. Without a single Irish person to assist us, we won the bottle of wine in the Emerald Isle themed quiz. After our brains had been tested, there was an Irish themed pub night consisting of loud and out of tune singing plus volunteers occasionally attempting different games. A high point of the evening was an Irish dancing game when a couple of Belfast girls came out and performed a very good traditional jig to music from Lord of the Dance. They got a resounding and deserved cheer from everyone.

It was a much longer evening than usual for us and we had a really good time. The next day Aurora would be sailing into the port of Muscat in Oman, with our arrival planned for mid-morning, and we would be staying there overnight. Deb and I had another trip organised to see the highlights of yet another destination where we had no idea what to expect.

Muscat, Oman
Sunday 18th March 2012 - Mother's Day

When we woke up the ship was still at sea, and we were due to arrive in Muscat at around 10:00. Aurora was enveloped in quite a thick fog, but strangely the wind was blowing. We hoped that by the time we got to our port the sun would have burned the fog away. During the morning it did clear a little as we moved towards the land but some lingered as we approached the Gulf State of Oman.

First impressions were not what I expected, and instead of a flat sandy desert, there were rugged hills of browns and reds. There seemed to be a lot of forts or small castles on top of the hills apparently protecting the city of Muscat and its port. Muscat itself was a mix of white stone houses and business premises but the most outstanding feature was a gigantic incense burner dominating the scene on a small hill at the edge of the city. Looking like a giant beehive, we initially had no idea what it was but when it was described to us later, we suspected it might possibly burn several kilogrammes of frankincense at a time with an impressive smell.

When we finally berthed, we saw another cruise ship on the other side of the harbour from us. This was the Costa Favolosa which looked to be very big and very new. I remember when Aurora and Oriana were new they used to be classed as giants, but now we were just a small ship alongside this floating hotel. Almost as soon as we had moored, it was time to leave the ship for our tour around the Muscat area. Our guide was called Ibrahim, a tall young man from the city who was making some money while home from university, and his pride for Muscat was obvious. He described the sights we were passing, and outlined where and what we would be visiting.

Our first stop was at the Muttrah Souk (market) which was like a small version of the Grand Bazaar in Istanbul. For those who have never seen either, these are huge covered markets selling everything you could want and a whole lot more.

Unfortunately our tour bus arrived at the same time as several others from both Aurora and the Costa ship, so it was busy to say the least. Inside the souk it was a crush of local shoppers and curious passengers surrounded by the hustle and bustle of traders. They were doing their best to get our attention to buy their clothes, perfumes, spices, fruit, vegetables, souvenirs... well the list just goes on.

Slightly claustrophobic from the crowds, we went into one of the small shops inside the souk that was selling incense burners. It was really an excuse for a breather but we allowed the shopkeeper to show us some smaller versions of the huge burner we had seen on the hill earlier. We decided to buy some as presents for our brothers but then had to go through the smelling session of the pungent incense mixtures.

Finally with burners and incense wrapped and tucked away in our bags we re-joined the crush to find more Omani treasures to take home. The clothes were also very interesting, and left Deb drooling over beautiful shimmering dresses on display. I could not stop myself asking about the traditional male Arab long white robes and chequered head scarves. Everything was ridiculously cheap but with around 20 coaches of assorted passengers, the market was just too busy to concentrate on making a choice so we gave up and went to find our coach. It was beginning to look a little chaotic with so many people on tours and we just knew they would all be with us at the other major attractions.

As well as being very hot, there was little shade while we waited for the coach to return. It was a relief to get back on and feel the air conditioning cooling us down. From the souk we went to visit the Bait Al Zubair museum which was originally just a family house. Over a period of time, the owner had collected weapons, jewellery, clothes, and all kinds of household items from all over Oman.

Although quite small, it had become a famous museum with a series of displays covering Oman's history and culture. The family must have been very rich as the gold and precious metals on show were impressive, and the vast display of clothing gave an absorbing insight into what the people wore (and still wear) in the different provinces. There was something for virtually everyone to get interested in, be it the ceremonial swords, perhaps the colours and materials of the clothing, or maybe the different size and shapes of the cooking pots. Outside, in the shade of the museum wall, there was a miniature model village showing typical styles of homes and forts to add just a little more information about what was already becoming a fascinating place.

As expected, all the tour parties seemed to arrive at the museum at the same time, meaning this smallish house was packed and I felt distinctly uncomfortable in such a crowd. It is a wonderful time-capsule of a museum, but the tour companies of Oman really must come up with a way of avoiding hundreds of people being at the same place at the same time.

Our guide hustled us back onto the coach as fast as he could so that we got away quickly and created a bit of a gap between us and the other coaches. With no more than perhaps ten minutes to cool down again we arrived at the Sultan's palace. ... Wow!

It was huge, and it was both imposing and stunningly beautiful. Imagine all the descriptions you have ever heard or read about palaces for sultans and this will probably match or exceed them.

The site was a rectangular complex surrounded by hills and

forts. At the time of our visit, it had completed buildings on three sides, whilst the fourth was still under construction. The main palace building stood at one end of the complex and was enclosed within a further walled compound. Most of us stood and drooled at the ornate gated entrance perhaps 50 metres from the palace building. So much of what we could see was made from pure white marble with shimmering gold that blinded us in the bright sunshine. It was absolutely stunning to see a complex of buildings with such amazing architecture and beauty. Sadly the sultan does not always live there but he uses the palace to show off to visiting dignitaries and world leaders. Of course, whilst I and many others stood open-mouthed, I was stunned to hear one of our tour group say that it wasn't very impressive. She must have been looking at something different. Although I might not be overly familiar with many beautiful buildings, this palace was as spectacular as anything I have ever seen for real, or in pictures.

The moaners never ceased to amaze me. They had been whinging at everything we had seen and done from the time we arrived at the market, and they continued long after we returned back to the ship. Was it what they were seeing and doing, or was there an underlying issue with the country? After taking countless photographs we started a search for our coach amongst the ever increasing convoy of buses. Soon we were relaxing in our seats and cooling down whilst travelling away from the city for a few kilometres, and listening intently as Ibrahim told us a bit about himself.

He told us about his life and explained the requirements of being a good Muslim with the obligatory prayer times throughout the day, and I found it fascinating to listen to a young man committed to his faith. He talked about his hopes for marriage and a home in the future, but said he was not ready for that quite yet. I think this was the only time we had a guide who opened up his life plans to us. One of the things he mentioned was the way Oman looks after its citizens providing a tax-free life with all the necessary support and services.

Our final stop was at the Grand Mosque. The building, its courtyards and grounds are vast and live up to its 'Grand' adjective.

Completed in 2001 for Sultan Qaboos, it is the largest mosque in Oman and one of the largest in the world. It can accommodate 20,000 worshippers at the same time, mostly on a single prayer mat that measures some 70 metres by 60 metres. It is certainly one of the biggest such carpets in the world.

The buildings and walls were made of marble, as were the approach promenades, smaller side paths, and steps. We were not able to enter at the time we visited, but by all accounts, the inside is as magnificent as the exterior.

It didn't matter how many coaches were at this attraction as it would never have been crowded!

Before long we were back in the coach and returning through the sights of Muscat towards the ship. It had been an inspiring tour and the young guide had done his best to bring his country to life for us. He continued telling us about Oman, and talked about a variety of subjects, such as the price of petrol being about £2 for 10 litres, and that most people work in the oil industry.

Deb remarked to me that a very high percentage must also work in the construction industry as there was building work going on everywhere. Ibrahim pointed out the largest car showroom in the world, and other 'largest this and that' to emphasise the status of Oman and its attempts to be the best. He continued to be a good ambassador for Oman, explaining that there is free education for everyone (male and female) for 12 years plus further years in university, free for high-achieving students, and part-paid for those not quite as educationally bright.

Everyone gets gifted a plot of land at the age of 23 to build a house for their family, and there seems to be a far more equal status for the women of this country compared to stories we had heard about other Arabic states.

All in all I really enjoyed the tour and recommend Oman as somewhere worth visiting if you get the chance, to see a modern Arab country that looks after its people with the wealth that oil had produced.

... So what did we do wrong in Britain with our oil 'wealth'? Unfortunately, the trip ended on a bit of a sour note.

Back at the docks, Ibrahim thanked us for coming to his country and asked if we had enjoyed the tour. A small group of passengers shouted back that they had hated every minute and that the country was horrible. There were gasps all around the rest of the coach and shouts of *"no!"* from many shocked people trying to distance themselves from these comments. I felt embarrassed that visitors to a country could make such rude and ignorant comments. The ship was full of moaners but this was going too far and shamed Britain.

Back on the ship we relaxed into the late afternoon and evening. We were the only ones at our dinner table with the others perhaps having a meal ashore. Aurora was staying in port overnight, and it was noticeably quiet with a lot of passengers missing. The cabaret session was an amazing couple of dancers who were runners-up in a Sky TV dance programme, followed by an equally spectacular session from Chris Watkins, the violinist.

After seeing the show we went to the deck party, but gave up after three quarters of an hour as hardly anyone turned up. Instead, we grabbed ourselves a large glass of red wine from the bar and sat on our balcony talking and reflecting until almost midnight.

As with most of the previous ten weeks, this had been another wonderful day.

A Sea Day to Abu Dhabi
Monday 19th March 2012

Early the next morning Deb and I looked out from our balcony as a number of dhows chugged their way from the other side of the harbour to start their daily work. Sometimes it felt unreal to be on holiday for so long while all around us people were carrying on as normal. I had really forgotten what work was all about, and I was just so happy.

Our next port of call would be Abu Dhabi in the United Arab Emirates, and as we left Muscat it was apparent that yesterday's fog still affected us. It didn't make sense to be sailing through this dense mist and yet still be feeling hot and dry. It turned out that this wasn't fog after all...

... it was a dust storm.

With the dusty atmosphere outside it was fortunate that there was quite a packed entertainment programme indoors. Firstly, Deb had her Zumba class while I had a walk, and then mid-morning there was a cookery show where the Captain and the Chief Purser competed to cook the best meal. It was based on the TV programme 'Can't Cook Won't Cook', with the ship's Executive Chef showing how it should be done. The hour-long show was a really good laugh with much mucking around and dodgy cookery skills a-plenty. The sea bass dish looked nothing like the professional chef's version, but the chocolate mousse was a success and Deb enjoyed the one that the captain presented to her at the end of the show.

After lunch and a snooze, I went to watch the entertainment team performing a show very similar to TV's 'Strictly Come Dancing'. This was once again a very good hour's fun with the entertainment team really putting their hearts and souls into the dancing.

... well most of them!

Following that it was a game of cricket in the dust storm. It was really too windy and dirty, but it was difficult to keep the enthusiasm under control when you gave a load of middle aged (and older) men a bat and ball. Oh, and as per usual, I was on the losing side again.

Another formal night started with the Portunas Club drinks party, plus the raffle for the specimen jar and bottle of champagne. We spoke to an officer we'd not seen before, and spent a pleasant 30 minutes chatting to him about such things as foghorns and dust storms, as well as his background. We didn't win the raffle prize but were sort of close, as it went to the cabin that we had originally booked before we were upgraded.

The evening continued with a full house at the dinner table and lots of chat about Mumbai, Muscat and upcoming ports and trips. Claire Sweeney was the night's cabaret artist and she was a good singer but more importantly very enthusiastic and bubbly with her audience interaction. Deb and I followed that with nearly an hour of dancing before having an early night. Actually it wasn't an early night; it was a normal night, as we had been going to bed regularly at around 11.00. It just seemed early when the ship was still buzzing.

Abu Dhabi in The United Arab Emirates
Tuesday 20th March 2012 – Our son Andrew's birthday

Although we hoped the weather would have improved overnight, we were disappointed to wake up to the same dust storm, and the wind had become much stronger. Everything was covered in a layer of brown sand and the wind roared throughout the ship if an external door was opened. Since we left Muscat yesterday we'd sailed northwest across the Gulf of Oman then through the Straits of Hormuz and into the Arabian Gulf. Unnoticed we had sailed past Iran and Aurora was able to forget about pirates for a few days.

As we finished breakfast Aurora completed the last few minutes of her arrival into the port of Abu Dhabi in one of the richest countries in the world. On the dockside there was a large party of local Arabs to welcome us. The men were all dressed in their traditional long white robes and some were proudly holding birds of prey to impress us while others danced holding long thin canes. There were women as well sitting on huge cushions sprinkled around an enormous carpet. They appeared to be preparing food to tempt the passengers. One or two older males were offering drinks (perhaps coffee) from a jug to accompany the food but most people leaving the ship were in too much of a hurry to stop and try the treats.

We had a busy tour this morning. It took us firstly to the Sheikh Zayed Grand Mosque, then on to a Women's Handicraft Centre, followed by a photo stop at the 6-star Emirates Palace Hotel as well as a drive past the ruling Sheikh's Presidential Palace. The tour would finish with a visit to a Heritage Village that portrays life through the ages.

As with Muscat, Deb and I approached Abu Dhabi with complete ignorance apart from the country being somewhere I remotely worked with during my days at Goonhilly. As we headed for the mosque it was obvious that the city had been built quite recently with stunning buildings be it housing, or the skyscraper business blocks. Architecture has been a major delight on this worldwide adventure and today was no different. There were good-quality wide roads everywhere, and the traffic was pleasantly quiet as our guide described the sights around us as well as the usual information about the country, the city, and its people.

Then we arrived at the mosque.
It is huge, stunning, mystical, beautiful, and in all ways magnificent. Made from a grey-white marble it still shone even with the dusty background. This was our first view at a distance, but as we got closer, climbed the steps, and then walked along the pathways to the entrance it became every superlative I could imagine. The ideas that must have been in the architects' minds have become something to make your eyes dance around to try and capture each major feature, and then to focus in to discover the details. Our jaws dropped in awe and most of us gasped several times as a new spectacle revealed itself around a corner, or through a doorway, or around the other side of one of the many pillars.
The scale is almost unbelievable with chandeliers worth £millions (you can only guess at their size), a single carpet covering the main prayer chapel that, was described as the biggest in the world, like the one in Muscat was. One feature is a solid gold prayer wall, but equally impressive are panels and pillars with designs created from marble of different colours and gold and silver leaf depicting flowers as well as mystical Arabic and Muslim shapes.
I thought the mosque in Muscat was special, but this was probably the most beautiful building I have ever had the honour of being allowed to see. I share different beliefs than

the users of this building, but I truly share their visions of beautiful architecture.

It is impossible for me to describe everything so I leave it to you to read about it for more information if you so desire. There were however a few other high points and moments of amusement that I can talk about.

Firstly all women entering the mosque have to wear full covering (head to toes) and visiting ladies are supplied with a traditional full-length black robe (Abaya) and headscarf (Shayla) to cover their heads. These are supplied clean for each person showing the care and desire to allow non-believers a chance to see the magnificence of the building. The fun thing was that when the women reappeared in their costumes, it was almost impossible to initially distinguish one from another. Most of the ladies had their photographs taken by amused, but admiring, partners as a reminder of the day. As a religious restriction, up until the moment that this covering is worn, ladies are not permitted to be photographed on the site. There were a few inadvertent mistakes with this rule, but we all tried to abide by our hosts' beliefs.

Just as a down side to the visit, two ladies on the coach refused to wear the clothing, and hence sat alone for nearly an hour on the coach while the rest of us had a truly unforgettable experience. The comments from most of the women were that it was not a major issue wearing the costumes as it wasn't for long; however, the idea of wearing it all the time wasn't very appealing.

A positive moment was for our friend Neil with his artificial leg. He has not previously been able to go inside any mosque because he cannot remove the shoe of the 'leg'. Here the enthusiastic custodians supplied him with a wheelchair (cleaned sufficiently for the purpose) so that he could enter and enjoy the spectacle. He was thrilled and wheeled himself around snapping his camera in all directions with a huge smile on his face. The only problem he faced was propelling the wheelchair along the thick piled carpet. Neil maintained his independent attitude and refused to allow anyone to push the chair, but I stayed with him to be sure he didn't get into any difficulties. The mosque is so organised that it has escalators and lifts to take users and visitors to underground toilets, and that was another bonus for Neil.

The visit to the mosque lasted about an hour and there were nearly 500 happy passengers in total from Aurora, plus a similar number of smiling faces from a Costa ship. I am sure we were all thrilled, and I suggest anyone coming to this area of the world makes a 'must do' note against this place. Ignore for a moment the religious aspects and then if you don't enjoy your visit, I suspect you come from a different world.

Leaving the Mosque we made a short drive to a Women's Handicraft Centre. Founded by the wife of a sultan (not sure which one) its aim was to allow women to use the traditional skills learnt at home, to come together with other women, and start a business selling the results of their skills. Visitors can watch the ladies at work performing such things as needlecraft, basket making and weaving. Alongside this small factory is an outlet to sell the produce (as well as some other bought-in bits and pieces) and finally there is an exhibition area showing examples of other crafts and traditional costumes. I innocently described it as being a bit like the Woman's Institute but run as a business. In reality it is one more step in the process of Arabian countries giving more freedom and equality to its women and has resulted in several more such ventures.

Our tour now became a little more of a drive-by of the sights, rather than a stop and visit, but these sights were rather special.

Firstly there was the Presidential Palace which is vast and

amazing with a similar level of imaginative architecture as the mosque we had seen earlier. This time it is a dwelling but it rates among the best you can ever see. Being for the Presidential Sultan, the building is so special that photography is not permitted so cameras on the bus were lowered to avoid the attention of the military guards watching our every move. Close by there was another building to thrill us. This was the 6-star Emirates Palace Hotel that is three or four times the size of the biggest hotel I have seen before.

 It has a special gate that is only used by the ruling Sultan as well as another similarly grand gate for the public guests. I dread to think what sort of facilities it has inside, but it certainly had a golf course and a football pitch visible outside. It is so special that it merited a stop to take photos through the fence. By this time Deb's camera had an exhausted battery so I made some token attempts to capture its grandeur on video. We had a little bit more sightseeing around the Corniche area of the city before eventually arriving at our last stop at the Abu Dhabi Heritage Centre. This was a small, but very interesting area, where examples of traditional Bedouin housing have been constructed. They range from tents, through palm leaf huts, to the earliest stone built dwellings. There were also some animals, including camels and goats, plus another handicraft centre showing more elaborate crafts creating pottery and glass as well as the simpler examples we saw earlier. Of course there were also the tourist traps of cafes and souvenir tents. These outlets were packed with Aurora and Costa ship passengers plus other tourists, scrambling over the bargains. Many, of both sexes, were considering buying the traditional costumes, and yes, I did think about it again for a moment.

Although absolutely sensational, it had been a long and busy morning, so it was quite a relief to get back to Aurora for lunch and a short rest.

In the afternoon we returned to the city on the shuttle bus to a shopping mall where we had a chance to see the glitzy shopping side of Abu Dhabi where prices are the same or higher than in Britain. It is a very rich country and the shops reflect that in their prices. At one side of the mall we discovered a Carrefour outlet where we bought some typical bits and pieces such as chocolate, deodorant, and dates, plus some art items for Deb.

... we know how to shop!

We had a quiet dinner with just Jimmy and Isabel, and then bought a bottle of wine to drink on the balcony. We sat and relaxed looking out at the still dusty sights of the city and reminisced on the last two and a half months. At around midnight the last of the shuttle buses had dropped off their final passengers, and Aurora set sail for the short trip to the city of Dubai.

Dubai (Day 1)
Wednesday 21st March 2010

After sailing northeast from Abu Dhabi overnight we were moored alongside in the city of Dubai before we had finished our breakfast. We had a two-day stay here at the huge purpose-built cruise terminal capable of dealing with several ships at once. This was the end of the fourth segment of our world cruise and many hundreds of passengers would be leaving and replaced by new ones before we sailed tomorrow. It was a bit disappointing to see that the dust haze was still with us, and although the visibility was improving, the cityscape of Dubai was just silhouetted against a grey background. We both had a taste in our throats from the dust and several people had mentioned sinus problems. For my part I was suffering from tiny nose bleeds.

No other cruise ships were with us at the terminal when we arrived, but a very well-known ship that we hadn't seen for several years was moored just across the port. This was the QE2 at its permanent mooring, and although it looked tidy in its Cunard colours, and the engine was producing power, this was a sad period in the life of such an iconic ship. Bought and intended to be a hotel, work to restore her was delayed as Dubai ran short of money, so she sat alone sulking at the way she had been treated. Apparently, restoration work had recently restarted and she would soon be reborn as a luxury hotel, so she will thrill and entertain people again with her beauty and style.

We had a tour booked for the evening but in the meantime we were going to take the shuttle to a mall and look around the city's shopping area. We left Aurora at about 09:30 for a 30-minute ride into the busy city centre. The shopping mall was just opening as the bus pulled up so while the shops raised their shutters, we had an excuse to enjoy a delicious cup of coffee and a cinnamon Danish pastry. This was the first drink we'd had on shore for some time and made a change from the coffee on board.

As we wandered around the mall it became apparent just how affluent this city and country was. Clothing stores were all top-of-the-range designer names or exclusive outlets that just oozed high prices. The clothing had two styles, being either Arabian smooth and silky elegance, or the crisp lines and materials of modern western-style dress. It seemed a bit strange that many of the women shoppers wore full black robes while looking at and considering the less than discrete colourful tight fitting western-style outfits. There was an occasional clue however to what they wore under the robes, or in private at home, as the hems sometimes lifted just enough to reveal a glimpse of a Jimmy Choo shoe.

Apart from clothing stores there were many other expensive outlets, and certainly no cut price shops, but there were some familiar names such as 'Boots', 'BHS', and 'Mothercare' to remind us of home. We wandered and window shopped for perhaps an hour but our only purchases were to replenish our Omega 3 and painkillers stocks.

The mall had an exhibition area with photographs of the current Sultan and his family. This was a reminder to locals and visitors that his power meant everything here and must not be forgotten. In this area of the world a ruling sultan or king is revered and even folding up currency notes is an offence as it defaces his image.

Having had enough of the shopping mall we looked at our maps and decided it might be possible to walk to the Dubai Museum that appeared to be nearby, so we took to the busy streets. Some 40 minutes later we retraced our steps after getting slightly lost, very hot, and quite thirsty without seeing any evidence of what we had been looking for. It was time to go back to the ship for lunch and a rest before our evening adventure.

At the port we spent a few pounds-worth of local currency on some pretty little souvenir objects, and after lunch we spent an hour or so in the sunshine plus a cooler period in the cabin. The ship was pretty quiet and even afternoon tea (just a drink and a single cake) was deserted although more people were out in the sun than had been for the last couple of dusty days. As the afternoon came to an end we showered and dressed up a little for our tour. This was to take us to a couple of souks that sold gold and spices, but the main attraction was an evening meal at a *"renowned Lebanese Restaurant"*. We had no experience of Lebanese food and would not be returning to Aurora until after 11:00 pm, so we had made sure we had a decent lunch.

Our guide on the tour was the same one we'd had the day before in Abu Dhabi so we were confident of having a good description of whatever we were going to see. Driving away from the quayside we could see the QE2 with her lights on, which showed she was still active, and we later discovered that she was already available to hire for private functions such as weddings.

After several minutes of driving with an excellent commentary from our guide, we arrived at the Gold Souk and the nearby Spice Souk. The stop involved a walk from a nearby coach park specifically reserved for tourist buses. Neil and Christine were on the same tour and although our guide was supportive of Neil with his walking sticks, he was being left behind as the group walked over uneven pathways and crossed roads. My instincts told me to stay with him and I kept quite close to him but far enough away so I could see where the rest of the group were going. We eventually arrived at the market and were given instructions by the guide for how to avoid getting lost, as well as confirming the return time.

Our meeting point was virtually the centre of the Gold Souk with streets radiating in four directions from it. These streets had further lanes at intervals on either side that progressively became narrower with more lanes again. It was crowded with shoppers, some like us on tours, but many were locals out to find a golden bargain. It was like a spider's web of little shops and most of them had brightly lit windows full of shiny gold chains, rings, and brooches with diamonds and other precious stones that sparkled at the shoppers to tempt them to stop and stare.

It was a dazzling sight.

If you were tempted to glance at something for more than a second, shop assistants would pounce and ask what you were interested in. The items did not display any prices, and we all knew that the first price suggested by the shop assistants would be ridiculous, and we would be expected to haggle, and sulk if necessary, until we reached a price agreeable to both of us.

Fortunately we were not tempted to even look at anything closely enough to attract an assistant, as our bank balance was far too low for the wonderful jewellery. Window shopping is permitted and it satisfied our curiosity at this amazing place. As well as the shops, there were young men offering fake, copy, or special deal watches, designer bags, scarfs and other amazing souvenirs......*so they said*. We ignored them and wandered onward until we reached the end of one alley where we started to notice the smell of the Spice Souk. Now the shop assistants were blatantly trying to get our attention to smell and buy their spices. Some thrust bags or pieces of vegetation under our noses to make it quite clear what they were selling but seemed quite upset when we politely refused to take the smallest sniff.

Of course, there were also more young men offering fake, copy, special deal watches.!

Our purses and wallets never opened and we came away quite satisfied with what we had seen and smelt but also quite dazzled. I remarked to Deb that there must have been £millions of jewellery on display protected only by a glass window. If this was a city scene in Britain, I think we would quickly be reading about smash and grab gangs in markets. Of course, in the Arab states, crimes are penalised to put people off for ever, with the saying of *an eye for an eye* taken very seriously.

Back on the coach we continued with an enjoyable scenic drive to old Dubai and then out onto the highway, with six lanes in each direction, taking us to the commercial area of Dubai. We started to pass skyscrapers that grew taller and shinier, and with increasingly spectacular light shows.

Special mention was made of the Trade Centre that was the city's first real show-off building, then Dubai's twin towers, and eventually the Burj Khalifa which was currently the tallest building in the world. It was so tall that from a coach you couldn't see the top unless you lay down on the floor, and photography was almost impossible.

With our cricked necks relaxed again, our guide outlined the next places we would be seeing and mentioned the Burj Al Arab and Jumeirah Beach Hotels that are classed as the most luxurious hotels in the world. This caused more excitement as it was not mentioned on the tour details.

Wait a minute; did he just say that this was where we were going to eat?

All our programme had said was that we would be eating our dinner at "one of the most popular Lebanese restaurants in the city" but didn't say that it would be at the iconic Jumeirah

Beach Hotel. Now the coach buzzed with anticipation and it was well deserved.

At the hotel, we jumped down from the coach and were led into the lobby of the most beautiful hotel building I have ever visited, and then onwards to a small restaurant where a band was playing music and a belly dancer was undulating around a stage area.

Over the next hour and a half we were treated to some delicious, if a little unusual, food and entertainment. Our biggest problem was that the food kept arriving in small dishes, mezze-style, and we had no idea when it had come to an end. It was a totally gobsmacking and amazing experience, and I could not believe what on earth I was doing in a place like this. Unfortunately, it seemed that one member of our tour party called the restaurant manager over to complain. She informed the host that the food was uneatable, and his restaurant was awful. We did not witness the incident but a member of the crew, who was with us, told the story, and the stupid thing was that this woman never even tried the food, so how she reached her opinion was a mystery. As far as I know this was the only dissenting voice as the rest of us enjoyed the food, the atmosphere, and the entertainment.

Several courses of food later, there was a choice of 'sweet' dishes where I was virtually the only one to attempt the slightly sour camel curd yoghurt and honey dish. We then declined the offer of coffee in order to go and take some photos of this amazing place. Many of the Aurora passengers were letting out giggles of hysteria while staring up at the ceilings, then left and right at the décor. Deb told me later that even the toilet paper was perfumed and had the hotel name on each individual sheet! Along with Christine, Deb went to the reception desk to ask for a business card, just to prove we had been there; the receptionist was very helpful and not only gave them both cards, but also a handful of pens to take home. The evening had been a wonderful occasion and after the return drive we had a glass of champagne in the Crow's Nest to celebrate a very special tour that would take some beating, ever!

Aurora stayed in Dubai overnight which meant we got a good night's sleep with none of the motion and sounds of a ship at sea. We had another full day to come in the city with a tour to look at the landmarks again, but this time in the daylight.

Dubai (Day 2)
Thursday 22nd March 2012

We awoke still in a bit of a euphoric state after the previous evening's experience. I looked out of the window and the dust storm was still with us, but perhaps things were looking a little clearer. From the balcony I could just make out some of the taller skyscrapers we saw last night, but from that distance they did look very similar to each other.

Our tour did not start until 10:00 so we had a leisurely breakfast and a relaxed stare down at the quayside where the cases belonging to the 500 or so people leaving today were being unloaded and moved to the hallway. The same number of new passengers would arrive later in the day, so the ship would once more have confused couples searching for the 'pointy end' for a day or so. We had company in the port today, with two other Costa ships moored in front of us. First there was our old friend the Favolosa accompanied by the Deliziosa, meaning between 7,000 and 8,000 passengers from three ships would potentially be running amok in Dubai today. We strolled down to the quayside wondering if we would have the same guide as for our last two tours. Sadly he was on the next bus to ours but the guide we did have was again very informative if a little less able to add humour to the trip.

The tour was described as 'Panoramic Dubai' and retraced much of the route we had taken in the dark last night.

We had another stop at the Gold Souk where Deb and I ignored the shops again, and went off to find a chemist so that I could buy a support bandage for my suffering tennis elbow. This did not waste much of our time and before long we were once more being offered *"copy, fake watches sir, or handbags, scarfs?"* from the hard-working touts. Ignoring them yet again we bought some postcards but spent less than £5 in two visits to this spectacularly glittery place.

Our next stop was somewhere new to us, at the Creek alongside the old part of the city known as Al Bastakiya. We had a chance to look at rather less bright and shiny houses plus dhow working boats and crude ferries that were moored or crossing the water. This was a wonderful photo opportunity, and we heard later than many passengers had thoroughly enjoyed a trip on the ferries to cross the creek.

We set off again along the main road where we saw the skyscrapers once more, and this time we were ready for the Trade Centre, Twin Towers, and the gigantic Burj Khalifa buildings. Our next stopping point was a shopping mall with a difference as it housed 'Snow Ski Dubai', an indoor winter play area of an enormous scale. It boasted a 400-metre ski run plus ride-on ski lifts, sledge rides, artificial snow areas for generally playtime, and gigantic plastic balls to sit inside and be tumbled down a snowy pathway. It was very expensive to use but also very popular for people to face sub-zero winter conditions for an hour or two, rather than the more normal temperatures of around 40°C. Our tour did not include using the facilities, but most of us stared in disbelief at the scale of the place.

This had been listed in our tour guide as a refreshment stop, but all we were offered was a can of tepid fizzy drink in a café outside of the main snow hall. It was not very appealing so we left our drinks unfinished and took the chance to look through the viewing windows at the snow and the happy people playing.

Back on the coach, we continued our journey to the glitzy quarter of the city which includes the Burj Al Arab and Jumeirah Beach Hotels where we had been the night before. Now we could see their daytime beauty and had a chance to take some proper (if hazy) photographs of these stunning buildings. The photo stop was at the Jumeirah Beach that is equally impressive with predominantly non-Arab tourists enjoying the golden sands and the clear blue water. Deb took a paddle and quickly returned as it was rather chilly compared to other places where she had dipped her toes recently.

A final stop was made at the Jumeirah Mosque which seemed small compared to what we had seen in the previous two or three days, but was once again very beautiful and serene in its design. As I was quietly taking in the tranquillity of the gardens, I was drawn into a conversation by a lady passenger who remarked on the beauty but asked why these people are so cruel. I had to politely tell her that I was not interested in listening to her opinions, as they were spoiling my enjoyment. Inwardly rather angry, I wished that people with negative thoughts would keep out of the very happy and positive moment in my life that I was enjoying. There would be plenty of time for negativity when we returned home to a country that has just as many ghosts from the past that can be dragged up.

After that slightly sour moment we all jumped back on the coach and returned to Aurora for our last few hours in Dubai. At the port Deb and I bought some more souvenirs and presents to use up the local currency before dragging our goodies back to the cabin to join the rest of our treasure mountain. It was beginning to look as if we would need to buy a new suitcase to carry everything home!

We grabbed a quick snack from the Sidewalk café and then had a restful period watching the scene ashore below our balcony. The last of the new passengers had arrived and Aurora cleared up the dockside gangways and made ready to sail on the final segment of our adventure.

It was hard to put into words the experiences of the Middle East compared to India or South Eastern Asia. We had visited so many countries in just a few weeks. We had witnessed old and new, poverty and millionaire lifestyles, decaying buildings and glitzy skyscrapers, all coexisting in the same city or small area. I would need to reflect long and hard about this area of the world before I could piece it all together enough to make sense of it in my mind.

There were just three weeks left now before we returned to the supposed modern society that these countries are all striving to match. Perhaps they should look carefully at what we have achieved to be sure they don't grow their society into the same chaos and greed.

Sector 5 – Dubai to Southampton

Four Sea Days to Sharm El Sheikh
23rd to 26th March 2012

There was now a series of sea-days from Dubai around the
Arabian coastline to Egypt. Our next port of call was Sharm El
Sheikh at the southern end of the Gulf of Suez, but before then
we had several days to make the most of the sunshine. We
would soon be moving back into cooler latitudes.

The first of the sea days was quiet but broken up by port talks
on our next two visits in Egypt. The first would give us another
chance to snorkel and see coral life in Sharm Al Sheikh,
followed the next day by a trip to see the Pyramids and cruise
along the Nile while the rest of the ship watched the Suez
Canal drift by.

I went for my brisk walk around the deck and Deb had her
Zumba class. She was suffering with the side effects of the
dust and had a sore throat and a cough and I felt annoyingly
congested and fed up with having to blow my nose so often.
The haze was still with us and the captain expected it to remain
for a day or two more. It appeared to be keeping the
temperature down a little which gave us some relief from the
heat of the last couple of weeks.

In the afternoon Deb went to her art class (working on a
Vietnamese street scene) while I went to cricket and we both
went to the individual quiz. We did quite well, but Deb missed
out by one answer to get her into the tie-break decider. She
wouldn't have won because Mavis was also in the tie-break.
Mavis was a very educated lady who played bridge, always
joined in with the individual quiz and also took part in the more
formal syndicate quiz late at night. She was a little infirm and
used a wheeled walking frame to make her way around the
ship. Not the best judge of gaps, she often crashed her walker
into other people sitting in the bar as we sat waiting for the

quiz to start. We got used to it and did our best to make gaps bigger if we saw her coming, and smiled in acceptance if we were too slow and received a shove in the back. Her claim to fame however was her ability to remember general knowledge and she won the individual quiz on several occasions, but usually in a tie-break.

On the many occasions when she shared the highest score with someone else, the winner was decided by a single tie-break question that was usually pretty obscure, with the winner being the closest to the correct date, time, or number of the answer. Mavis had a knack of plucking answers from nowhere to win these challenges and I never saw her lose one. Once the question was to guess how many hours the footballer Rio Ferdinand was late for a drug test. She had no knowledge of football, or the player, or the incident, but managed to come up with the exact number of hours, to the amazement of everyone in the bar.

She was a lovely lady, and always put a smile on everyone's faces.

Dinner was a bit special that evening as it was Brenda and Micks 44th wedding anniversary so we all had a glass of wine to help them celebrate. The food was all right as well!

The evening entertainment was Adrian Walsh, an Irish comedian. He made us laugh but he was another who had probably had 45 years or more experience in the business, and much of the material, though funny, was predictable and mostly based on *"do you remember when we..."*.

After the show we had a drink with Brenda and Mick as we took on another quiz. We ended up joint top and so had a tie-break question to separate us from two other teams. There was no sign of Mavis this time! The question was "how many strings are there on a harp?" Deb guessed at 48 but I insisted there were many more so we changed our answer to 102.

The correct answer was 47, and if I hadn't got involved, we would have won, I should have known better and to always trust Deb in these situations!

The next morning the sun was much brighter as the dust had virtually disappeared which meant that the temperature went up again. It was Saturday and after breakfast Deb went to Zumba and I spent an hour updating the blog before I took my now regular walk around Prom Deck for a mile or so. That gave me a chance to break into a sweat on the three-and-a-bit laps and quite often I saw the same people on each lap. Some were wide awake as I passed on lap one, but fast asleep with their open mouths by the time I finished. Others ignored the world around them while reading in their own personal little bubble. This was a common occurrence on the ship as a lot of us liked to escape from the rest of the passengers by reading a book or listening to music, and switching off from the people passing by and just mentally being as one for a little while.

There were times on my walk when I became slightly frustrated with one or two couples. They tended to stroll, hand in hand, doing the same walk as myself and several others.

There was nothing wrong with this, except that as they came to the narrow parts of the deck, they failed to notice the queue of more energetic walkers behind them trying to overtake.

In hindsight it was rather sad that I was finding fault with these passengers. One day I will probably be the same and slow down my pace, so I apologise if any of them noticed my frustration when I eventually passed them.

By now we had returned to a routine with a port talk before lunch and a spell in the sun in the afternoon until it was time for art for Deb (attempting a view of Muscat) and of course cricket for me. There was a spectator today from Germany and a couple of us were trying to explain the game to him. He was not impressed by 'in and out' or 'overs and runs' and his reaction to the idea of watching a five-day Test Match was not repeatable. In the end he suggested that this was a very British game and similar to many of the British things that we do. I believe he was politely saying we were a bit weird, but at least we were having fun, and had perhaps been 'taking the mickey' with him as well.

On the way back from cricket we saw some whales playing in the sea alongside the ship. While the adults demonstrated spouting and wallowing, a couple of the more athletic youngsters performed leaps into the air and splashing back into the water. There was even an occasional somersault as well. What an absolutely terrific moment.

The evening was a formal one and involved the final "Welcome on Board" party with free drinks and the captain's jokes again. The complementary drinks do help to us to keep smiling and play along with the game for the new passengers. We found a couple of new officers that we had not spoken to before, and it appeared that they would be on our tour to the Pyramids. It was always useful getting to know crew members for these circumstances in case of problems.

… not that there would be any of course.

We had a full house at dinner, and it was the usual good meal with plenty of humour as we caught up and discussed our day. Our waiters were like old friends by now and they regularly shared a joke with us. Each night at the end of the meal young Meghnath brought little biscuits or sweets to accompany our coffee, and he knew we would refuse them unless they were chocolates. Of course when it was the special chocolate nights, he couldn't disguise the delight on his face as he came to the table with a bowl of treats, knowing we would accept them, and even ask for more.

The evening entertainment was a pair of young Scottish men (apparently finalists from TV's 'X-Factor') with music involving multiple instruments. More music so Deb and I opted out. There were always plenty of other things to keep us amused around the ship.

Sunday 25th March was another quiet, warm and sunny day in the Arabian Sea. Deb was not very well as the dust had got to her and she had a chest infection. The doctor prescribed (at a cost!) some antibiotics to help her get over it.

That dust storm had quite a serious effect on many people and left several passengers coughing for Britain. While Deb was at the surgery I went for my walk and then we had a cup of coffee before going to a port talk on Haifa in Israel. We didn't know what to do in Haifa as we had decided to avoid the long trip necessary to get to Jerusalem. There was little to do locally especially as it would be a Saturday when a lot of places would not open. It looked like it would just be a walk.

After lunch we had an hour in the sun. It was hot and humid again making it hard to stay out too long. Back to the cool cabin for the Aurora daily Sudoku puzzle and crossword, before art class and cricket.

Success!

I was on the winning cricket side for the first time since my initial game several weeks ago.

Feeling rather elated at my sporting prowess it was time for the individual quiz. We didn't win, but I did witness a moment of drama. An army officer and his wife had joined Aurora in Dubai and they regularly joined in with the quizzes. One question that posed no problem to anyone was *"what is the name of the islands invaded in 1982"*. As the answers were being given out one cocky passenger responded with 'Las Malvinas'. I quickly glanced at the soldier's face and saw a look of both surprise and out-and-out anger. I believe if the soldier had been sitting nearer the said idiot, his manhood might have been as risk. Never make jokes about patriotism in front of a trained killer from the armed forces.

The cabaret artist that evening was Matthew McGurk, an illusionist. We had seen him somewhere before but that did not affect a good show with a couple of tricks that impressed me. I have a small knowledge of magic and thoroughly enjoy seeing tricks that I can't figure out at all. We could have followed that show by going to a Tom Jones tribute act, but once again, *"if you don't like the original, why watch a tribute act?"*

Our evening was completed by another quiz (close but not close enough) and then half an hour listening to 'Caravan' in the Crow's Nest over a glass of wine.

During my meditations for the day, I looked at the changing demographics of the passengers.

When we left Southampton on that chilly winter's evening in January, the passengers on board were, in the main, adventurers like ourselves. They had come to see unusual places like the Panama Canal, and distant cities like San Francisco. Long sunny days in calm blue seas were not their primary reason for coming aboard Aurora. Several days of the North Atlantic are not something to look forward to at that time of year. There were, of course, those who had cruised round the globe ten times and more, and the 'million nautical mile club' but they are a quite different species. For these people the rationale is simple: it's January so it must be time for a world cruise. I envy them, and I certainly understand why they do it, and if I had the same freedom of choice I would jump at the opportunity to repeat the experience.

After San Francisco there was a different type of passenger on board, with a lot of people looking for a three-week holiday to Australia or New Zealand, and they were not just Americans. Many people flew from Britain to avoid the Atlantic and joined the ship to enjoy the thrill of arriving in Australasia, or to enjoy the calmer sectors of the cruise. They probably did not experience the best of the weather on that sector of the voyage, but there were some amazingly spectacular ports of call.

In Australia we gained the people of that country who were out for a three-week late summer break to Mumbai, or maybe going just as far as Darwin or Singapore. These people treated the trip like a convention with regular get-togethers for a chat. At 7:00 in the morning several of them would chatter while they walked up and down in the swimming pool...

... quite odd really.

Breakfast for the majority was at 7:30 when real talking could begin. Throughout the rest of the day, they would group on deck in the sunshine to discuss anything that might have been forgotten earlier. When they got bored with sitting in the sun, they would repeat the pool walking ritual until a meal beckoned. To round off the day while waiting for the show to start in the theatre they ensured their views were loudly shared with the Brits sitting around them.

Bless you, but you really do talk very loudly, and for a very long time. Some might suggest that's better than being a moaning Brit, but let me tell you those Australians could give us a good run for our money complaining about the colour of grass or the wetness of water.

As many of them had left by the time we reached Dubai Aurora gained more out-and-out holiday-makers. They were mostly from Britain, many taking advantage of the amazing last-minute bargains to be had on a cruise back to Britain across the Mediterranean while visiting some magical countries. Before we got to Sharm El Sheikh these new passengers were keeping rather quiet. They were probably finding it strange that the ship was not partying every evening with wild discos till dawn. After surviving winter at home, they generally seemed to love having some warm sunshine with the use of a swimming pool to cool themselves when there weren't too many Australians walking up and down. There were a good number of Aussies left, but they were much outnumbered now!

For the 600 or so of us who had been on board throughout the entire trip, our days had settled into a way of life where we enjoyed talking with each other, and also to the transient passengers.

We got our pleasures from seeing a sunset or passing ships, and we also had the joy of our memories of where we had been that these other newer sailors had missed. So many dreams had been fulfilled, so many gasps had been uttered, and so many discussions had followed a visit where sometimes the small things had totally thrilled us.

Our clocks went back in the early hours of Monday 26th March, and with the change to British Summer Time at home we were now just two hours ahead. We had woken up to another hot and humid day and no sign of land to be seen.

So, let's look at where we were that day.

Since leaving Dubai in the area of water described as 'The Gulf' we had sailed back into the Arabian Sea via the Strait of Hormuz. We then passed Oman (Gulf of Oman), continuing past Yemen and into the Gulf of Aden (just north of Somalia) as we entered the Red Sea with Eritrea to our port side and Saudi Arabia on our starboard side. A little later we passed Sudan before getting into the vicinity of Egypt for our stop at Sharm El Sheikh. If it was a geography test I would have failed it before coming here but now I was actually interested in what was just a few miles away from my cabin. The experience of visiting or passing by so many different countries is mind boggling.

There had been a change in the state of the sea and it had become a little livelier than in the Indian Ocean. Our sea legs were firmly fitted by now and it made a pleasant change to see a few 'white horses' in the back garden.

Deb was soon off to Zumba (chest a little better today, thank you for asking) and I was out on the deck to walk my mile and a bit.

There were two port talks today with one on Izmir during the morning and another on Istanbul in the afternoon. We already had a tour booked to Ephesus from Izmir, but we needed something else for our visit to Istanbul. Our stop there would be a day and a half and we only had a river cruise booked for the second day, hence the port talk was quite important to help us make a decision. We also enjoyed listening to Jo, our port lecturer, as she was so informative, even when she was talking about places familiar to us.

Deb's art work had now moved on to a dhow scene in Muscat, or was it Abu Dhabi, or Dubai? She was still enjoying the new challenge. As for me, who needs cricket? Yes we lost again but I came away with no new bruises and it was tremendous exercise and fun for an hour each day.

In the evening we watched a show by the Headliners that we had seen before, but it was still very good. There was no quiz that evening as there was live football coverage in Masquerades. I am a football fan but I didn't come on holiday to sit in the bar and watch a game for two hours. We sat in Andersons and had a chat with Mick while Brenda was at the cinema, and the captain came along and joined us for a while. He was really very approachable and actually chatted, rather than just fulfilling his obligations to 'engage' with passengers.

Final Sea Day Before Egypt
Tuesday 27th March 2012

We were still in the Red Sea powering north towards Sharm El Sheikh, but there was a slight change this morning as we were going slower than we have done for the last couple of weeks. We'd finally left the piracy region, and so longer had to sail at high speed to outrun them.

It was another warm day, although the sea was a bit bumpy and various bits of the ship rattled with the movement, but nothing serious enough to affect passengers.

Deb went to Zumba, and I went for my walk. When I had finished, I went to spy on the Zumba class, and I want to warn all men with normal male coordination – avoid this exercise! It is fast, and involves moving the body in all directions with hand clapping and swinging, plus leg kicks and sidesteps, all to a Latin music track. This is most definitely something designed for women, or very wiggly men. When the session ended, Deb and I went together to listen to Jo's port talk on Athens, and followed that by a spell in the sunshine.

The sea actually became quite lumpy as the day went on, and the wind grew significantly stronger than we had been used to for a long time. It didn't really affect us much except for trying to find a spot in the sun after lunch where we could avoid being blown around. The aft deck was perfect and I sat and listened to my music and tried to get the insides of my arms to change colour. They never go beyond a dirty grey colour no matter how long I expose them to the sun. The rest of me was well-coloured though, but not as much as the wrinkly men who stayed in the sun for most of the daylight hours, looking a little like gnarled walnuts.

Cricket was a very close match but I was on the side that came second again. There was one amazing moment where I dropped quickly to my right to catch the ball brilliantly then rolled over in a perfect parachute-landing style before standing to an ovation and the applause of my friends.

In my dreams!

In reality I dropped my arm to valiantly attempt the catch with a flapping hand, missed, then collapsed to the floor on my backside, rolling further with flailing limbs until my left knee and hand found the ground and I came to a halt. Struggling back to my feet like a new-born calf, I was shaken and embarrassed by the laughter from these men who used to be my friends.

The evening was formal dress code again, and we were looking forward to the second performance by the comedian Adrian Walsh. It all promised to be a good evening as there would be some dancing to follow, and of course we could have a walk on Prom Deck again now that the anti-piracy restrictions had been lifted.

It's funny how things can change in a couple of hours. I had a few niggles with my knee and finger from the cricket but thought nothing of it until I tried to get up after dinner and promptly sat back down again. My knee had decided that it was not interested in standing and told me off for playing stupid games at my age. There was a bit of alarm around the dinner table for a while, but I eventually convinced the knee that I was not staying in the dining room, and I hobbled painfully away, embarrassed once more, and slightly annoyed. The evening was not totally spoiled as the comedian was really on very good form but the dancing was out as I now felt considerably older than my years. After a few minutes of watching the others enjoying themselves Deb went to the bar and asked for some ice to ease my knee. Having convinced the bar staff of what we needed, we returned to the cabin with a huge bag full of ice to attempt a little bit of treatment. On the way back to the cabin the ice prompted several people to ask if we were throwing a party.

The ice deadened my knee enough to allow me to get to sleep but it was a fitful night of waking and moving carefully to see if the pain got worse. To be honest the pain in my little finger was affecting my comfort more than a stubborn and swollen leg. I soon realised that our snorkelling trip was almost certainly off, and I thought the trip to the Pyramids might also in jeopardy.

You idiot!

Sulking in Sharm El Sheikh
Wednesday 28th March 2012

I woke up and as I expected the knee, although better, was not going to allow any trip out today. After breakfast Deb went to the tour office to let them know, and I hobbled down to the Medical Centre to get my sadly swollen knee checked out. Thinking back to the cricket the day before I remembered the fall when I tried to stop the ball. That movement had caused my knee to twist in addition to jarring my little finger.
What a plonker!
The doctor said that the cartilage had taken a bit of a battering, and would need to be inspected properly when we got back to the UK. For now, I received a very tight bright green neoprene support and some anti-inflammatory painkillers to help it recover. My little finger was possibly broken so it was splinted to its neighbour to stop it moving around. I was also told to use the lifts for a few days, and to avoid walking too far and for too long.
Goodbye to the Pyramids trip.
I felt extremely annoyed with myself and very upset for Deb. We spent most of the morning sulking in the pleasant sunshine that was hot but not as overpowering as it had been recently. The ship was deserted with the major activity being some Army squaddies playing in the swimming pool. Presumably they had been part of our extra protection on board during the pirate threats.
Later, while we were sitting on our balcony before lunch, we heard the call to prayer from the local mosque summoning the faithful.
It was an eerie sound that we had heard in previous years but although we had visited several countries recently where it might have been expected, this was the first time we had

heard it on the cruise.

Looking out at the bay it initially reminded me of Oman with hills and small mountains all around. These hills were mostly the yellow colour you'd expect of a desert, but there were also layers of darker and even red soil. Only at the actual coast was there any sign of habitation. The hills continued towards the horizon making it an imposing sight. In the haze, the distant mountain peaks became ghostly giving the vista a magical affect.

The bay was all that we could see so I cannot comment on what the true touristy bits were like but I do know they are well serviced by pleasure craft. Just in front of us was a marina for fleets of pleasure craft worth £millions and as we arrived maybe 30 or more left to go down the coast a little way to where they entertained the tourists. There must have been a huge business here just to buy, sell, service, and repair the boats, let alone the actual money-making end of the chain.

The boats have different experiences on offer, with glass-bottomed ones to see the coral reefs and tropical fish, others to take passengers on a relaxing cruise around the coast line, plus more specialised ones available to pull water skiers, para gliders, and no doubt also help with other types of extreme sports.

The weather was good and temperatures crept into the mid to high 20°Cs with unbroken blue sky all day. I could see why so many northern Europeans find this place so attractive with its long summer season.

The hotels that were eventually visible as we left the port appeared to be only two or three stories high, but I don't know if this is the typical. From what I saw, it didn't look too over-developed, and so I can only say that it looked to be a nice place.

What a pity my stupidity meant we could only see it from the ship.

As we sailed away, the sunshine gave one last magical touch to the view. It produced a beautiful orange tint to the hills and rocks, and the sea glistened like millions of diamonds. There was also the sight of the little flotilla of pleasure boats returning home.

We decided to treat ourselves to an al fresco meal in the Pennant Bar that evening to drown our sorrows. It was wonderful with delicious and superbly cooked food, plus absolutely perfect service. It was the first time we had ever eaten there in the dark, as in the past we had been in the Mediterranean with its lighter summer evenings. The meal, and a fine bottle of red wine, helped us forget our disappointment at missing the Egyptian tours, and we spent quite a long time happily reflecting back over the cruise. Our heads were full of memories of stunning cities, and landscapes that were so magnificent that no suitable adjectives exist to describe them. We truly loved visiting countries where the simple way of life is so refreshing, and discovering the differences that exist between the continents, and their cultures.

Tomorrow we would miss the trip to the Pyramids so the view of the Suez Canal from Aurora was all that will be on offer to us.

Through the Suez Canal
Thursday 29th March 2012

At around 3:30 this morning 280 passengers left the ship, and quietly boarded the tenders to start their expedition to see the Pyramids. I was disappointed that Deb and I were not with them, but we had had so many good days with wonderful experiences that we didn't dwell too long on the ones we missed.

By the time we got up Aurora was already in a convoy of ships sailing northwards through the Suez Canal. After breakfast we sat for a while in the Crow's Nest looking out at the vast expanse of totally calm water in one of the lakes of the Canal. In front of us I spotted four of the other ships in our convoy, and earlier I had seen two others following us. The ships travel two miles apart, at a maximum speed of just nine knots.

On our port side there were built-up areas with small villages dotted about. Earlier, in the area around Cairo, there had been some green fields that made a change from the desert conditions we'd seen so far on this sector. At times it was possible to make out military aircraft hangers disguised as sand dunes, which were reminders of the conflicts that had occurred in this area, and which could flare up again at a moment's notice. In the hazy distance there were more of the sandy-coloured hills and mountains that had been a common sight for the last few days. On our starboard side there was just barren desert. As described to us in the port talk, the Suez Canal is impressive but not in the same league as the Panama Canal that had amazed and delighted us oh-so-many weeks ago. Most of the passengers took a few minutes to absorb the atmosphere and the scale of this huge waterway. There were far more people than usual in the Crow's Nest, all making the most of its vantage point, and it was also quite chilly outside, bringing passengers inside instead of hanging over the ship's rails.

The captain made several announcements as we made our way towards the Mediterranean, explaining what we were seeing and what was coming up. Soon we were in the huge lake with ships in the southbound convoy anchored all around us waiting for our convoy to pass.   Virtually all the ships were container or freight ships, but I spotted the Costa Victoria in the distance. From our vantage point it looked a very confusing sight with ships seemingly all over the place, but in fact we were travelling through a huge parking and passing area where changes in the convoy order are possible (I don't know why this is required), enabling a safe and ordered crossover between the two directions. Once our convoy had left, the southbound one would reform and continue towards the Gulf.

About an hour later we left the huge lake where it had been just water almost as far as you could see in all directions, and now the canal became a narrower lane of water again. On our starboard side it was still just desert but I did notice a mosque next to a lookout post. On our port side was a small town and a ferry crossing point where the locals were friendly enough to wave at us.

Just on from there was a small army camp complete with guns pointing skywards. Close by a series of pontoon bridge sections stood ready to be used by the army in case a rapid crossing to the other side was necessary.

We were now in the northern section of the canal and only had about 40 miles to go which would take about four hours at the maximum speed allowed.

Back in the cabin, while Deb went to Zumba, I sat on the balcony where there was plenty to see. Towns were rare, with many of the buildings military ones, but occasionally there were small settlements and even one with what looked like a luxury hotel with a swimming pool and lush green grounds around it. We were passing a continually-changing landscape that was sometimes desert, then lush vegetation, or military barracks, and small towns. It all seemed to be on our port side however as the starboard view remained mainly sand. There was a heavy military presence all along the Canal which gave it a bit of a sinister feel, but many of the soldiers seemed quite friendly and whistled and waved to us as we sailed by.

While I continued to admire the views, Deb had moved on to her art class. I was having a really lazy morning but with the temperature only just creeping up to the mid-teens, I'd no intention of sleeping in the sunshine.

After lunch, it became a little warmer so we had an hour out on the deck. We timed it perfectly by returning to the cabin just as a serious shower arrived very suddenly. It started with a dust storm but that quickly changed to torrential rain and winds of up to 50 mph.

By late afternoon we were at the end of the canal at Port Said. There was no intention of anyone getting off here, as we docked simply to recover the passengers who had gone to the Pyramids. However, the local traders saw us and immediately set up their stalls on the quayside.

The captain eventually announced that because the tour buses were late coming back, we could have an hour ashore but would not be allowed to go beyond the port gates. He didn't think many people would want to get off the ship but several hundred of us bounced down the gangway in search of souvenirs and a chance to stretch our legs.

As the afternoon turned to evening, we could hear another call to prayer, and were treated to the strange sight of perhaps 50 huge balloon dolls maybe four metres high being inflated around the port area as if to welcome us. Not the most common sight and all in vain, as we were merely waiting for the outstanding passengers to return, and then we would be cutting loose for the trip into the Mediterranean and on to Cyprus. This was very much to the captain's joy as he'd earlier told us he'd had enough of Egypt for some reason. I think he was perhaps looking forward to getting to Southampton and driving to Derbyshire at the speed of several thousand gazelles for a break with his family.

We ate in the Orangery that evening, and had a quiet time by avoiding the show. We would have like to have seen the illusionist again, but the show was a double-bill with the second half being the return of the Tom Jones tribute act that we had no intention of seeing. So we didn't go at all.

The passengers finally got back from the Pyramids at 8:00 pm, nearly three hours late.

Goodbye Egypt, maybe we will see you again one day.

Limassol in Cyprus
Friday 30th March 2012

Back in the Mediterranean Sea and well on the way back home, we arrived in the Port of Limassol in Cyprus. It was cold again at about 12°C with a forecast suggesting the mid-teens for the afternoon. But the sun was still shining on us and we had decided to simply go for a walk in the shopping area of the city rather than taking a tour.

Later that day we would have a face-to-face interview with the Israeli immigration authorities before we arrived in their country. I assumed that this would be the last of these checks, as European authorities are much less stringent.

After breakfast we got our bits and pieces together (Euros as currency at last) and, with my support on to protect my knee, carefully made our way down the gangplank to another dock in another country. The shuttle bus took us to the centre of the shopping area next to what was described as an exhibition centre, but we discovered later that it was just a fancy souvenir shop. The local representative helped us to decide what to do as she directed us towards the Old Fort as a 'must see' as well as pointing out the way to the shops.

We had no intention of doing very much so we strolled to the Old Fort and had a pleasant half an hour just wandering around the higgledy-piggledy maze of stairways and corridors.

The building had had a bit of history as a church as well as a fortress, and now housed an exhibition of recovered pottery, pewter cookware, military bits and pieces, remnants of walls and pillars, and the tombstones of long-dead people. Some items dated back as far as the 7th Century so there was quite a good range of things to see although Deb made a rapid exit from the crypt when she realised where she was.

Back out in the street we found an ice cream parlour and

enjoyed our first proper cornet since Brisbane. We had been warned to avoid 'scoop style' ice cream in a lot of our previous stops, because of suspect hygiene standards in some of the countries we had visited. Anyway, the Cyprus 'fruits of the forest' cornet was delicious. It was then time to get down to the serious business of shopping, and yet more souvenirs were added to our collection.

We had a short mental shopping list of plasters (to strap my little finger) and hairspray for Deb. These were not easy to find, as the only chemist we saw was halfway down a road that was being dug up and hence wet, muddy, and sticky. After buying our bits we splodged our way back to tarmac where Deb did her best to scrape the Cypriot mud from her shoes. So, what else did we spend our money on here? Not much really, there was the usual fridge magnet for our worldwide collection, several postcards, a little pot, some smelly soap, a tea towel set and a bag of macadamia nuts. We wrote the postcards whilst having a cup of coffee, and sent them on their way. These would be the last cards we sent as we'd almost certainly arrive home before any sent later were delivered. With nothing left to tempt us we returned to Aurora, dumped our treats, had a couple of nuts, and then went to lunch. We were a bit naughty and had a hot dog and chips, which is almost unheard of for us. After that there was a chance for a couple more nuts, before spending half an hour in the sunshine. Later we heard the announcement calling us to go for our immigration inspection. The Israeli officials were very pleasant and efficient so the queue was quickly being processed, and we were soon back in the cabin suitably cleared to enter another country.

With an increasing stash of souvenirs, I decided to try and organise a bigger hire car for our return journey from Southampton, but the upgrade quote was going to cost us an extra £100 for a single journey. While the lady on the phone was checking for an alternative, she successfully managed to cut me off so we forgot the idea, stayed with what we had booked, and prepared ourselves to cram everything in somehow.

The next little housekeeping job I had was organising a dentist appointment which took no more than a simple three-minute phone call.

The evening dress code was casual but there was also a fancy dress party. This resulted in loads of men looking silly in Arab costumes, and Deb described the scene as something from an OPEC conference.

I wonder if the Israeli immigration people became suspicious about the sudden increase in Arabs on the ship!

After much consideration I had decided not to buy one of the Arab robes because it would never have got worn at home, and I certainly wouldn't have worn it that evening.

Perhaps as I get older, I prefer being amused by others rather than amusing them as I had done for so many years on previous holidays. Deb on the other hand tried her best with the Vietnamese clothes she's bought, complete with a coolie hat! It was quite authentic.

Tomorrow we would be in Israel at the port of Haifa. Once again we had no plans for any official tours and just wanted to enjoy a walk around in yet another different city.

Haifa, Israel
Saturday 31st March 2012

Many apologies to all the readers who are fascinated by this country, but I can't get enthusiastic about it. Either Deb had the same thoughts, or my negativity had rubbed off on her, but we really hadn't any plans to go and see or do anything today. There was a long stop here as many hundreds of passengers were on their way to Jerusalem, Bethlehem, Nazareth, or the Sea of Galilee, and each trip was between eight and eleven hours. For some passengers the combination of Pyramids and Jerusalem in the space of three days would totally exhaust them.

Deb put a machine full of washing on, with the hope that it would be the last, but probably just one more would be needed to keep us in clean underwear. I never did find anywhere to buy suitable underwear in all of the places we had been. Saying that, I did buy some in Abu Dhabi but the large size (labelled up to 37 inches) turned out to be more like a posing pouch for a skinny teenager!

For any enthusiasts, there was an American Naval Ship (Number 72) across the harbour from where we could hear many 'piping aboard' whistles during the early morning. Whilst in the city there were a number of young men with shaven heads looking as if they might have been sailors having a break. After we'd had a cup of coffee and a cake in the Orangery, the last of the washing was finished and we went for a walk into the city of Haifa. To be honest it was the quietest city we had been to, proving how seriously the people respect the Jewish Sabbath. The only shops open were small corner ones or restaurants and bars. We didn't have any shekels so we had no intention of buying anything. We walked to Mount Carmel and the Baha'i Shrine and Gardens. This was a beautiful series of terraced gardens on the side of a hill with the tomb of the founder of the Baha'i faith in a golden domed mausoleum half way up. Because of the Sabbath restrictions, we could only go up to the first terrace level but it still allowed some wonderful photo opportunities.

We returned to the ship, and I was pleased to find that after an hour and a half of walking my knee seemed to be holding up, with the swelling not getting any worse. It was lunchtime, so we topped ourselves up and then had an hour in the rather cool sunshine of a spring day in Israel.

At the end of the afternoon, I was relaxing on the balcony when I became aware of loud music coming from somewhere. After a while I realised it was coming from the nearby US warship, and I have to say their musical choices were somewhat distasteful for a religious afternoon. It was predominantly rap music with a serious number of explicit words. I'm no prude but I thought the US Navy would have been a bit more careful of what their ship was broadcasting around the harbour.

That just about covered our day in Haifa except to say that it was a very large sprawling city with few new buildings visible in the port area. The port guide in our cabin pointed out several museums close to the docks, but being a Saturday, they were closed. We had been warned at the port talk that Haifa was not a port to visit and just look around, but one for access to Jerusalem and the other holy places. That was certainly the case, so if you get the opportunity to come here on a cruise, either write it off as a day to do the washing, or go on a trip to the amazing attractions on offer.

Our holiday had now got to a point where Deb and I could estimate what clothes were required for the rest of the evenings, so we started packing away unwanted items. Our dinner-mates had said that they were doing the same thing, and I imagine several cabin wardrobes were looking a little less stuffed than they had been.

This was quite a sad moment as we realised that our adventure was nearing its end.

Our evening started with an Italian buffet meal in the Orangery followed by a show from Lee Wilson, another comedian of pensionable age, and one we had seen before. His jokes hadn't changed much either. It was a very good act for those who hadn't already seen it, and a lot of people were laughing throughout. Unfortunately, very few of the jokes were new to us and he made the show worse for us by singing Country and Western songs to fill up the time.

Afterwards we went to Carmen's for a completely different show from the entertainment officers. A group of them were singing songs from musicals, and although the five of them were not employed by P&O primarily for their singing skills, they gave us a most enjoyable hour and their voices were really very good. The show also included a quiz to guess which shows the songs came from so there was something for most people here......*we lost of course.*

The next day would be a sea day, but we had our Round the World Lunch (part 2) so we were looking forward to being quite full up and hopefully slightly tipsy in the afternoon.

Sea Day Towards Turkey
Sunday 1st April 2012

Aurora was sailing away from Israel with Lebanon and Syria to our starboard side and Cyprus on our port. We continued westwards for a while before turning to the north and sailing between some of the islands along the coast of Turkey to the port of Izmir where we would dock the following morning.
It was a pleasant morning with the sun peeking through the patchy clouds onto a reasonably calm southern Mediterranean Sea. The temperature was in the low teens and our acclimatisation back to British temperatures was well under way.
Deb had Zumba with Cruise Director Natalie, who then took part in a sponsored walk, or run, around the Prom Deck. This event, in aid of Sport Relief, was to complete the marathon distance, meaning more than 80 laps of the deck. It was featuring Natalie and Gavin from the entertainment team but others were sharing the distance as a team, and several of the passengers took part as well. If it hadn't been for my knee I would have happily joined in, but common sense prevailed.
Deb and I went to the final port talk of the cruise, on Lisbon. We were not sure if this would be of any value as we have been there several times, but perhaps it was more about seeing Jo's final talk rather than the content.
Well done Jo, you were a breath of fresh air compared to some port presenters we had seen before.
Lunch was the second formal affair for the passengers going completely Around the World. It turned out to be a lovely event with fine wine, delicious food, superb service and the company of the ship's crew to chat with us. Our table guests were the same as for the first lunch with six of us from our dining table, plus Sam and Bob. We had the Food and

Beverage Officer hosting our table, hence a number of the conversations had complaints as their theme (in jest mostly). The majority of the talk centred on our experiences with a chance to ask each other what we had loved most about the cruise, and generally laughing at our adventures.

Through lunch and during all the afternoon the marathon walk continued, finally finishing just after 6:00. Natalie was one of the last to finish the 7½ hour ordeal and she was shattered. Gavin had supported her after he had finished a bit earlier, and they both had very tired and aching legs.

To make matters worse, they had just a couple of hours before they started work again to entertain us.

It was formal dress evening and Deb and I had a very light dinner, in fact I just had a starter and a plate of chips. Oh, plus a fruit salad as a sweet, and coffee and a macaroon!

The show was by the Headliners performing 'Blame it on the Boogie' which was a really colourful happy-clappy 45 minutes. We met up with Brenda and Mick after that for the quiz in Masquerades that was all about guessing the names of sweets from cryptic clues. We did quite well, but no prizes. The quizmaster was Gavin, who had entertained us on many evenings with his own very personal style. He had many different themed quizzes including pictures, video clips, sound clips and some unusual trivia questions. Always good for a laugh, and a very good singer, I hope to see him on our cruises again one day.

Izmir and Ephesus, Turkey
Monday 2nd April 2012

We had a tour starting at 08:15. I got up early and put the kettle on for the early morning cuppa and discovered it was raining. Apart from odd short sharp showers, this was the first rain we'd had for weeks.

This was our first visit to Izmir, which is the third largest city in Turkey (after Istanbul and Ankara), and it looked really huge with masses of apartment blocks all along the waterfront and up into the hills. The dock is like so many others, with the buildings nearby really needing a good makeover or preferably demolishing.

Our tour was to the archaeological site of Ephesus, where we had a magical visit on our first cruise back in 2000. The captain's words this morning described the getaway being at the "speed of a thousand turkeys"; perhaps we should have made his day by shouting *"gobble, gobble"* as we bounced down the gangplank! We found our coach and met our guide for the day. He was called something complicatedly Turkish that he tried to tempt us with, but eventually decided that "George" would do.

This was to become quite confusing.

As we set off we were all given little radio receivers to wear to hear his commentary. The only other place we had used this terrific system was at the Sydney Opera House...

... sorry I just had a quick flashback to that wonderful day. George (our guide) chatted to us about his city and country while we drove for about an hour to Ephesus, and he proved to be very amusing and really knew his stuff. It was only going to be a short tour of the site at the old city of Ephesus, but it didn't take us long to become immersed in its history and fascinated by the stories as we walked down through the ruins.

Deb and I loved it the first time and this had been an opportunity to revive the memories from nearly 12 years earlier.

The experience this time was just as sweet.

If you are planning to go to Turkey, be sure to go to Ephesus if you can. Try to get a local guide to show you the best bits and explain the history. Just like our George, they use their knowledge to bring the site to life. One of his gems of wisdom was a simple statement that put what we were seeing into context:

"The city is 4,000 years old and was completely buried before work started nearly 150 years ago to uncover it. Since then, they have only managed to reveal about 10% of the city".

Just to whet your appetite for Ephesus, the tour took us about a kilometre down a marble-tiled street that runs from the top of the site to the bottom. This street is the focus of any visit to the site, and is lined by spectacular marble pillars and remains of temples, buildings and shops. I dare anyone making their way down the street not to occasionally sigh with delight.

At the bottom end of the street was the façade and entrance to the Library of Celsus, said to be the third most important historical library in existence. It is huge and simply stunning. Commissioned by Tiberius Julius Aquila and completed in 117 AD, the library was a mausoleum to his father Tiberius Julius Celsus Polemaeanus who was the governor of the Roman's Asian territories with its capital at Ephesus.

When you have had your fill of the library, you pass through the remaining city gate, and move on a few metres to be presented with one of the largest amphitheatres left from this period. It is mentioned in the Bible, as the apostle Paul is supposed to have lived in Ephesus for a time. Sitting on the stone seating you can see the stage area below where lions were said to have fought with gladiators but looking further you see an avenue of marble pillars that marked the road to the sea. You can almost imagine the Roman Emperors waving to crowds from their chariots.

We were only at the Ephesus site for about an hour and a half, and we came away with just a photograph taken of us at the top of the site, plus some packets of the apple tea which Deb loves so much. Back on the coach I heard the majority of the passengers say that it had been a wonderful tour. Our cheerful guide then gave the all the ladies a gift of a small lucky charm bracelet to say thank-you for being his first tour of the year…
… the final smoothie of the cruise!

It had been a lovely morning that reminded us of the excitement we felt on our first visit so many years ago. No doubt some of the passengers would complain that it was too far to walk, or too slippery, or the buildings were too old, but I truly believe that most of them left with happy memories of Ephesus.

Everyone was back on the ship by just after 1:00 and Aurora soon cast off her ropes and started her journey further up the coast of Turkey. In the evening we would pass through the Dardanelles before entering the Sea of Marmara to arrive at the mystical city of Istanbul in the morning. This is one of our most favourite places, and we looked forward to an overnight stop in the port just as we had done 12 years earlier.

The evening was casual dress code and the entertainment was supposed to have been a singer by the name of Victor Michael. It turned out that he had a sore throat and was replaced by the comedian Lee Wilson, so we gave him another chance. If it wasn't for the singing (why do comedians need to sing?) it would have been a reasonable act. We still remembered a lot of his jokes, but some were new and there were a few jokes that may have crossed the decency boundary as well, so that improved things a little...

... wash my mouth out!

Later we had a go at another quiz, this time based on TV Theme Tunes. We were proud to say that we didn't watch enough TV to be able to do it.

We were useless!

We could see some of the monuments on the banks of the Dardanelles as we walked back to our cabin, but as usual we were passing through in darkness. I know a lot of servicemen and their families have great respect for this part of the world, and the captain was hoping to make the return journey before sunset so there could be a chance to see a little more.

Istanbul, The Jewel in The Crown of Turkey
Tuesday 3rd April 2012

Today was our second stop in Turkey, in the magical city of Istanbul.

An amazing sight greeted us this morning at 6:45 as we woke up and looked out of the window. There was a view of the Hagia Sophia, the Sultan Ahmed Mosque (Blue Mosque), and Topkapi Palace, three of the most beautiful and visited places in Istanbul and all saying "hello" to me and Deb. We managed to time our look at the perfect moment to see this magical view that would only be there for an instant?

It seemed a good idea to have our morning cuppa on the balcony but that idea was quickly abandoned...

... it was blooming cold.

The captain had seen fit to park the ship with our side towards the shore which was very nice in some ways but disappointing for the picnic we planned to have that evening. We had intended to sit on the balcony with some nibbles and a bottle of champagne, looking out at the view of the Bosphorous and Golden Horn waterways. Never mind, we would have to sneak the bottle and the nibbles out onto the aft deck when it gets dark.

No tour today as we wanted to go and do our own thing. Once breakfast was over, we got ourselves ready and strolled along the quay towards a 'hop on hop off' bus to take a leisurely look at the city.

That was a big mistake.

An open top bus in just 12°C was not the most pleasant way to spend an hour and a half. We both had jumpers but like many of the other intrepid passengers we wished we had brought hats, coats, scarves and gloves as well. On the plus side, the trip was thoroughly absorbing and we saw several areas of

Istanbul that we hadn't seen before. We eventually arrived at the main touristy bits that we had seen first thing from the ship, so got off the bus for a stroll.

Our intention was to start at the Hippodrome, wander via the Grand Bazaar and Spice Bazaar to the Galata Bridge, and eventually make our way back to the ship. But before we started our walk we made a detour for a cup of coffee with Brenda and Mick to warm ourselves up and to get our bearings. It was so cold that I spotted Brenda warming her hands above the coffee cup. Realism was setting in and we remembered that this was April and a long way from the equator. With just over a week left before we would be home it was time to get used to winter.

Eventually slightly warmer, we went our separate ways through the city. This was our third time in Istanbul and it was just as crowded with tourists as in the heat of high summer. Coaches dropped off groups of people talking in many different languages, which showed the universal attraction of this intriguing city.

We had no intention of actually visiting the major attractions as the only one we really wanted to see again was Topkapi Palace which was unfortunately not open to the general public today.

Instead we walked along the Hippodrome past its ancient pillars and then turned down a side road in the general direction of the Grand Bazaar. We had no real idea of where we were going, but while people kept coming towards us with carrier bags, we assumed we were heading for some form of shopping area. After perhaps half an hour, we were rewarded with the sight of the Grand Bazaar entrance.

The Grand Bazaar is an experience that few people can ever forget. You walk through overpowering crowds of shoppers and tourists exploring shop after shop in row after row of a market that seems to sell everything. The brightly-lit stalls, the constant chatter of shoppers and traders, and the array of souvenirs, jewellery, leather coats and day-to-day necessities are mind-numbing.

As we expected, many of the smaller stalls were openly selling counterfeit goods but they were rarely without a queue of customers trying to strike a deal. On our first visit back in 2000, the experience was a little intimidating as we had continual unwanted attention from the traders, and there was a lot of begging as well. The authorities had cleaned up the city significantly since then, and hassling was no longer allowed unless you entered a shop or made conversation with the traders. Begging was outlawed, and although it was still going on, it was far less obvious.

We didn't buy anything in the market, just being there was enough, and we simply walked straight through from one end to the other and came back out into the sunlight, and the busy back streets of the city.

The shops and stalls now changed from brightly lit attractions into real business premises where we saw many of the same items for sale, but in bulk. This was more of a wholesale area rather than a retail market. We saw the same bracelets that our guide gave to the ladies yesterday, and while in the market they were perhaps $2 or $3 each, here in these backstreet shops they were closer to the same price for ten. When we were back on the ship we saw the same items again, this time priced at almost £10 each.

We still didn't buy anything.

Eventually we emerged into the open area near the Galata Bridge which spans the Golden Horn waterway of Istanbul. Our noses told us we were close to the Spice Market so off we went to investigate. It was another narrow, crowded lane, only this time we were passing between shops selling spices of all colours and smells. As with the souk in Dubai we were being tempted to sniff the products by the very pushy traders but it was a moment to savour rather than to buy, so we politely declined the offers.

The stalls were selling other things apart from just spices, with lots of chocolate, sweets and nuts on offer. Finally we were tempted to bring out the wallet and purse. Although we were hoping to find some more macadamia nuts, they were illusive so instead we bought some hazelnuts (called Findik nuts in Turkish), as well as some Turkish Delight of course.

Exploration over, we crossed the bridge and looked at the various restaurants that crowd the lower pedestrian deck. The waiters were doing their best to entice us in and although tempted, they were predominantly for fish lovers of which I am not one.

Still a little peckish, we were now in the back streets on the other side of the waterway. At last we saw a little café and bakery where we bought some cheesy pastries to nibble at as we continued our walk. Initially we had no idea what they were but we thoroughly enjoyed them, and realised we should have bought more. Instead we stopped very close to the cruise terminal for another cup of coffee and just sat watching the world go by.

We could have walked more, done more, and seen more but this had been a lovely relaxing morning. Istanbul had not let us down and its busy bustling streets and tourist traps brought back memories of 12 years ago. The bazaars were incredible even if the traders still found ways of hassling innocent tourists who probably just wanted to absorb the atmosphere. The sounds, smells, and yes even the hassling, all added up to an experience that just shouldn't be missed.

On board again, we lay in the sun for over an hour. It was not hot but a sheltered spot kept the chilly wind at bay and I fell asleep as usual while Deb read her book. We spent the rest of the afternoon in our cabin reading or staring down at the quayside as passengers came and went.

At afternoon tea, in addition to a drink and cake, we sneaked out some sandwiches and rolls for our picnic, to have with the nuts, sweets, and champagne when the sun set later.

We had no plans to watch the show that evening, even though it sounded as if it might be good. Our thinking was that by the time the bottle of bubbly has been downed it might be late enough to crawl back to the cabin, but who knows, we could always make a bit more of a night of it in the bar afterwards.

When our stomachs suggested it was time to eat, we found ourselves a deserted spot at the end of the 'horseshoe' of the aft terrace deck. The champagne, sandwiches, chocolates and nuts were delicious, and we sat and watched the dusk turn to night with spotlights coming on to light up all the mosques. It was beautiful. Just before darkness came, the call went out for evening prayers and the air was filled with eerie cries to remind the faithful of their duties.

As we were sipping our final mouthfuls of champagne, we saw some plumes of smoke rising above the area of the bazaars. We thought little of it and even when we heard sirens, we assumed it was just a fire. With the drink finished, we chatted about our adventures and considered the future. It was going to happen sometime, and the inevitable question finally popped up: would we ever do a world cruise again?

As we became cooler we went inside and as expected, we didn't go to the show except for briefly popping in to the back of the theatre to see what was happening. On stage was a belly-dancer trying to make a passenger look a fool. Unfortunately the passenger concerned had been the same one chosen by every comedian, or cabaret artist, throughout the cruise.

I will refer to him and his wife as Jack and Jill. We met them early in the cruise while learning to dance and became friends. Jack was a very chatty person who quickly learnt people's names and greeted everyone when passing or sitting nearby. The pair stood out in a crowd, were quite good looking, always dressed well and they did everything they could possibly do. As well as the dancing, at which they were very good, they went together to the art classes, and I believe crafts and bridge might also have been on their timetable. Each evening they went to the theatre where they sat in the front row, and later they would be in Carmen's for dancing or the second cabaret show, once more in a front seat. Male singers would pounce on Jill and sing ballads to her, and if a comedian, illusionist, or juggler needed someone to help them, Jack was singled out and he gladly took part.

A number of the passengers made comments about them and they were the centre of some discussions at our dinner table. They had gained a reputation that wasn't totally positive. I have to admit I was a little tired of seeing Jack on the stage laughing and being laughed at. He usually gave a good performance each time, and in hindsight I suspect I was seeing myself when I was younger, and maybe I was just a tiny bit jealous. When we were younger, Deb and I always sat at the front on holidays at holiday centres, and we often got chosen (or volunteered) to join in games and shows just like Jack and Jill. I also remember overhearing comments about us always being involved.

So, if you recognise yourself as being Jack and Jill or someone like them, don't worry about it, carry on enjoying yourselves while you can. The time will come when your faces won't fit or you prefer to watch others make a fool of themselves, but I warn you that you will miss the attention. Perhaps sometimes though, be prepared to say *"NO"* or take a seat further back and watch someone else become the comedian's stooge. If it still looks good then return to the front row, enjoy the time, and ignore the comments.

It was time for bed.

Aurora remained in port overnight and we were to stay in Istanbul until lunchtime. We had booked a trip on the Bosporus the next morning to see the city from the water for a change.

Another Morning in Istanbul?
Wednesday 4th April 2012

Things had been going so well, but this was Aurora, and she still seemed to be a little jinxed on this cruise.

As I said earlier, while we were having our picnic the previous evening, we spotted plumes of smoke and heard sirens but assumed it to be just a fire. No, it turned out to be a series of bombs.

Very early in the morning the captain took the only sensible decision, and as soon as he had confirmed that all passengers and crew were back on board, he slipped the ropes and we sailed out of Istanbul at about 7:00 am. The announcement was heard by a few bleary eyed passengers like us who were just getting up, plus the other early birds who were already eating their breakfast, but many did not know what had happened until sometime later.

At least we had enjoyed one day in this wonderful port and had achieved what we had planned to do ashore. Unfortunately, as with earlier mishaps, we seemed to find it difficult to succeed with tours that involve the water. After breakfast, the jeans we had chosen to wear earlier were exchanged for shorts, and the coats put back in the cases. It was cold again this morning, but we wouldn't need to wrap up for a cruise on the windy Bosporus. With most of the entertainment team still in their beds, we waited now for Natalie to surface and plan out the day's activities and hoped they hadn't been celebrating on shore too much last night.

We did have one small perk as a result of sailing early, as we would now be seeing the Dardanelles and the memorials to the Gallipoli battles in daylight. We had always passed this spot at night before, so it would be a first for us.

Our day was very quiet, with the temperature being cool

enough to keep us out of the sun for most of the time. Deb had an art class in the morning (painting mosques in the mist of Istanbul – she called her offering '*Mistanbul*') and I just sat and read to keep myself awake – well, for most of the time anyway. There was a brief burst of excitement when some dolphins were spotted swimming in the distance as we sailed through the Sea of Marmara, and we saw a lot of ships and birds.

During the late afternoon we sailed passed the memorials to the Gallipoli conflict. With a significant number of Australians and New Zealanders on board as well as the British, it was quite poignant. The captain gave a solemn description of both the conflict and the memorials, plus a respectful reading of the *"at the going down of the sun...we will remember them"* poem. As we passed the final memorial, he sounded the ship's horn to honour yet more young men who never grew old. My family had been very lucky with no casualties in either of the world wars, or in the conflicts since, but I cannot fail to have a deep respect for the young men and women who didn't live to enjoy the rewards that their sacrifices enabled.

That evening we went to watch Victor Michael, the classical tenor. His voice had recovered and he turned out to be a tremendously talented singer. Afterwards we had a pleasant drink in the Crow's Nest with Mick and Brenda after just losing out in the Motown quiz. Caravan was playing in the Crow's Nest and it was a really enjoyable selection of music to listen to while we chatted until quite late.

Piraeus and Athens, Greece
Thursday 5th April 2012

The slightly more-than-usual amount of alcohol last night probably accounted for my mistake of setting the alarm and being woken at 6:45 am for no good reason. Aurora was still some way out at sea then, and even after a cup of tea and breakfast we still managed to get back to the cabin before the captain made his *"Welcome to the port of Piraeus"* chat. Our tour today was due to leave at 9:30 and so there really was no rush.

The port of Piraeus was very busy with ferries continually passing by the ship as they sailed to and from the Greek islands. Some were little tiny foot-passenger ones but many were huge roll-on-roll-off ferries taking freight, cars and their drivers. Aurora was berthed just a little way from another large Costa ship (Costa Pacifica) and the extremely small Orient Queen that dates from the late 1960s. It was a wonderful reminder of what cruising used to be like before the big floating hotels of today.

We went down to the Curzon Theatre to get our tour stickers and were soon on our way. There was a slightly strange arrangement at Piraeus, as we had to use a shuttle bus to go no more than 100 metres to the terminal building, followed by a walk almost as far to get to the actual tour bus. Our guide greeted us and his name was "George" (obviously a popular name for guides in this part of the world!) but he also gave us his Greek name which we all ignored. He was good but probably not the quickest with the English language that we had had over the last three months.

After a 30-minute run into Athens with various bits and pieces being pointed out along the way, we began to remember just how busy the traffic was in this city. George told us a story of the government making it a rule that cars with registrations ending with an odd number could enter the city on one day, and the even numbered ones the next. He said it eased the traffic for a while but eventually everyone bought two cars with both combinations of number so making the problem even worse.

Our first stop was at the old Olympic Stadium which we had seen and smiled at on two previous cruises. On our first visit in 2000 we could go right into the stadium and walk on the track, but today visitors can only view it from behind a barrier. This was sad, and as I suggested earlier, there would be a lot of demand from sports fans to get closer to these venues if such tours could be organised.

From there we went up to the Acropolis and its various temples. This was the highlight for us and for several thousand other people. With two large ships in port, plus land-based tourists and children on school trips, it was pandemonium, but George said today was quiet! He explained the layout of the site, its history and details of the renovation work that was going on. His talk was enough to satisfy the new people as well as reminding others like ourselves of just how special this site is to the world. There were a few verbal digs at Britain over the Elgin Marbles and other items that had made their way out of Greece, and I can understand the Greek standpoint here. Maybe the time had come to discuss the possible return of those very valuable Greek heritage items.

Deb and I could see the difference over the 12 years, and it was quite noticeable that a lot of work was still going on. Scaffolding obscured a lot of the buildings, reducing the number of superb photo opportunities, but it was still a wonder of the world that attracted and enthralled people every day. This work will take at least another 25 years to complete so my generation will never see the Parthenon without scaffolding and in its eventual restored glory.

After an hour and a half at the Acropolis we drove back into the city and arrived at the old Plaka area where we had the rest of the time to explore. We went off and found a small taverna where we sat outside and had a light lunch.

Deb ordered a Greek salad and I decided on a cheese pie shaped like a Cumberland sausage. While we waited for our food we had a coffee and tucked in to the complimentary basket of bread and olive-based spread that appeared on our table. Then the 'light snacks' arrived and they were enormous! There had been a couple of showers earlier in the day, but now the rain became much heavier so we were glad to have chosen a table well under the awning. The rain enticed others in and the quiet restaurant became busier while we tried to eat our way through the generous 'snacks'. Another couple from our tour, plus a pair of the girl singers from the Headliners Theatre group came in while we were eating. Our meal finished with a complimentary dessert, so that also had to be eaten before we could leave to go and explore the shops.

There were a few items that caught our eye and joined our collection of souvenirs, but in reality we just wanted a walk and a look around. We went into the nearby Cathedral but couldn't see very much as it was under renovation with yet more Greek scaffolding.

Deb commented that compared to the very opulent and 'in your face' mosque décor, this was very restrained and maybe concentrated on the religious aspects rather than the *"bigger and more beautiful is better"* buildings of the Muslim faith that we had seen. This was only an observation from a couple of non-believers of either faith, so please do not be upset if my words seem offensive, these buildings belong to you, not us.

Our visit over (and it had been yet another superb day) we returned to the ship and had a rest before waving goodbye to the Costa ship leaving before us, and then to Greece, as we eventually returned to the sea. Over dinner it was obvious that the topics of conversation were now focussing more towards going home. The adventure had moved into its last week with just Lisbon to break the journey before arriving back in Southampton. It seemed we had been lucky with this stop, as the ship had received reports that demonstrations were planned for Athens that evening, and the Greeks don't seem to muck around when they want to demonstrate.

Now, what can go wrong in Lisbon?

The evening entertainment was a female singer (Alana Shirley) who had been in various West End shows. We gave her a miss while we recovered from our long day walking around Athens. It was also a Country and Western themed night with the passengers' line-dancing group performing their skills in Carmen's...

... we missed that as well.

There were three days at sea now before Portugal and we hoped that the Mediterranean would give us just a little bit more sunshine and warmth before we turned northwards next week.

Sea Day from Greece
6th April 2012 - Good Friday

We woke a little later this morning and although it was a bit warmer, it was very foggy. The ship's foghorn occasionally sounded a warning to others that Aurora was coming through. After a late and leisurely breakfast, we looked at our on-board statement to see how the finances were going, and spent over an hour trying to make sense of the way that the various refunds from cancelled tours had been applied to our account. Other people who have cruised before will understand the confusion surrounding interim statements.

Anyway, what should have been a simple task ended with a confusing visit to the reception desk, which still didn't clarify what they had done. So I eventually created a simple spreadsheet on the laptop to track all the transactions. Once things were tabulated in order I finally made sense of what the statement was telling me.

Everything was clear
... I think.

Deb had long gone to Zumba and I was in the Crow's Nest working on the laptop and feeling a little guilty because there was a Good Friday religious service going on. It had all the very special elements that are associated with the faith on this special day, and reminded me of Easter time when I was a child. Unfortunately the serenity of the service was broken by the noise of glasses clinking in the bar and the intermittent blast of the foghorn. Others like me probably appeared as unwanted witnesses to their faith while we sat in silence listening to their service.

Life must go on for all the passengers, and on a cool day like today, places to sit inside were at a premium so believers and doubters were sitting together. The service was quite pleasant, and I tried to respect the moment.

Deb came up to the Crow's Nest for her art class just after I closed the laptop and had decided to rest my eyes a little. After letting her know that all was well with our account, I left her and her paintbrushes and went for a coffee, before going back to the cabin for a read. This was really a lazy time. When the art class was over Deb showed just a little bit of panic as she had been asked to choose two pieces of her work to go on public display.

I was so glad she took up the art class and was very proud of her work.

There were a lot of 'talks' today in the theatre. One was about the achievements of a Round the World yachtsman, another about Musical Movies. A third one was by Jonty Hearnden, a presenter on TV's 'Cash in the Attic' and 'Antiques Roadshow', about his love of antique furniture. We just went to the antiques one as we recognised the presenter's name. It was OK but I thought I'd probably enjoy his next talk more as it was to be about his career on television.

I think somebody needed to educate Jonty about his references to Aurora being a 'boat' or he is liable to upset his employers who may not invite him back to the 'ship'.

The fog had lingered for most of the day and the wind was making it rather chilly. The crew had finally closed the roof over the Crystal Pool to give people somewhere to doze, but there were also some truly determined sunbathers around the open deck, while other passengers lay fully clothed and curled up under towels. I personally preferred the comfort of an inside public room or our cabin, but each to their own.

There were treats today in the Orangery for afternoon tea where there were hot cross buns...

... Maybe a bit small but very nice.

Another pleasant discovery was the realisation that the cold water in our bathroom taps was now COLD for the first time since we reached the Caribbean several weeks ago. The only really cold water we had had since then came from a fridge. Dress code tonight was 'Smart with a Jacket', and there was only one more such evening, plus two formal and two casual ones remaining. Clothes were starting to be put away in cases all over the ship during days like today when there was little to do outside.

In the evening there was another violinist (Craig Owen) in the theatre, and a dance show in Carmen's by the entertainment team. We decided to go to the dance show first and then to the violinist later if we were still awake.

So our evening began by watching 'Dance Explosion' by the entertainment team with more than a little help from some of the Headliners troupe, and it was terrific. It was a competition to see who could best dance their version of an iconic dance from the past. As an example, one pair did their version of the famous Dirty Dancing scene...

... they were good!

I won't say any more to avoid spoiling it for others who might see the show in the future.

From Carmen's we went straight to the theatre to watch the violinist. Deb and I agreed that he was very good, but after the previous male fiddler his act was a little tame, and he seemed very unsure of using a microphone to chat between tunes.

It had not been a very active day but we were ready for a late night cup of hot chocolate and bed.

Overnight the clocks went back again leaving us just one hour ahead of home and only a few days left.

Mid Mediterranean Sea Day
Saturday 7th April 2012

The sky was clear this morning but a chilly wind was blowing us around a bit (Force 6 to 7) and the back garden had a lot of white horses running around it. Aurora was bumping along, but nothing too unpleasant. Our TV display showed us to be just south of Sardinia's western tip and north of the border between Tunisia and Algeria.

After breakfast we went to the Crow's Nest for me to update my blog while Deb did a puzzle before going to Zumba. She had her art class to follow while I just relaxed. What a life. My only challenge today involved getting another book to read as I had finished the Rick Wakeman biography that had amused me for a couple of days. My colleagues at work had bought me an e-reader for my retirement present, and that had proved to be a wonderful gift. Unfortunately I didn't realise how much I would use it, and failed to load enough books to keep me going for three months. Downloading on board was possible but the internet connection was expensive, not very reliable, and certainly not fast.

There was another religious service in the Crow's Nest this morning as part of the Easter weekend celebrations. Most of the passengers not directly involved respected the service but a couple behind me chattered throughout. I wonder what these people were taught about respect for others as they were being brought up.

With Zumba over and Deb gone to her art class, I had a stroll and a cup of coffee and then looked for another book to read. I thought the weather was far too cold and windy to sit out on the deck but, as yesterday, a lot of people were trying to absorb warmth from the sun either under cover or by the open pool. They really had to be a hardy set of people to sit outside in this weather, or was it perhaps that they had inside cabins and being outside was essential?

After lunch we had a talk from the captain and it was most enjoyable. He talked about himself and his past unlike some of the captains we've listened to who have only talked about their work and the ship. Captain Neil Turnbull was a fascinating person with a wealth of experience and a dry humour that most of us found entertaining.

There was a little bit of bad news for our visit to Lisbon: our tour had been cancelled due to a lack of demand. It wasn't too disappointing as we would be quite content with a stroll around the city.

Before dinner we had the final, final, Portunas Party and enjoyed a few glasses of bubbly, courtesy of P&O. We chatted to the First Officer that we met with many weeks ago, before he went on leave. Full marks to Andrew Wolverson for remembering us! There was another draw to win the champagne and wine carafe and our dinner table friend Roger was the winner. Well done to Roger, and we looked forward to helping him and Laura drink their prize!

After dinner Deb decided to go to the cinema to watch 'The Artist' which didn't appeal to me, so I added a bit more to my blog while having a drink on my own. When the film finished, we got together again and went to Carmen's to watch a show by Fogwell Flax. He's a comedian and impressionist that we had seen somewhere before but couldn't remember where or when. His act was good but just a little familiar and hence predictable.

It was time for bed with just one day to go before Lisbon, our final port of call.

Sea Day Passing Gibraltar
Sunday 8th April 2012 – Easter Sunday

Easter Sunday at sea, and for the first time that I can
remember we didn't give or receive any Easter eggs.
At 8:00 we were just south of Almeria in Spain. It was a
brighter day with the state of the sea back to 'slight' after
yesterday's slightly wilder 'moderate' conditions. The wind had
reduced but was still whistling around the open decks as we
walked to breakfast.
We were in quite a busy shipping area and we spotted vessels
ahead, to the left and right of all types, colours and sizes. One
going the other way on the African side of the waterway was a
cruise ship but we had no binoculars handy to identify what
cruise line it belonged to. There was always interest from
passengers in identifying passing cruise ships, especially when
many people could say
"We were on her last....."
Someone said it was the Queen Mary 2, but I thought she was
elsewhere at that moment.
Later that day we would be sailing past Gibraltar before turning
right and heading northwards to Lisbon, and then towards
home. A lot of British people have a soft spot for Gibraltar and
some had expressed their disappointment that we were not
stopping there. It is a special place, with a character that is
different from neighbouring Spain, but I personally feel it
survives on its history and it is no longer as

British as some want it to be.   Aurora could have stopped at Gibraltar but I am glad that P&O chose Lisbon for our final port as that city doesn't pretend to be anything other than itself. Although few people openly said it, there was an acceptance that the journey around the world was in the home straight, and many conversations turned to *"Our next cruise is..."* rather than remembering the last three months. I was ready for the return now and, deep down, looking forward to seeing home, our family and our friends. We didn't have another cruise booked for the first time in several years, but we had a number of things on our calendar for the summer. I was quite sure that it wouldn't be long however before we got that twitchy feeling when last-minute deals might just tempt us away to a big white floating hotel again.

There was an invitation to a photo-call later in the afternoon when all the 'Around the World' passengers were asked to assemble on the aft horseshoe decks for a panoramic photograph of the 600 or so of us.

Mid-morning, while I was having a cup of coffee in the Orangery, I looked towards land and saw a beautiful scene of the coast of Southern Spain covered by a blanket of fog. But looking beyond the coast there was a mountain range lit up by the sun with their peaks covered in snow. As well as being picturesque, it was a reminder that we were most definitely back in Europe and it was still only early spring. I believe that some of the passengers saw snow on the mountains of Cyprus, and the temperature had cooled even further over the last week, but this was the final proof that the best was behind us.

The afternoon weather surprised us and we had the treat of a restful snooze in the sunshine. It was not hot but the spring warmth was very pleasant.

This spurred me on to greater things and I had a game of cricket as well. Probably the last chance before Biscay would put an end to the games, so it was good to say *"hello"* to my geriatric cricketing friends for a final time.

Following on from my bit of exercise (we won!) Deb and I joined the other 602 'Round the Worlders' for the group photograph.

This was just a bit special.

One obstinate lady sunbather refused to move, so the photographer positioned all the crew in front of her. This had the bonus of blocking the sun from her as well...

... silly woman!

It was quite impressive to see the wraparound horseshoe decks filled with intrepid passengers. We had been thrilled by so many places, and survived some strange experiences, but the majority of us had laughed our way around the world.

There was a lovely dinner that evening and we had the bonus of the champagne won by Roger.

The entertainment was superb with the Headliner's brilliant 'Destination Dance' show. This is fast, athletic and a treat to watch. It was made even more of a challenge for the troupe as two of them had quietly left the ship during the previous week. The reason for their disappearance was never explained but laundry rumours (never denied or confirmed) suggested there had been a dispute between them and the management that would no doubt impact on their future careers. The remaining singers and dancers had to work even harder than usual to cover for the missing two, and deserved the ovation they got at the end of their last show for us.

Thanks, and well done Headliners, you were absolutely

brilliant!

We ended the evening with another music quiz from Gavin where we lost in the tie-break question about the date of a Boyzone single. Slightly miffed, we had a couple of drinks in Andersons, and chatted about what we would be doing when we got home, and how we could ever top this experience.

Last Stop Lisbon (Portugal)
Monday 9th April 2012

Aurora had arrived in the lovely city of Lisbon in Portugal. We had been here four times before this visit and have a lot of wonderful memories of the city. Previously we had been on organised tours, trams, a lift, and spent considerable time just walking and window-shopping. Today we had no plans other than to go in on the shuttle bus, then wander around, have a cup of coffee and see what took our fancy.

The weather looked promising and although it was cool to start, the captain suggested that it would get quite warm later in the day.

After breakfast we shuttled into the city to a square known as the Pracados Restauradores, which was not where we were expecting to be dropped off. On our previous visits the bus had stopped at the Black Horse Square, but this was out of use while some major road works were going on. Today's drop-off point was in a beautiful square and not far from the areas of the city that we were familiar with. There were wide pavements bordering some wonderful buildings with lots of cafés, clothes shops, and stalls selling fruit and tempting cakes. We strolled along to the narrower streets and soon found Black Horse Square, as well as the ornate Elevador de Santa Justa, an iron lift giving visitors a short ride up to the higher Barrio Alto area of the city. Once we'd got our bearings, we just window-shopped and noticed that clothes appeared much cheaper now than on previous visits, but still very much more expensive than Vietnam, Mumbai, etc. We didn't buy much, but we did of course stop for coffee and delicious baked creamy custard tarts while we watched the locals, and many Aurora passengers, passing by.

Our visit was not long, and we were back on Aurora by midday as it was very apparent that the temperature had risen and the sunshine was tempting us to make the most of it.

As the end of the afternoon approached, the captain announced that we were ready to go, with just 900 miles left to sail before we would arrive at the Mayflower terminal in Southampton. He also warned us that there would be a Force 8 storm in the Bay of Biscay, with seas of five metres or more. These were the conditions that we started the cruise with, and there would be a repeat performance to end it.

The Great British Sailaway got underway on the aft decks. We had only joined in with this maybe two or three times in 12 years, and would not be leaping up and down, waving flags, or singing this time either.

During the evening we treated ourselves to a final intimate meal in Café Bordeaux. The dinner was excellent, as we knew it would be, and made even more enjoyable by Caravan performing in the background as we sipped a bottle of wine. The waiters attended to our every need as we chatted and smiled for an hour or so savouring a simply wonderful meal.

Our plans for the rest of the evening were to watch Roy Walker, a comedian who had appeared on TV's 'The Comedians' many years before, as well as hosting his own 'Catchphrase' show. We'd seen him before and knew that he would amuse us.

Our meal took longer than we thought meaning we were too late for the first show in the theatre, so we went to Carmen's to watch Jonty Hearnden with his second show. Unfortunately, Roy Walker's act was overrunning in the theatre so Jonty had to delay his start time to allow his audience to arrive. He finally got going and talked about his career in TV as well as discussing the many antiques-based programmes that fill the programme schedules. The talk was entertaining but concentrated too much on him, and his co-stars, rather than the special moments that occur in the shows.

Because Jonty started late, he also finished late, and we missed the beginning of Roy Walker's second show. We are not the sort of people who like going into a theatre after a performance has started so we didn't see his show at all. Never mind, I'm quite sure we will see him another time, assuming we continue going on cruises.

We had a late-night cup of hot chocolate and then went for a read in the cabin before bed. The sea had certainly become angry and Aurora was beginning to move unpredictably, and creaking as she lifted up and crashed back down through the swell.

A Not-So-Nice Sea Day
Tuesday 10th April 2012

The ship was moving far more erratically than I liked. The captain's words of yesterday were correct and we were heading into some stormy seas.

After breakfast we did our usual thing and went to the Crow's Nest where I updated my blog and Deb sat reading until it was Zumba time. As she prepared to go, the religious service was just about to start behind us, and with the movement at the top of the ship making me uncomfortable, I left with her and went back to the cabin. I was no longer interested in working on the laptop, or reading the last few chapters of my book. Although I might have grown my sea legs through being away for such a long time, I discovered that I had not grown my sea stomach.

I went outside for a walk around the deck and that settled my stomach and cleared my head a little. A bit later there was to be another immigration inspection ready for our return to Britain, so I went back to the cabin to await the call. The ship's motion quickly convinced me that I needed to be somewhere else, so I grabbed our passports and manifest paperwork and went to look for somewhere with less movement. I can handle rough seas that make the ship pitch and roll quickly, but today the conditions were making Aurora move slowly up and down and side to side, and my stomach couldn't come to terms with it.

Setting up a temporary camp at the back of Carmen's, I waited until Deb's Zumba class ended. Carmen's was much lower down in the ship than our cabin, and the sea's motion was less noticeable.

Before the class ended our immigration manifest numbers had been called, so when Deb finished, we joined a queue to meet the British officials. This was not at all painful and the gentleman concerned actually smiled and chatted for just a few seconds, unlike the US officials who snarled at anyone trying to make conversation.

The rest of the morning was spent packing another suitcase and my stomach tried to survive until lunchtime. Oddly, even while feeling a bit queasy I was able to eat some fried chicken and chips without feeling any worse. After lunch there was a show by the Entertainment Officers to display their singing talents.   Their singing (or reciting of a poem in Gavin's case) was very good, and the finale was a comedy rendition of "If I were not aboard this ship....."

I think this was enjoyed by everyone. At the end the audience gave them a well-deserved round of applause.

The Entertainment Officers had worked very hard and were very good at their jobs. Some of them were with us all the way around the world, but there were several personnel changes when Natalie took over, and personally I thought the entertainment improved from then on. Perhaps I was biased but I thought she was extremely good in her role as Cruise Director.

By now the sea was really angry with anyone who was not a 'salty sea dog' and the swell was approaching the predicted five metres. Our cabin TV information page displayed the sea as being 'rough'.

I dragged Deb up to the Orangery for a cup of tea but all I really wanted to do now was to curl up on the bed. And that was what I did, until Deb asked if I wanted to go to the final cocktail party as it was time to get ready. I did have a shower but decided I was not interested in a drink, and especially not high up in the Crow's Nest.

So Deb went to the party without me while I went for a walk. I had already decided dinner was also out of the question, but then I changed my mind at the last minute and went to get dressed (formal night) and go to dinner.

Simply putting cufflinks into my shirt became the final straw. This was only the second time I had ever been seasick.

At least being sick stabilised my stomach for a while, and I put on some tidy clothes and a jacket and went outside on Prom Deck to sit midships where the movement was minimal. I quickly began to get cold so I went inside and waited for Deb to come by after her meal. Seeing my discomfort, she asked what I wanted to do, and kindly accepted my plea to simply go to the cabin and ignore the show.

That was the end of our day except that I eventually ate two bread rolls and butter which Deb had gone and picked up from the Orangery buffet. That was my dinner and supper combined, and it went down pleasantly as my stomach finally required something. I was soon curled up asleep while Deb read her book, and mine still waited to be finished.

Final Sea Day
Wednesday 11th April 2012

Our last day, and as I woke up I was slightly happier to see that the weather, although still rough, was not as bumpy as last night, and with less rolling and pitching. The night had been bad with Force 8 to 9 winds and extremely high waves making the ship crash and bang as well as wobbling around.
I was hungry and had an unhealthy fried breakfast that was absolutely delicious.
Not brave enough for the Crow's Nest yet, we sat in Charlie's and read our books until Zumba took Deb away for the final time. I stayed and finished reading my book and then returned it to the library before watching the end of the Zumba in Carmen's. We went from there to the Orangery for a cup of coffee and a Danish pastry.
It was then time to complete what we could of the packing. Before lunch we went and looked at the display of paintings from the art class and Deb's pictures hung proudly amongst the others. She was pleased with her efforts on board Aurora, and intended to continue with her new hobby at home.
The ship felt so much better now that we had come out of Biscay. Aurora still creaked and wallowed along but had just about got the better of the sea at last.
After lunch our luggage joined the growing display of multi-coloured shapes and sizes of cases in the corridor outside the cabins. Ours had imitation flower garlands tied to them in the hope that it would make them easier to find the following morning. Of course that assumed the garlands stayed on through the bashing they would get on their way to the baggage reclaim hall!
Our dinner was more about wishing the best and exchanging email addresses with our table-mates rather than the food.

There was also a sad farewell to our waiters who had looked after us so well. The young assistant waiter, Meghnath, was staying on for a few more cruises yet, but Paul was going home to Goa from Southampton for a couple of months rest before returning to Oceana later in the year.

Thanks guys.

The evening show was a triple-bill: a violinist and two comedians, who each gave us a 15-minute performance. As for the rest of the evening there was a quiz and a final couple of quiet drinks around the different bars. It was a sad time as we said *"goodbye"* to the many friends that we had made, and to the beautiful ship had been our home over the previous 14 weeks.

Southampton and Home
Thursday 12th April 2012

Smiles are few and far between on the last morning of any
cruise. Some passengers had taken up the offer of a very
cheap deal to stay on board and go to the Caribbean, but most
would leave Aurora.

There was a short delay with the disembarkation process but
we were off by about 10:00 and quickly collected our cases
from the busy luggage hall. Outside we squeezed our bags into
a taxi and made our way to the hire car depot and less than
half an hour later we were in a car and back on the road
towards home.

Deb and I said very little as our heads were full of memories
and sadness to be ending such a life-changing experience.
Unusually we did not stop except to refuel the car and to drop
into a supermarket close to home to grab some basics. Early in
the afternoon we turned into our drive and started unloading
our luggage.

We were home after more than three months of absolutely
magical adventures and it would take several days to come
down from the biggest high either of us have ever had.

It was time to move on to the next phase of our lives with
retirement, but our first priority was to let all our friends and
family know that we were home, and to tell them that we
hoped to do it all again as soon as we could!

Home Again, and the Final Blog Entry

All through our cruise I kept a diary, which I copied-and-pasted onto a blog every couple of days or so. What follows is the final entry.

Monday 16th April 2012

It's early evening and I'm in our sitting room, relaxed after four days at home. I have started to dig my allotment, and have cut the field at the back of our house that we call 'the lawn'. I have also watched Deb working herself into exhaustion washing, drying, and ironing our holiday clothes. We have been to Shropshire to see Deb's mother, her brother and his wife, and our son came for dinner with us on Sunday. That doesn't complete the family reunions, as we go to Cornwall very soon to see my brothers, and we still have to organise a trip to Andover to see our daughter and her husband. Various friends have seen us and their opening comments have been *"you look well"* and *"how was it?"* Our reply has been that we both feel very well, and it has been the most amazing, memorable, fabulous experience that either of us has ever had.
As we showed the family in Shropshire some of our photographs it brought back memories roughly in the order that they happened, and it reminded us of some of the major experiences that we had already started to forget.
When the photographs become actual prints rather than just bits of digital memory on the laptop, and as the video starts to be laced together, we will be able to relive, and remember, so much more of the magic that we have been exposed to. We also have a set of P&O's official DVDs of the five world segments to help reactivate the memories.
I have had many comments on the blog from people saying

that they lived the cruise with us through my words, and I feel humble that they shared a little of our dream – a dream from which we have finally woken. The words I tapped into the laptop at the time, and those that Deb also produced and shared on the 'Crow's Nest' cruising network forum will remind us of our feelings and how they correspond to the photographs and the little souvenirs that have already found homes around the house.

We've already made our minds up to try and have a similar cruise again in the near future. We have our Ruby wedding anniversary in three years' time, and Deb and I both have landmark birthdays in four years, so these are a couple of target dates. To make this possible, we will have to seriously reconsider our financial position to find a way of making the trip possible. One thing that is not an option is to go back to work. My decision to retire was made to let me concentrate on doing what I wanted to do, rather than what other people needed me to do for the past 40 years or so, and I know Deb feels the same way.

If money restricts us to having just this one journey to see the multitude of paradises that exist around the globe, then so be it. We have seen more in three months than most people will ever see. We have "ooohed" and "aaahed" and laughed, and yes shed a tear or two as we travelled to luxury skyscraper cities one day, and then backstreets full of poverty the next. We have seen commercialisation gone crazy in some countries, and also seen people in a country just a few hundred miles away who dream of maybe one day having some of the same. I have seen smiles on faces of people with no money for new clothes, and I have seen richness beyond belief in countries that battle it out to build the tallest tower or the biggest mosque, and yet the people there don't seem any more contented than those families living in poverty in the middle of a forest.

We wanted our cruise around the world to be the holiday of a lifetime, but it turned out to be so much more than that. It will be hard not to bore our friends and family with our excitement and yet we will always want to share our experiences. So to the hundreds of people who have read my blog, I give you my thanks for bothering to work your way through my spelling and grammatical nightmares. It is difficult resting a mouse on the arm of a chair, typing in a sometimes rocking and rolling ship, and not to rely on spellcheck to find mistakes.

... that's my excuse anyway.

And if any of you ever get the chance to go around the world then grab it with both hands – and don't forget to let us know how it went.

Coming up to Date
Spring 2016

Four years on and the fantastic experience of that World Cruise had not diminished. In fact, we attempted to book a similar adventure twice, but my body let me down.

Remember the ache in my groin?

Well, a couple of months after our return, it was diagnosed initially as a hernia?

As a part of our retirement, Deb and I moved home in 2013 from Staffordshire to a little village in Herefordshire. Here the summers were taken up looking after a rather large garden in between various DIY projects around the house, plus a few cruises of course.

That ache continued to be unresolved, and turned into a long saga. After various delays and meetings with surgeons, it resulted in me having a new hip in 2014.

We had to cancel a World Cruise booked for the spring of 2015. The booking was transferred to January 2016, but although the hip was now wonderful, the original ache had still not gone away. The idea of a hernia was resurrected and I was scheduled to have an exploratory operation in January 2016. So we postponed our worldwide adventure for a second time.

Our travel adventures were restricted by my hospital visits but we managed to fit in a few cruises to satisfy the itch to be on a ship. We returned to Aurora for a sensational cruise to the Baltics, and it was with the same captain, Neil Turnbull, who actually remembered us. In a way, we also saw my Jack and Jill characters too, as a large canvas photo of them adorned the walls of the Photography Shop... absolutely typical!

There was also a glorious cruise to the Adriatic plus a couple of last minute bargains but our minds were set on having that second world cruise.

Summer 2021

Deb and I settled comfortably into retirement, and got used to not working. Our days were full of things that we wanted to do and at the times when we wanted to do them.

In 2017 our repeat global circumnavigation was finally achieved. It was on Aurora again, but we went the other way around the world sailing eastwards. The adventure was equally spectacular, and we made some wonderful new friends, that have remained in contact with us. The story of that cruise is chronicled in another book with the title of '**Searching for New Sunrises**'.

In the January of 2018, we took another long cruise, and met up with our new friends again. Our voyage to us south initially and explored the Amazon River, then relaxed in the warmth of the Caribbean Sea, and Central America. We extended to cruise by staying on Aurora when we arrived back in Southampton, and all six of us took the following cruise that went north to the Arctic Circle. That adventure was truly mind blowing, and of course I turned our memories into another book. This one is called '**From the Furnace to the Freezer**'. That was to be our final long duration cruise. It was time to concentrate our finances on a comfortable retirement.

In the Autumn of 2019, we moved home again. This time we returned to Cornwall, and a retirement village just outside of Truro. The temptation of the sea could not be ignored completely, and in the following Spring we repeated the adventure of going north to Norway and the Northern Lights. Our return coincided with the worldwide crisis of Covid. We were almost immediately put into lockdown. Our village includes a dedicated Care Home, and many of the patients died from the virus. 2020 was a year to be forgotten, and even our hopes of exploring Cornwall had to be abandoned.

Now in June 2021, we are slowly immerging from Covid, and

life will hopefully begin to resume some normality. We have a short cruise booked for September, when we will try out one of the new Saga ships where all the cabins have a balcony, and the holiday experience is virtually 100% inclusive.

... and yes, there will be more books about cruising soon.

Other Books by The Author

Cruise Related:
'A Cornishman Goes Cruising'
'A Cornishman Cruises to the Western Mediterranean'
'A Cornishman Cruises to Venice'
'Searching for New Sunrises' – (Around the World Without Wings the Sequel)
'From the Furnace to the Freezer'

Autobiographical:
'Time for Tea and a Cheese Scone'
'Would You Like Some Plums?'
'You Need a New Hip'
'A Cornishman Grows Up'
'Cornishman and his Goonhilly Years'

Printed in Great Britain
by Amazon

45777503R00215